Wolfgang Taubmann (Ed.)

Urban Problems and Urban Development in China

MITTEILUNGEN
DES INSTITUTS FÜR ASIENKUNDE
HAMBURG

------- Nummer 218 -------

Wolfgang Taubmann (Ed.)

Urban Problems and Urban Development in China

Hamburg 1993

Gefördert von der Volkswagen-Stiftung.

Redaktion der Mitteilungsreihe des Instituts für Asienkunde:
Dr. Brunhild Staiger

Textgestaltung: Dörthe Riedel
Gesamtherstellung: ZEITGEMÄßER DRUCK, CALLING P.O.D

Titelfoto: Pudong/Shanghai, Aufnahme W. Taubmann, Oktober 1991

ISBN 3-88910-117-8
Copyright Institut für Asienkunde
Hamburg 1993

VERBUND STIFTUNG
DEUTSCHES ÜBERSEE-INSTITUT

Das Institut für Asienkunde bildet mit anderen, überwiegend regional ausgerichteten Forschungsinstituten den Verbund der Stiftung Deutsches Übersee-Institut.

Dem Institut für Asienkunde ist die Aufgabe gestellt, die gegenwartsbezogene Asienforschung zu fördern. Es ist dabei bemüht, in seinen Publikationen verschiedene Meinungen zu Wort kommen zu lassen, die jedoch grundsätzlich die Auffassung des jeweiligen Autors und nicht unbedingt des Instituts für Asienkunde darstellen.

CONTENTS

Contents	5
Preface	9

Chi-Keung Leung and *Anthony Gar-On Yeh*
Urban Development in China in the Midst of Urban and Economic Reforms — 11
1 Introduction — 11
2 Economic Reforms — 13
    Rural Reform — 13
    Open Door Policy — 14
    Urban Reform — 15
    Housing Reform — 15
    Land Reform — 17
3 Impacts of the Economic Reforms on Urban Development — 18
    Urban Population — 18
    City System — 20
    Regional Distribution of Cities — 20
    Economic and Employment Structures of Cities — 21
    Rural Urbanization — 23
4 Issues of Urban Development in China — 24
    Floating Population — 24
    Urban Land Use and Development Control — 25
    Transport — 26
    Environmental Pollution — 27
5 Conclusion — 28

Dirk Bronger
Urban Systems in China and India - A Comparison — 33
1 Relevance of the Problem — 33
2 The Concept of Comparative Research: Objectives and Constraints (Note) — 35
3 The Demographic Dimension — 36
    3.1 Urbanization/Metropolization Quota — 36
    3.2 Urbanization/Metropolization Process — 40
4 The Functional Dimension — 41
    4.1 Functional Primacy: The Concept — 41
    4.2 Functional Primacy in China and India I: Present Situation — 42
    4.3 Functional Primacy in China and India II: Interdependencies between Metropolization and Regional Structures — 52
    4.4 Functional Primacy in China and India III: Dynamics of Primacy — 59

Contents

Thomas Scharping
Rural-Urban Migration in China 77
    Overall Dimensions 77
    Trends in time 78
    Structure of rural-urban migration 81
    Causes and effects of migration 83
    "Temporary" urban-rural migration 86
    Conclusions 89

Wolfgang Taubmann
Rural Urbanization in the People's Republic of China 94
1 Introduction 94
2 Rural-urban barriers 95
3 Characteristics of rural urbanization in China 96
4 Employment opportunities in non-farm economic activities 98
5 Rural enterprises - development and structural problems 100
6 Relationship between *zhen* or township development and rural enterprises 101
7 Social and occupational differentiation of the rural workforce 103
8 Rural urbanization and spatial mobility 105
9 Possible development strategies 111

Kok Chiang Tan
Changing Rural-Urban Relations in China 128
1 Introduction 128
2 Pre-Reform Rural-Urban Relations 128
3 Recent Reforms 130
4 Nature of Rural Development 132
5 Limitation of Rural Urbanization Programme 135
6 Rural-Urban Integration 138

Peter C.J. Druijven
Trends of Urbanization in the Pearl River Delta 143
1 Introduction 143
2 Demographic Processes and Their Impact on Urbanization 146
3 Selective Impact of Industrialization 150
    3.1 Introduction 150
    3.2 The Special Economic Zones of Shenzhen and Zhuhai 152
    3.3 The Old Capital of Guangzhou 154
    3.4 Inner Delta Cities and Counties 156
4 Spatial Problems 161
5 Concluding Remarks 164

Bingyu Shen
**Social Transformation in Rural China -
An Alternative Pattern of Urbanization** — 167
1 The Problem — 167
2 Background — 168
3 Methodology — 169
4 General Situation of Bixi Xiang — 170
5 Changes in Bixi Xiang — 170
   5.1 Economic Changes — 170
   5.2 Value Changes — 174
      5.2.1 Shifts Away from Traditional Ethics — 174
      5.2.2 Changes in the Institution of Marriage — 174
      5.2.3 Changes in Attitudes toward Childbirth — 175
      5.2.4 Changes in the Sense of Time — 177
      5.2.5 Changes in Cultural Life — 177
      5.2.6 Changes in Material Life-Style — 179
6 Discussion — 180
   6.1 It Contributes to More Rapid Economic Growth — 180
   6.2 Social Stability is Retained During the Process of Urbanization — 181
   6.3 Small Towns Serve as an Intermediary between City and Countryside — 181
   6.4 A Reservoir of Manpower is Provided — 181
   6.5 Women's Social Status is Elevated — 182
   6.6 Family Planning Occurs More Spontaneously — 182

Thomas Heberer
Recent Development of the Urban Private Economy in China — 184
Introduction — 184
Latest Developments — 186
Individual economy and employment problems — 188
Private economy and urban supply — 190
Providing Funds — 191
The function of the private economy for urban development — 192
Prospects — 195

Zhongmin Yan
**Suburbanization of Megalopolis and Spatial Change of
Urban-Rural Fringe. A Case Study on Shanghai** — 205
1 Introduction — 205
2 Shanghai's Urban Fringe: Structural Changes and Actual Land-Use — 206
3 Functions of the Urban Fringe — 211

Zhaoliang Hu
Beijing in "Open Door Policy" - Breakthrough, Scope and Challenge   214
1 The Space of Beijing   214
2 Breakthrough to an International City   217
3 The Regional Economy   218
4 The Rapid Growth of the Urban Population   220
5 Severe Shortage of Water Resources   221
6 Difficulties for City Planning   222

Contributors   224

Preface

This publication comprises selected papers presented at an international symposium on "Urban Problems and Urban Development in China", which took place in Shanghai at East China Normal University (ECNU) from September 26 to 30, 1991. The conference was sponsored by the Volkswagen Foundation and organized by Professor Wu Jianfan, then ECNU, now Shanghai University, and by the editor.

Main aspects of urban development and urban systems in China are discussed in the first two articles. Chi-Keung Leung and Anthony Gar-On Yeh/Hong Kong elaborate the impact of the most important economic reforms on Chinese urban development. It is specially discussed how the weakening means of control (migration, distribution of resources) have influenced the growth of cities after 1978.

The growth and structure of city systems under comparative aspects are examined by Dirk Bronger/Bochum. He points out that even under conditions of socialist societies the so-called "functional primacy" cannot be avoided. Consequently in India and China an unequal regional development can be observed.

The paper by Thomas Scharping/Cologne describes the development, scope, structure, and motivation of rural-urban migration. He tries to examine critically the validity of different sample surveys and data collection methods. So far the Chinese research on migration does not fully include the economic consequences or the social costs and benefits of migration.

The papers on rural urbanization mainly concentrate on the urbanization process in the hinterland of big agglomerations. Wolfgang Taubmann/Bremen tries to characterize the decisive processes of rural urbanization. His paper specially focuses upon the correlation between rural industrial development and the growth of small towns.

Kok Chiang Tan/Guelph investigates the changing urban-rural relations under imperfect market operations. As the urban-rural barriers are still in existence, the agricultural population tries to expand rural industries. The pro and contra as well as the prospects of the rural industries and the rural-urban integration are discussed.

Peter Druijven/Groningen proves the thesis of "reversed polarization" by analysing the urbanization process in the Pearl River Delta. His main conception is that the extent of the city system's "primacy" is reduced because of the accelerated growth and ensuing urbanization in the rural area, at least as far as his research area is concerned.

Mrs. Shen Bingyu's/Beijing findings are based on a case study (Bixi/South Jiangsu). She states a change of traditions and values in consequence of the transition from agricultural to non-farm activities.

Thomas Heberer/Trier studies the role of private economy with regard to urban development and the supply of the citizens as well as its influence on the emergence of new social structures in the urban society.

Mrs. Yan Zhongmin/Shanghai, the senior of the Chinese urban geographers, analyses the process of suburbanization in Shanghai in relation to the different dominant functions and their locations. She stresses the disadvantages of an uncoordinated development of the urban fringe that might result in grave social, economic, and ecological problems.

Hu Zhaoliang/Beijing examines the development of the Chinese capital and its chances of growth under the conditions of the open-door policy.

My thanks go to the Volkswagen Foundation for its generous support of the conference.

Bremen, December 1992   Wolfgang Taubmann

Urban Development in China in the Midst of Urban and Economic Reforms

by

Chi-Keung Leung
and
Anthony Gar-On Yeh

1 Introduction

Urban development, particularly urban system development, in most countries, is influenced by market forces. Cities which produce goods and services that are in demand and are attractive to live in will have faster growth than those which do not. Government generally has little direct influence on urban development. However, in the centrally planned economy of the People's Republic of China, government plays an important role in urban development.

Before the adoption of economic reform in 1978, politics and public policy were the two most important factors in shaping urban development in China (Lo, 1987). They exerted strong influence over the growth of urban population (Xu, 1984a), urban system development (Chang, 1976; Xu 1984b), and provincial distribution of urban population (Yeh and Xu, 1984). In the pre-1978 era, because of the "anti-urban" sentiments, urban population growth was slow and was maintained at an average annual growth rate of 2.8%. This was in sharp contrast to other countries in Asia which were urbanizing at a rapid rate of over 5% per annum. The policy of controlling the growth of large cities led to the development of small and medium-size cities and a balanced urban system. The policy of dispersing industries from the coast and controlling the growth of large cities has caused an increase in urbanization level and primacy of cities in the interior provinces of Northwest China. The development of large cities in China was contained mainly by the national policy to "strictly control the size of large cities, properly develop the medium-sized cities, and actively encourage the growth of small cities".

The ability of government to exert strong influence on urban development is mainly through population control and resource allocation. A household registration (*hukou*) system was established in 1954 to stop unauthorized migration from the countryside to the cities and rampant growth of the large cities. It divided the population into "agricultural (*nongye renkou*) and "non-agricultural" population (*fei nongye renkou*), in line with the food rationing system which was to regulate the monthly quotas of foodstuffs, consumables, and consumer durables (Kirkby, 1985). The household registration system required all residents to register with their neighbourhood police station. In collaboration with lower-level civilian officials, police ran late-night household registration checks to ensure that people did not move into the neighbourhood without proper registration. These were effective systems in controlling the population in cities because, without a proper household registration, one had no access to many highly subsidized and otherwise unavailable consumer necessities such as grain, cloth, oil, pork, bean curd, and soap, hence could not survive in the cities. The predominantly publicly-owned housing was not accessible as was the over 90% of all state- and collective-controlled jobs (Whyte and Parish, 1984). The urban system was further tightened by a migration law in 1958 that limited the entry of peasants into cities, except those who had obtained work permits from the labour bureau. The household registration system was also effective during the Cultural Revolution (1963-73) in sending youths to the countryside. There was an absolute population decrease in the large cities, with a net decrease in the total population of the city system (Yeh and Xu, 1990a and 1990b). Some of the extra-large and large cities were even depopulated to become large and medium-sized cities.

City size distribution and spatial distribution of cities were influenced by resource allocation at different periods of time. In the First Five-Year Plan (1953-57), the Soviet model of economic development with its emphasis of heavy industries was adopted. There was concentrated development of heavy industries in the industrial bases in the Northeast and large coastal cities in pre-1949 China. However, to reduce regional disparity, a policy that favoured the decentralization of industries from the established Northeast bases and the coastal port cities to the inner part of the country was stressed (Wu, 1967; Lardy, 1978; Leung 1980). As a result, large cities continued to develop and a number of key-point cities were developed in the interior and frontier provinces.

The failure of the Great Leap Forward and the Soviet withdrawal of assistance from China in 1960 led to a serious stagnation of the economy. By the early 1960's when the Sino-Soviet relations were at the lowest point, the so-called Third Front Construction was initiated by the Central Committee of the Communist Party to divert industries from the hitherto emphasized "periphery" to the Third Front area consisting of Sichuan, Guizhou, Yunnan, Shaanxi, Gansu, and the western parts of Henan, Hubei, and Hunan (Leung, 1986; Chang, 1989; Linge and Forbes, 1990). The Third Front Construction affected not only new enterprises but also existing industries in the coastal cities that were vulnerable to attack in case of war. The establishments of Dukou in Sichuan and Shiyan in Hubei were examples of the outcome of such a policy.

Resources allocation also played an important role in shaping the social areas of the cities (Xu, Hu and Yeh, 1989). Because of the housing allocation system, residential location is mainly governed by one's employment and the location of production/working units in which one is employed. Clusters of social areas were found in Chinese cities, and their characteristics were determined by the production units and the population composition and characteristics of those employed by them.

Before the economic reform in 1978 the Chinese government, with population control and resources allocation, was remarkably successful in shaping the urban system according to its policy and ideology. The growth of large cities was successfully curtailed, small towns were developing rapidly, and the number of cities and city population were successfully shifted from the coast to interior and border locations. These were the results of a highly centralised government. Many of the means needed to achieve these results may not be available in other countries. Without tremendous central control over human mobility and economic resources, it would not be possible to control the population and to allocate resources to the desired place successfully. It was the control over jobs, housing, and the necessities of daily life that made it possible to exclude people from cities. It was the centralized ownership of industry that made it possible to shift resources from larger, coastal cities to cities in the interior. All this has been changed with the adoption of the open policy in 1978.

2 Economic Reforms

In December 1978, the Third Plenary Session of the Eleventh Central Committee of the Chinese Communist Party (CCP) announced its Four Modernizations plan in agriculture, industry, national defence, and science and technology (Leung, 1983). This involved reducing the dominance of central state planning, permitting a more market-led economy and adopting an "open door policy" to open up China to the world market and foreign investments. Before the reform, all production units and enterprises were state- or collective-owned, with practically no private sector. The 1978 economic reforms opened the economy to foreign investments and market processes, reintroduced commodity economy (*shangpin jingji*) and private individual economy (*geti jingji*), with individuals owning their means of production and earning their living through their own labour. Since the adoption of the "modernization" policy, a series of economic reforms followed, and those that affected urban development in China include rural reform, open door policy, housing reform and land reform.

Rural Reform

The early reforms mainly have affected the rural areas where communes have been replaced by a production contract responsibility system. Rural land has been distributed to households according to their size; these bear sole responsibility to fulfil a predetermined production quota. After meeting the production quota, they are free to produce whatever they like and can sell their products to the free market. Households can also contract to run agricultural production units such as duck farms, fish ponds, or orchards. This reform has aroused the enthusiasm of the farmers for it allows "more pay for more work", hence rural production has increased tremendously. There is an increase in the number of "specialized households", which make use of their special production skills. Households that prefer to engage in non-agricultural activities are allowed to sublease their plots to other people. The surplus labour freed from agriculture due to the increase in the productivity of the farmers has stimulated the development of small enterprises in the rural areas, giving rise to rural urbanization.

Open Door Policy

Foreign investment was considered inductive to economic development in China. The 1978 economic reform has led to the development of special economic zones and special districts for attracting foreign investments.

To attract and manage foreign investment effectively, four special economic zones (SEZs) - Shenzhen, Zhuhai, Xiamen, and Shantou - were established in 1979. The SEZs represented a major attempt to attract foreign capital, enterprises, and technology in strictly demarcated zones where experiments with new economic policies in dealing with foreign investments can be conducted (Jao and Leung, 1986). The SEZs had the initial objectives of producing goods for export to earn foreign exchange. They also acted as social and economic laboratories where foreign technologies and managerial skills might be observed. They offer a range of inducement to foreign investors, including tax "holidays", early remittance of profits, and good infrastructure.

Despite some criticisms, the SEZs were considered to be successful and could be used as a model for other cities in China. In 1984, fourteen other coastal cities were opened for investment. These "open cities" offered similar concessions to foreign investments as the SEZs, although they were not provided with the same level of central government funding for infrastructure development. Apart from establishing special economic zones and coastal open cities to attract foreign investment, other areas were designated as special economic regions for foreign investments. In 1988, three "open economic regions" were designated: the Changjiang (Yangtze) Delta Economic Region (around Shanghai), the Zhujiang (Pearl River) Delta Economic Region (around Guangzhou); and the Minnan Delta Economic Region. They are attempts to spread the benefits of the open door policy from the SEZs to other parts of the country.

The designation of special economic zones, cities, and regions along the coast for foreign investment is understandable because they are more accessible than interior cities and regions to foreign investments, and most of them are familiar ports where foreigners formally had lived and traded with China.

Since the adoption of the "open door" policy, foreign capital equivalent to US$ 27 billion has been utilized in the period 1979-85 (Philips and Yeh, 1990). Of this 72 per cent has been in the form of external loans, and 27.8 per cent has been direct investment. Hong Kong provided most of the direct foreign investments, followed by Japan and U.S.A. Because of the policy of designating SEZs, coastal open cities, and open economic regions along the coast, foreign investments are unevenly distributed spatially. They are highly concentrated in the coastal provinces, particularly along large cities such as Beijing, Shanghai and Guangzhou, and the special economic zones of Shenzhen and Xiamen (Philips and Yeh, 1990), which hence are the main target areas of current urban reforms.

Urban Reform

An urban reform was officially launched in October 1984, when the Third Plenary Session of the Twelfth Central Committee of the Chinese Communist Party adopted the policy of reform of the economic structure. It tried to introduce the rather successful rural economic reform to the urban sector. It consisted of expanding the autonomy of enterprises, giving material incentives to workers, loosening planning and price controls, replacing state investment by credit finance for industrial development, encouraging small-scale private enterprise and allowing market forces to determine the distribution of goods and services. Enterprises were allowed to retain and allocate investment, to plan production, to hire and dismiss employees, and to determine bonuses and prices. These reforms were mainly aimed at enterprises but because most of the enterprises are located in the urban areas, they were referred to broadly as urban reform.

Prior to the official announcement of the 1984 urban reform, Shashi was designated as the first pilot city to carry out pilot comprehensive economic structural reforms in July 1981. Since 1981, 74 cities such as Chongqing, Wuhan, Shengyang, Dalian, Nanjing etc., have been approved to be pilot cities for economic reforms. Twenty of them experimented with institutional reform, 27 with banking reform, 14 with housing system reform, and 13 with market-responded production reform (State Statistical Bureau, 1990).

Housing Reform

Housing shortage is a big problem in most cities of China. This is partly because housing had been considered as a non-productive item with little funding allocated in the past, and partly because housing rent, with heavy subsidies, was set so low that it could not even meet the maintenance cost. Since 1982, a new policy of "commercialization of housing" has been gradually experimented, with "purchasers" being granted the rights of use of premises (Lin, 1986). In 1982, a demonstration project for housing commercialization was initiated in the four cities of Changzhou, Zhengzhou, Siping, and Shashi, where a small number of new housing units were sold to individuals. Under the housing commercialization scheme, an individual pays one-third of the construction costs of a residential unit, with the government and the buyer's working unit each paying an equal share of the balance. The amount paid by the purchaser goes to the state which then reinvests it in constructing new housing. Since 1985, it is said that housing commercialization has been extended to 80 cities, including the three major cities of Beijing, Shanghai, and Tianjin (Fong, 1988).

The aim of housing commercialization is to establish an equitable and efficient housing system; to reduce the amount of subsidies to those who can afford it; to increase the source of income for constructing more housing; to integrate housing into the economy and make real property part of the economy; to improve the living environment through better maintenance by owner occupiers; to offer choices in housing according to income, needs, and preferences; to rationalise the use of land by taking into consideration the economic value of land at different locations. Housing commercialization has been introduced mainly in large and medium-sized cities. The special economic zones are also pioneers in housing commercialisation (Philips and Yeh, 1987).

Recently, apart from housing commercialization, a series of housing reforms are also experimented with in some cities. These reforms vary from city to city. In general, they include the increase in housing rent, the raising of funds for constructing more housing, and the sale of flats to those who can afford them. Housing reform is addressed to two types of people: people working in government departments and state and collective enterprises, and people working outside this system.

Housing reform for people working in the government departments and state and collective enterprises is most difficult because of the large number of people involved. A huge amount of funding is needed to implement housing reform. To rectify previously low housing rent, rents for housing managed by the city housing bureau and enterprises are increased, and at the same time, small amounts of subsidies are provided to the residents. The increased housing rents are put under a housing reform fund to be used exclusively for future housing maintenance. New housing units allocated to work units and enterprises can be sold to their employees at a preferential price. This is to speed up commercialization of housing and to recapture capital to increase housing construction. Existing housing units managed by the city housing bureau and enterprises can also be sold to the residents. Such type of housing is sold mainly to employees who are eligible for allocation of government or enterprise housing. The price of a housing unit is calculated according to the average construction cost per sq metre, which varies according to different locations in the city, being most expensive nearer to the city center. Residents who buy their rented housing units can enjoy a 10% discount from the preferential price. Home purchasers can either pay in one payment with 20% discount or pay by instalments.

Provident fund schemes are used in some cities to help workers to buy their own housing. Workers have to pay 5% of their salaries as provident funds which will be matched by their enterprises. The provident fund can be transferred when the employee changes his employer. The provident fund can only be used to pay for home purchase and major housing maintenance. If the provident fund is not adequate to pay for home purchase, housing loan can be obtained from the central provident fund. In order to raise funding for the construction of housing to ameliorate the housing shortage in some cities, housing construction bonds are also issued. Families who were allocated new housing units managed by the city housing bureau and enterprises will have to purchase housing construction bonds before they can move to the allocated housing units. They also have to pay the housing rents. Elderlies and poor families can be exempted from buying the housing construction bonds.

Two types of housing are sold to people working outside the state and collective system, or enterprises involving foreign capital. They are foreign remittance commodity housing and housing financed by foreign investors. These types of housing are sold at full cost with some profits. Foreign remittance commodity housing are sold to overseas Chinese, returned overseas Chinese and people from Hong Kong, Macau and Taiwan. They have to use Foreign Exchange Certificates or overseas currency to buy such housing. Housing financed by foreign investors are houses built by foreign investors for sale or for let.

The existing housing reform only attempts to recapture housing investment for new housing and to bring housing rent to a level that can meet maintenance cost. The long-term objective is to recapture investment from all housing so as to provide funding for the construction of more housing for the people.

Land Reform

Land is owned by the government and is normally allocated free to users without any charges. However, this has changed with the economic reform. Land use fees are charged and recently even land use rights can be transferred and sold (Walker, 1991). Several cities have started charging annual fees for the use of land. Shenzhen started charging land use fees in 1981, Guangzhou in 1983 and Fushun in 1984. Land use fees are charged mainly for land use involving foreign investment. In Shenzhen, an annual land use fee is levied according to the type of use, location, and lease period (Yeh, 1985). Depending on the use, land is leased from a period of 20 to 50 years. The cheapest annual land use fee is for industrial use to attract foreign investment in industrial development. Tourism and commercial land use has the highest land use fees. Special preferential treatment is granted to educational, cultural, scientific, technological, medical, health and public welfare land use. Projects involving the most advanced technology and non-profit making projects may be exempted from land use fees.

Further land reform has been carried out in the Shenzhen SEZ. A "Land Management Reform in the Special Economic Zone" in 1987 proposed that publicly owned land can be leased to developers through open auction or competitive bidding. The maximum term of lease is 50 years which can be renewable through negotiation when the lease expires. Leaseholders are allowed to sell, assign, transfer the land use right. The selling of land use rights through open bidding was started in Shenzhen in September 1987 (Tang, 1989), and the first land auction took also place in Shenzhen on 1 December 1987. A similar type of land reform for the sale and transfer of land use rights was carried out in Shanghai and Haikou. The transfer of land use rights was made official in the First Session of the Seventh People's Congress in 1987. The clause "The right to use of land may be transferred in accordance with law" was added to Article 10 Section 4 of the Constitution which stated that "No organization or individual may seize, buy, sell land or make any other unlawful transfer of land". This amendment was approved by the National People's Congress on 12 April 1988. This opens a new era of lawful transactions of urban land. In addition, in 1988, the State Council announced the "Regulations on land use tax collection in cities and towns", which enabled cities and towns to collect land use taxes. This marks the end of free land use in China.

Prior to the introduction of the paid land use system, because land was allocated free, land users very often would try to acquire more land than needed. It is hoped that through the new system, land can be used more efficiently. In addition, local government revenue can be improved through the sale of the land use rights and the collection of land use taxes. This can help to strengthen the tax base for constructing and maintaining the urban infrastructure.

3 Impacts of the Economic Reforms on Urban Development

Urban Population

There has been a marked increase in urban population since the adoption of the economic reforms in 1978 (Fig. 1). The increase in urban population is partly due to the increase in rural-urban migration but mainly due to the increase in the designation of human settlements as cities and towns and the enlargement of the boundaries of cities and towns. In 1979, the "city leading county" (*shidaixian*) system was implemented. As a result, many counties were abolished and turned into cities without boundary and name changed and some counties were merged into cities. There was a relaxation of the criteria of establishing cities in 1983 and many counties and towns have been upgraded to cities (Yeh and Xu, 1990b). The number of cities has been increased from 194 in 1978 to 450 in 1989. In 1984, with the changes in the criteria in designating towns and township seats granted town status if its non-agricultural population exceeds 2,000, many townships (*xiang*) became towns. The number of towns increased dramatically from 2,781 in 1983 to 6,211 in 1984, adding 73.2 million people to the urban population. Of the 73.2 million population, 89.8 per cent was agricultural population. Because of the inclusion of a large amount of agricultural population in its definition, urban population in China is often considered to be over-inflated (Chan and Xu, 1985; Ma and Cui, 1987).[1] Non-agricultural urban population would be a better estimate for the actual urban population in China. Based on the non-agricultural urban population, the urbanization level of China has increased from 12.9 per cent in 1978 to 19.0 per cent in 1989 (Fig. 1); this is much lower than the 51 per cent given in the official definition of urban population which includes a large percentage of agricultural population. Urbanization is steadily increasing, but is still low compared with other developing countries.

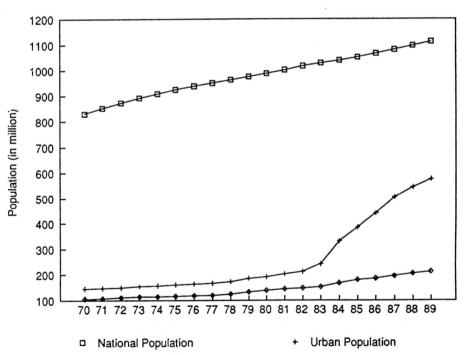

Figure 1: Urbanization of China 1970-89

City System

The most spectacular impacts of the economic reform was the increase in the number of cities. There was a more relaxed attitude towards the establishment of cities. The granting of city status was also a mechanism to facilitate local authorities in attracting foreign investment. As a result, the total number of cities rapidly jumped from 194 in 1978 to 450 in 1989 and the city population (non-agriculture population in city proper) from 84.1 million in 1978 to 146.3 million in 1989. A relatively large number of medium and large cities were added to the city system.[2] As a result, there is a decline in the proportion of large cities in the city system and an increase in the proportion of small cities (Fig. 2) (Yeh and Xu, 1990b).

Regional Distribution of Cities

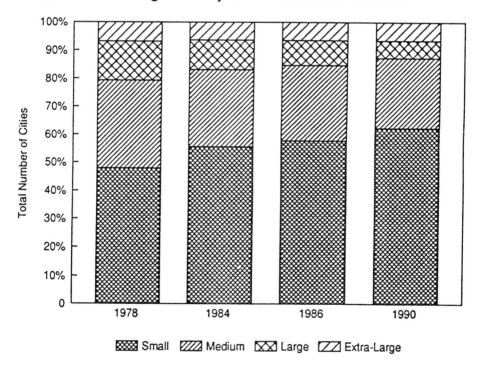

Figure 2: Changes in City Size Distribution 1978-90

The open policy has reversed the previously much emphasized city and economic development in the interior and frontier provinces. As a result, new cities and population were added to the coastal provinces. The trend of decentralization to interior and frontier provinces was reverted after 1978, with more new cities established in the coastal provinces than in the past.

With continued economic development in the coastal provinces resulting from the open policy, more towns will be upgraded into new cities in the future, reversing the past trend of decentralizing cities to the interior and frontier regions. Unless there is a major shift of the existing policy, there will be an upsurge of new cities in the coastal provinces because the majority of the rapidly growing towns are located in the coastal provinces such as Guangdong and Jiangsu. Furthermore, some towns located in these provinces such as Dongguan have already been granted city status to have more autonomy and flexibility in attracting foreign investment. Apart from the addition of new cities, the open policy also favours the development of existing cities in the coastal provinces which have a better accessibility and economic base for foreign investment. Cities in the special economic regions and open coastal cities are benefiting more from the urban reform and have higher economic growth rates than inland cities (Xie and Costa, 1991).

Economic and Employment Structures of Cities

The economic reform has changed the economic structure of the cities. More people are working in the tertiary sector and in non-state owned enterprises. With the rising living standard of the population, and the need for a better network to sell the products of reformed enterprises, the tertiary sector is growing rapidly. In the 74 main surveyed cities of the State Statistical Bureau, the percentage of the tertiary sector in the city's GNP increased from 19.1 per cent in 1978 to 32.6 per cent in 1988 (Table 1). Employment in the tertiary sector increased from 24.4 per cent to 33.9 per cent (Table 2). Changes in the economic

Table 1: Percentage of GNP in City Proper of 74 Main Surveyed Cities. By the State Statistical Bureau

	1978	1988
Primary	4.7	4.0
Secondary	74.9	63.6
Tertiary	19.1	32.6

Source: *Forty Years of Urban Development (1949-88)* (1990), pp.164-172.

Table 2: Labour Force in City Proper of 74 Main Surveyed Cities (in per cent). By the State Statistical Bureau

	1978	1988
Primary	24.3	11.2
Secondary	51.5	54.9
Tertiary	24.2	33.9

Source: *Forty years of Urban Development (1949-88)* (1990), pp. 138-142.

structure of the cities are faster in the special economic zones where there are more free market mechanisms than in other cities. In 1989, 45.9 per cent of the labour force was employed in the tertiary sector in SEZs, as compared to 31.6 per cent in the 74 economic reform cities and 36.7 per cent in the coastal open cities (Table 3).

Table 3: Labour Force in City Proper in 1989 (in per cent)

	Primary	Secondary	Tertiary
74 Economic Reform Cities	17.1	51.3	31.6
14 Open Coastal Cities	9.3	54.0	36.7
4 Special Economic Zones	8.5	45.6	45.9

Source: *China Urban Statistics 1990*, p.63.

Despite the existence of non-state enterprises, the majority of the people in the cities are still working in state enterprises (Table 4). There is only a slight increase in the percentage of people employed by other forms of employment, such as individual enterprises and enterprises with foreign investments. There are great variations among the cities with different degrees of economic reform. There is a much higher percentage of people working in non-state-owned enterprises, particularly individual enterprises and enterprises with foreign investment in the special economic zones than in other types of cities (Table 5). There are 29.8 per cent of the people in the special economic zones working for non-state and non-collective industrial enterprises and 18.9 per cent for non-industrial establishments. In contrast, there are only around 2.9 per cent and 2.0 per cent, respectively, for the coastal open cities which is already higher than the national norm. This is mainly due to the degree of economic reform and the utilization of foreign investment in the coastal open cities and special economic zones.

Table 4: Types of Employment in City Proper (in per cent)

	1984 State	Collective	Others	1989 State	Collective	Others
Non-Industrial Establishments	73.0	26.5	0.5	73.3	25.4	1.3
Industrial Establishments	69.2	30.0	0.8	69.2	28.8	2.0

Source: *China Urban Statistics 1985*, pp.451, 459; *China Urban Statistics 1990*, pp.593, 603.

Table 5: Types of Employment in City Proper 1989 (in per cent)

	Non-Industrial Establishments			Industrial Establishments		
	State	Collective	Others	State	Collective	Others
74 Economic Reform Cities	71.9	26.7	1.4	67.0	30.8	2.2
14 Coastal Open Cities	73.9	24.1	2.0	68.4	28.7	2.9
4 Special Economic Zones	55.3	25.8	18.9	37.1	33.1	29.8

Source: *China Urban Statistics 1990*, pp.593, 603.

Rural Urbanization

The new rural policies introducing the responsibility system have increased productivity by granting incentives to those who work harder. Farmers can sell their surplus products at the free market after fulfilling the contracted quota. Along with the increased agricultural productivity and the revived market towns, the rural industries are a significant source of income and employment opportunities for the peasants (Chang and Kwok, 1990). They employ a growing number of rural surplus labour producing goods and services for the rural economy and a steady demand for raw materials. Rural savings are reinvested in rural enterprises. The free markets and rural industrialization initiated a rapid growth of small towns in China. Rural urbanization was praised by Fei Xiaotong (1984) as the solution of China's rural surplus labour problem by allowing the rural inhabitants to leave their farmlands without leaving their villages (*litu bu lixiang*). Rural urbanization was phenomenal in China. The number of towns increased from 2,176 in 1978 to 11,481 in 1988. In some growing regions, such as the Pearl River Delta, small towns are growing faster than the cities, reverting the urbanization trend of most developing countries where cities are growing faster than towns (Xu and Li, 1990).

4 Issues of Urban Development in China

Economic reform, particularly the introduction of foreign investment, market economy, and private enterprises, has had great influence on urban development in China since it has been adopted in 1978. Economic reform has weakened the pre-1978 mechanisms of population control and state resource allocation that were effective in shaping urban development into a form desired by the government. The household registration system has been relaxed and there is increasing mobility of the people. The availability of free markets and the proliferation of individual enterprises outside the state system are rapidly eroding the household registration system which was effective in controlling population growth in the cities. The state is less relied on for providing employment and services. People can earn more outside the state system in private enterprises and enterprises involving foreign investment. The Chinese government no longer effectively controls urban development. Kwok (1988) observed that large cities were developing more rapidly than the government policy of "controlled development of large cities, rational development of medium-sized cities, and active development of small cities". There have been rapid changes in the urban system due to economic reform, particularly the weakening of previous mechanisms that were effective in controlling urban development. As a result, the following pressing issues have to be faced:

Floating Population

The most remarkable feature in urban development in China is the growth of the floating population (*liudong renkou*) in the large and medium-sized cities. The floating population is normally not included in the city statistics. In some cities they can be as large as 20 to 25% of the resident population. The percentage of the floating population in Guangzhou is the largest, being 38% of the resident population (Zou, 1990). There are two types of floating population - the transients who enter and leave the city within a few days or weeks, and those who may live there for an indefinite period of time. The building industry engages the largest proportion of floating population, followed by retailing. The Institute of Urban and Rural Economic Development in the Ministry of Construction has conducted a detailed study of the characteristics and problems of the floating population in the large cities (Li and Hu, 1991). They found that there is a rapid increase of the floating population in the large cities. The duration of stay of the floating population has increased. Most of them come to work in the cities, either self-employed or employed in the building and retailing sectors. Most of them are from villages and they are mainly male with low educational background. The presence of the floating population is alarming in some of the large cities. They have increased the crime rate and overloaded the cities' transport, infrastructure, and housing. The existence of the floating population partly results from the relaxation of the household registration system, and partly from the inefficiency of the household registration system in restricting non-registered people in the city. Non-registered people can bypass the household registration in getting their daily necessities from the free market.

Urban Land Use and Development Control

In the past, the internal structure of Chinese cities was strongly influenced by urban planning and state investment. These, however, are of diminishing importance when there are more and more firms and factories owned by individuals and financed through foreign capital. Although a "City Planning Act" was enacted in December 1989, it has not been effective in controlling land development. It mainly required the city government to prepare master plans which, however, are too broad for controlling site-specific development, leaving too much discretionary decision to the building administration and local district governments. The existing land use zones are too broad. Disputes may occur between the applicant for land development and the authority which grants the planning permission. It is difficult to reject a building on the basis of the existing land use zones because they are too broad. The actual location, type and intensity of development may not be what the planners had intended to achieve in the master and detailed plans. For example, a site zoned for public building may be used to build tall office buildings irrespective of whether it is a suitable site for office building and whether there is a need for cultural and recreational building in the neighbourhood. In the past, most of the offices, shops and commercial activities were owned and operated by government departments. All non-residential and non-industrial lands were considered as public building land. This is different from the concept of public building land in the Western free-market economy. Most of the land that is considered to be "public building" land in China would be regarded as office and commercial land in other countries. Because of the increasing private and foreign investments in the cities, land zoned for public buildings may no longer be under the control of the city government. Land zoned for public buildings may be developed into commercial offices and hotels for higher profits by government departments and state enterprises which want to make more money, leaving inadequate amount of land for other public buildings to meet the demand of the community for sports, cultural, and recreational facilities. The existing land use zone is too general. It cannot make sure that a certain type of land will be available at the right location and available at all. For example, land zoned for public building may be used to build offices and hotels irrespective of whether they are located at the right location. This is the reason why office buildings and hotels seem to be erected randomly in the city. If all public building land is developed into offices, there will not be any land left for public buildings for sports, culture and recreation. A new form of land development control is needed to cope with the new development. Shanghai as well as other cities are now experimenting to introduce zoning regulations to control the type and intensity of land use in the city. With the experimented zoning regulations, it is hoped that the objectives of the master and district plans can be better achieved and there is less dispute over the type and intensity of development in the planning permit application process. The building administration and local district governments will have less discretion over the type and development intensity of a site. It is hoped that an orderly and efficient land development can be achieved, avoiding incompatible land use.

Transport

Another major urban problem that has surfaced in the midst of China's urban and economic reform is that of city transport. The problem manifests itself in a number of ways, notably inadequate infrastructural development, rapid increase in motor vehicles, conflicts in urban land use and between public and private transport.

Take the case of Guangzhou as an example. Between 1949 and 1986, the city's road length increased from 228 km to 474 km, or by more than 200%, whereas road space expanded from 1.85 million square metres to 5.37 million square metres, or by nearly 300%. However, during a similar period from 1949 to 1988, Guangzhou's bicycles and motor vehicles have increased by 82 times and 81 times to 1.9 million and 0.158 million, respectively, and passenger travel volume by 27 times to 1.1 billion trips per day. Moreover, while the growth rate of the vehicular fleet was round 10-12% per annum in the 1970s, the same rate has increased to 22% per annum in the 1980s. Table 6 illustrates that since the open policy of the late 1970s, despite infrastructural development measured by road length and road space expansion, there has been a steady deterioration in terms of traffic volume by road length or road space.

As the city expands, and new areas of development such as the Tienhe and Huangpu districts are established, conflicts over land use and traffic arise between old and new city districts. To put it simply, the (old) central city is densely populated and developed, whereas the new districts are more spacious and located at some distance from the central city. This generates uneven cross-traffic, sharp peak hour demands, and increasing commuting or journey distances and time. All of these make the provision of efficient public transport in socialist China not an easy task.

Table 6: Growth of Traffic Volume and Road in Guangzhou

Years	Traffic volume at main junctions (average no. of cars at peak hour)	Growth Rate (%)			Road Capacity Rate/ Traffic Volume Rate	
		Traffic Volume	Road Length	Road Space	Length/ Volume	Area/ Volume
1976	818	100	100	100	1.00	1.00
1978	1.046	127	106.5	104.9	0.84	0.83
1982	1.925	235	108.4	116.2	0.46	0.49
1984	2.828	346	110.3	126.4	0.32	0.37

Source: Li Ping and Gan Hui-man, "On Urban Roads in Guangzhou and Improvement", in: *A Strategic Study of Guangzhou's Basic Infrastructural Development*, Guangzhou: Guangzhou Cultural Press, 1988, pp.77-89.

The worsening situation of the passenger transport can be attributed to the failure to resolve conflicts between public and private transport. In China, regarding the functions and characteristics, bicycle transport may be considered as some form of private transport. Yet it is a mode that has been nationally subsidized and heavily interwoven into the social fabrics. In Guangzhou, passenger trips are classified as motorised (32.02%), bicycle (29.95%) and walking (38.03%). Passenger trips made by bus and trolley bus account for only 21.63% or roughly two-thirds of the motorised trips, or 72% of the bicycle trips daily. Thus the more efficient motorised trips are not being fully utilized or developed, and the significant role of the bicycle poses problems on efficiency, safety, transport planning, and traffic management. Increasingly, the modern form of private transport in the form of motor-cycles and private cars is being introduced and further complicates the issue.

The traffic congestion problem is getting worse in the cities. There is an increase in the range of commuting because of the increasing separation of residences from work places. Moreover, the transport system is not growing fast enough to cope with the increases in passengers and motor vehicles. The situation is characterized by inadequate provisions of roads and a shortage of traffic control systems and facilities.

Environmental Pollution

Environmental degradation is an increasingly important problem in China. Although the Environmental Protection Act was initially adopted on a trial basis as early as 1979 and finally adopted in 1989, it was not effectively implemented, particularly in the small cities and towns. Environmental pollution is better controlled in the cities than towns. Many rural enterprises discharge water without any treatment (Chang and Kwok, 1990). The air pollution problem also becomes increasingly severe.

In the Pearl River Delta, one of the fastest growing regions in China in the post-1978 era, the threat to the environment does not come from the major cities in the region but from the rapidly growing small cities and towns (Yeh, Lam, Li and Wong, 1989). Despite the increase in population in Guangzhou in the first five years of the 1980s, the water quality of the Pearl River section downstream of Guangzhou has only shown a very minor deterioration trend (Huang, Wang, Cheng and Yang, 1988) because the increase in domestic sewage has been offset by a reduction of as much as 23 per cent in the discharge of industrial effluents during the same period as a result of tightening environmental control measures in Guangzhou. The industrial sector in Guangzhou was growing at a rate of 12 per cent per annum in this period, but environmental control measures had been able to reduce the amount of industrial effluent generation per industrial production unit by 16 per cent in these five years. Environmental control is much more relaxed outside the major cities of the Pearl River Delta region. The main threat comes from industrial development in small and medium-sized cities and towns and rural industrialization (Ma and Qiang, 1988). In the eyes of the industrialists, one of the attractions of the small and medium-sized cities and towns are their less stringent environmental control measures. Hong Kong and Macau are the major sources of foreign investment in the Pearl River Delta. Some of their polluting industries such as tannery and dyeing which are becoming more and more costly to operate because of the tightening of environmental control are moving their factories to the Pearl River Delta. Some industrial enterprises in Guangzhou also move to the countryside for similar reasons. Rapid industrial development in the small cities and towns has produced large amounts of industrial wastes, creating problems that are often beyond the capacity of the local authorities to handle. This has resulted in unabated pollution in many areas, rendering prime agricultural land less productive and causing oxygen depletion and eutrophication in receiving water bodies and subsequent contamination and reduced production of aquatic products (Shen, 1983).

5 Conclusion

The post-1978 economic reforms have opened the highly centralized controlled economy to a mixture of centralised and market economy. An increasingly number of people no longer rely on the state for income and housing. The pre-1978 mechanisms of population control and state resources allocation that were effective in controlling urban development now are less effective in shaping urban development. One of the main manifestations of the weakening central government in this respect is the marked increase of the floating population in the cities. The massive rural-urban migration that has plagued many large cities in the less developed countries may be becoming a major problem in China.

China is in the midst of economic reforms. It is uncertain how much more free market mechanism will be allowed in the future. The existing form of free market demonstrates that there is an urgent need to improve urban management. In the past, urban development to a large extent was controlled by the state through fund allocation. With the free market, the city governments have less control over the location and timing of development. Without good urban management, the land use pattern will be chaotic leading to inefficient use of the land and traffic congestion.

A lot of research on topics concerning urban development, such as urban economy, urban economic issues of regional industrialization, internal structure of cities, rural-urban migration, city size distribution (particularly the role of cities versus towns), and urban and regional planning, as suggested by Ma and Noble (1986) and by Pannell (1990), still has to be done in China. Geographers and planners could contribute not only by analyzing the past and current situation but also by proposing new ways of dealing with the new situation. For example, what is the most appropriate internal structure of cities that can meet the needs of the changing urban economy but avoid some of the known problems of the western cities? How to determine land prices when there is little land transaction? This presents a great challenge to geographers and planners.

Notes

1) The definition of urban population is most problematic in China, particularly since 1983 when many counties were abolished and turned into cities and 1984 when many townships were abolished and turned into towns (Chan and Xu, 1985; Ma and Cui, 1987). Urban population reported in the Statistical Yearbooks of China refers to the total agricultural and non-agricultural population within the administrative boundaries of the designated cities and towns, excluding the counties under the jurisdiction of the cities. This over-inflated the urban population of China because part of the agricultural population has been included. If this definition is used for the estimation of the urbanization level, the urbanization level of China would have increased from 17.9% in 1978 to an astonishing 51.7% in 1989. Over 63% of the urban population in 1989 has been agricultural population not involved in urban activities. Non-agricultural urban population in cities and towns is a better indicator for the urbanization level in China because it is less affected by changes in the boundaries of cities and towns and more involved in urban activities (Ma and Cui, 1987).
2) Cities are classified into four categories based on the non-agricultural population in the city proper (*shiqu*) and suburban districts (*jiaoqu*) (State Council, 1984). Extra-large cities are those with a non-agricultural population of over one million; large cities are those with a population between one million and 500,000, medium-sized cities between 500,000 and 200,000, and small cities less than 200,000.

References

Chan, Kam Wing and Xueqiang Xu (1985): "Urban Population Growth and Urbanization in China Since 1949: Reconstructing a Baseline", *China Quarterly*, No.104, pp.583-613

Chang, S.D. (1976): "The Changing System of Chinese Cities", *Annals of the Association of American Geographers*, Vol.66, No.3, pp.398-415

Chang, S.D. (1989): "The Changing Pattern of Chinese Cities 1953-84", in: Chi-Keung Leung, Chi-Yung Jim and Dakang Zuo (eds.), *Resources, Environment and Regional Development*, Hong Kong: Centre of Asian Studies, University of Hong Kong, pp.302-331

Chang, S.D. and R.Y. Kwok (1990): "The Urbanization of Rural China", in: R.Y. Kwok, W. Parish, and A.G.O. Yeh (eds.), *Chinese Urban Reform - What Model Now?*, New York: M.E. Sharpe, pp.140-157

Fei, Xiaotung (1984): "Small Town, Big Problem" (in Chinese), Jiangsu Province Small-Town Research Group, Compendium 1, Nanjing: Jiangsu People's Press

Fong, Peter K.W. (1988): "The Commercialization of Housing in a Socialist State: An Attempt to Solve China's Urban Housing Problem", *Planning Quarterly*, pp.32-36

Huang, X., J. Wang, G. Cheng, and Z. Yang (1988): "Water Quality of the Zhujiang River (Guangzhou river Beach) in Early 80's", in: P. Hills et al. (eds.), *Pollution in the Urban Environment: POLMET 88*, Vol.2, pp.438-443

Jao, Y.C. and C.K. Leung (eds.) (1986): *China's Special Economic Zones: Policies, Problems and Prospects*, Hong Kong: Oxford University Press

Kirkby, R.J.R. (1985): *Urbanization in China: Town and Country in a Developing Economy 1949-2000 A.D.*, London: Croom Helm

Kwok, R.Y. (1988): "Metropolitan Development in China: A Struggle Between Contradictions", *Habitat International*, Vol.12, No.4, pp.195-207.

Lardy, N. (1978): *Economic Growth and Distribution in China*, Cambridge: Cambridge University Press

Leung, C.K. (1980): *Railway Patterns and National Goals*, Chicago: University of Chicago, Department of Geography, Research Paper No.195

Leung, C.K. (1983): "China in Readjustment: An Introduction", in: C.K. Leung and Steve Chin (eds.), *China in Readjustment*, Hong Kong: University of Hong Kong, Centre of Asian Studies, pp.3-9

Leung, C.K. (1986): "Spatial Redeployment and the Special Economic Zones in China: An Overview", in: Y.C. Jao and C.K. Leung (eds.), *China's Special Economic Zones, Policies, Problems and Prospects*, Hong Kong: Oxford University Press, pp.1-18

Li, Mengbai and Xin Hu (1991): *The Impacts of Temporary Population on the Development of Large Cities and Measures in Dealing with Them* (in Chinese), Beijing: Economic Daily Press

Lin, Zhiqun (1986): "On the Policy of Housing Commercialization", *Building in China*, No.1, pp.1-9

Linge, G.J.R. and D.K. Forbes (1990): "The Space Economy of China", in: J.R. Linge and D.K. Forbes (eds.), *China's Spatial Economy: Recent Developments and Reforms*, Hong Kong: Oxford University Press

Lo, C.P. (1987): "Socialist Ideology and Urban Strategies in China", *Urban Geography*, Vol.8, No.5, pp.440-458

Ma, Laurence J.C. and Allen G. Noble (1986): "Chinese Cities: A Research Agenda", *Urban Geography*, Vol.7, No.7, pp.279-290

Ma, Laurence J.C. and Gonghao Cui (1987): "Administrative Changes and Urban Population in China", *Annals of the Association of American Geographers*, Vol.77, No.3, pp.373-395

Ma, Shiaoling and Binhuan Qiang (1988): "Environmental Management of Village and Township Enterprises in Guangdong Province", in: P. Hills et al. (eds.), *Population in the Urban Environment: POLMET 88*, Vol.1, pp.125-128

Pannell, Cliften W. (1990): "China's Urban Geography", *Progress in Human Geography*, Vol.14, No.2, pp.214-236

Philips, D.R. and A.G.O. Yeh (1987): "The Provision of Housing and Social Services in China's Special Economic Zone", *Environment and Planning C: Government and Policy*, Vol.5, pp.447-468

Phillips, D.R. and A.G.O. Yeh (1990): "Foreign Investment and Trade - Impact on Spatial Structure of the Economy", in: Cannon, T. and Jenkins, A. (eds.) (1990), *The Geography of Contemporary China: The Impact of Deng Xiaoping's Decade*, London: Routledge pp.224-248

Shen, Tsan-Hsin (1983): "Ecological Balance in the Pearl River Delta", *Asian Geographer*, Vol.2, No.2, pp.1-10

State Council, PRC (1984): *Regulations on City Planning* (in Chinese), Beijing: State Council

State Statistical Bureau (1990): *The Forty Years of Urban Development*, Beijing: China Statistical Information and Consultancy Service Center

Tang, Yunbin (1989): "Urban Land Use in China", *Land Use Policy*, Vol.6, No.1, pp.53- 63

Walker, Anthony (1991): *Land, Property and Construction in the People's Republic of China*, Hong Kong: Hong Kong University Press

Whyte, M.K. and W.L. Parish (1984): *Urban Life in Canada*, Chicago: University of Chicago Press

Wu, Y.L. (1967): *The Spatial Economy of Communist China*, New York: Praeger

Xie, Yichun and Frank J. Costa (1991): "The Impact of Economic Reforms on the Urban Economy of the People's Republic of China", *Professional Geographer*, Vol.43, No.3, pp.318-335

Xu, Xueqiang (1984a): "Characteristics of Urbanization in China - Changes and Causes of Urban Population Growth and Distribution", *Asian Geographer*, Vol.3, pp.15-29

Xu, Xueqiang (1984b): "Trends and Changes of the Urban System in China", *Third World Planning Review*, Vol.6, No.1, pp.47-60

Xu, Xueqiang, Huaying Hu, and A.G.O. Yeh (1989): "Factorial Ecological Study of Social Spatial Structure of Guangzhou" (in Chinese), *Acta Geographica Sinica* (1989), Vol.44, No.4, pp.385-399

Xu, Xueqiang and Si Ming Li (1990): "China's Open Door Policy and Urbanization in the Pearl River Delta", *International Journal of Urban and Regional Studies*, Vol.14, No.1, pp.49-69

Yeh, A.G.O. (1985): "Physical Planning", in: K.Y. Wong and D.K.Y. Chu (eds.), *Modernization in China: The Case of the Shenzhen Special Economic Zone*, Hong Kong: Oxford University Press, pp.108-130

Yeh, A.G.O., K.C. Lam, S.M. Li and K.Y. Wong (1989): "Spatial Development in the Pearl River Delta: Development Issues and Research Agenda", *Asian Geographer*, Vol.8, Nos.1 & 2, pp.1-9

Yeh, Anthony Gar-On and Xueqiang Xu (1984): "Provincial Variation of Urbanization and Urban Primacy in China", *The Annals of Regional Science*, Vol.23, No.3, pp.1-20

Yeh, A.G.O. and Xueqiang Xu (1990a): "Changes in City Size and Regional Distribution 1953-86", in: R.Y. Kwok, W. Parish, and A.G.O. Yeh (eds.), *Urban Reform - What Model Now?*, New York: M.E. Sharpe, pp.45-61

Yeh, A.G.O. and Xueqiang Xu (1990b): "New Cities and City System Development in China 1953-86", *Asian Geographer*, Vol.9, No.1, pp.11-38

Zou, Deci (1990): "The Review and Prospect of Chinese Urban Planning from 1980s to 1990s", *China City Planning Review*, Vol.6, No.3, pp.3-16

Urban Systems in China and India - A Comparison

by Dirk Bronger

1 Relevance of the Problem

Meanwhile a large number of articles as well as books exists stating the fact that the urbanization of the earth is to be considered one of the most fundamental global processes of change in the history of humankind. However, a general comparison between the urbanization processes of the "Industrialized Countries (I.C.)" and the "Developing Countries (D.C.)" reveals the fact that this radical change covering all spheres of life, has taken quite a different course between these two: Caused by a rapid population growth in the second half of this century from 2.5 billion in 1950 to around 6.3 billion at the end of this century, i.e. by 2 1/2 times, the growth of the *urban* population will amount to 4.6 times within this period (Tab. 1-III). But whereas the growth rate of the total population will be roughly 2 : 1 in favour of the D.C.s, the growth of the urban population of the D.C.s will be more than 3 times higher than that of I.C.s within this fifty year period (Tab. 1-III).

The most striking difference of this process is to be seen in the fast-growing concentration of the population within very large cities, i.e. the metropolises: Whereas the growth of the metropolitan population (in places with more than 1 million inhabitants) in the I.C.s is forecasted from 105 to 350 mio., i.e. by 3.3 times, it will rise from 56.5 to about 910 mio., i.e. by more than 16 times in the countries of the "Third" World! (Tab.1-I & II). Whereas in 1940 just two out of 100 lived in a metropolitan city here, in 1980 this proportion already comprised 10; at the end of this century almost every fifth (Tab.1-VI) or nearly every second urban dweller will live in a metropolitan city (Tab.1-V).

To sum up: The actual population "explosion" of the "Third" World Countries has taken place in the metropolitan cities. Moreover, these figures prove that *"metropolization"* is an entirely independent problem within the context of the global process of urbanization. Already because of severe financial constraints the state governments in general and the urban authorities in particular cannot cope with the gigantic socio-economic problems, both internal and external, caused by such an explosive growth. *Internally* there is to be noted a marginalization of the constantly expanding population strata of the metropolises accompanied by widening income disparities. A serious consequence is the steadily increasing percentage of the slum and squatter areas - of much higher dynamics than the overall demographic "explosion" - within these cities.

Table 1: Urbanization/Metropolization Process 1950-2000 - D.C - I.C.

No.		1950 D.C.	1950 I.C.	1980 D.C.	1980 I.C.	1990 D.C.	1990 I.C.	2000 D.C.	2000 I.C.
I	Metropolitan Population (absolute figures - in mio.)	56.5	105.3	327.6	243.4	571.9	301.3	908.1	350.0
II	Growth of Metropolitan Population (1950 = 100)	100	100	580	231	1.012	286	1.607	332
III	Urban Population (absolute figures - in mio.)	275.0	443.7	977.6	822.4	1.430.6	950.0	2.206.0	1.065.3
IV	Growth of Urban Population (1950 = 100)	100	100	355	185	520	214	802	240
V	Metropolitan : Urban Population Ratio (figures in %)	20.5	23.7	33.5	29.6	39.9	31.7	44.8	32.9
VI	Metropolitan : Total Population Ratio (figures in %)	3.4	12.7	9.9	21.4	14.2	24.9	18.7	27.4

D.C.: Latin America, Africa, Asia (excluding Japan), Oceania. I.C.: North America, Europa (including Soviet Union), Japan.

Sources: UN (Ed., 1980): *1977 Compendium of Social Statistics*, New York; UN (Ed., 1982): *World Population Trends and Policies: 1981 Monitoring Report*, Vol.I, New York; UN (Ed., 1985): *World Population Trends and Policies: 1983 Monitoring Report*, New York; UN (Ed., 1986): *World Populations Prospects. Estimates and Projections as Assessed in 1984*, New York; various individual (= country-based) sources (author's calculations).

However, a definately much more essential component of the phenomenon "metropolization"[1] than the already high percentage of population (*demographic primacy*) is to be seen in the concentration not only of the political and administrative functions but also of the economic, social and cultural activities on the capital region - in short, the *functional primacy* of the metropolis. Apart from the four subcontinental states of China, India, Indonesia and Brazil, all vital functions are concentrated in the mostly sole metropolitan region (including the larger capitals); when related to the strong and disproportionate growth of the population (see: App.2A & B) this becomes even more pronounced.

This overconcentration of all the major functions of life in a single or, as in China and India, in relatively few metropolises produces serious consequences *externally*: a serious development gap between the metropolitan city on the one hand and the vast majority of the remaining regions within the country concerned on the other. In concrete terms this means the stagnation of almost all the other regions forming the dynamization of the regional development incline between the centre (metropolis) and the periphery. This stagnation even includes the vast majority of the higher ranking regional centres. These often neglected centres, particularly the smaller ones cannot even properly perform their essential functions - to ensure that the rural population is supplied with its basic needs - quite apart from providing development stimuli for "their" region.

To sum up: The dynamics of metropolization and the regional disparities in the respective country's development which are directly and causally linked with those dynamics have become a major feature of the spatial structure, while their consequences have become a serious development problem for the "Third World" Countries. The aim of this paper is to attempt a comparative analysis between China and India regarding the demographic dimensions of the "urbanization", i.e. of the larger cities (> 100.000) in general and the functional dimension of the phenomenon of "metropolization" including the spatial consequences of this process.[2]

2 The Concept of Comparative Research: Objectives and Constraints (Note)

International comparisons in which subjects are compiled and discussed are widespread. The phenomenon of "urbanization" is no exception; comparative studies on this topic are numerous. Concerning the demographic aspect we may cite the "UN Demographic Yearbook" and the "World Development Report" as particularly well-known series. In the latter the degree of urbanization, i.e. the urbanization quota is named a so-called "development indicator".

The usefulness of such studies lies in the fact, that such comparisons make problems and even figures more transparent. For example the figure of 14.2% metropolitan population in relation to the D.C.'s population in total (Tab. 1-VI) reveals first that this proportion in China still is comparatively quite low, i.e. just over one third (5.46% - see Tab.2) and second that out of the 27 provinces - leaving Beijing, Tianjin and Shanghai aside - only one, the industrialized province of Liaoning exceeds this figure (Tab. 3). The disadvantage or even the danger of such studies lies in the fact that they suggest a comparability which is at least questionable. Again the example of the urbanization quota may show this: The pertinent area on which these figures are based, are (almost) never given. Yet this would be a precondition of the validity and comparability of any conclusions. To cite the best-known source of such frequent "confusing" information: The population figure of Manila given in the "UN Demographic Yearbook" is based on 38 sqkm, whereas the one of Beijing refers to 16.808 and that of Los Angeles to an area of 88.000 sqkm. However, this necessary information is not given in this compendium! Moreover, such aspects as the determination of the population figure of towns and cities and thus the degree of urbanization/metropolization in order to make a cross-country comparison significant are seldom discussed in the literature concerned.[3]

Similar basic difficulties regarding a cross-country comparison of urban systems exist also for India and China - leaving aside the numerous constraints to define the urban population of China itself, a subject already extensively discussed.[4] In contrast to the more or less limited "urban area" in India, the population figures of Chinese cities refer to a much bigger area including an often considerable agricultural umland.[5] Even the "city proper" area in most of the cases is considerably larger than the one of the "urban agglomeration" in India (see: App. 1A + 1C - col.5: 1B + 1D - col.3). Consequently already the city area includes a respectable amount of agricultural population; in the case of Beijing this proportion amounts to 22%, in Tianjin to 26% etc. (see: App.1A, col.6:7). Taking these difficulties into account the figures for the non-agricultural population (App. 1A + C, col.7: 1B + D, col.4) could be compared best.

Regarding China's past in view of getting data for the urbanization/metropolization process (Tab.2), we are faced with a number of additional difficulties:

- Frequent and sometimes extensive changes in urban area. They refer to almost all the cities, however in a quite different dimension from city to city.[6]

- Regarding these aerial changes quite contradictory figures are to be found in the literature concerned (see esp. App.3A - for Shanghai & 3B for Shenyang).

- The non-agricultural population for urban places, recently compiled continuously since 1949[7] does not exist according to order of cities/towns.

Because of these circumstances I had to use the "urban population living in urban places" published according to order of cities/towns by Ullman already in 1961. This figure admittedly is a bit higher than that of the above-mentioned compilation by Ma/Cui (1987). - In contrast to the "Chinese puzzle" the territorial extensions of the Indian metropolitan cities, even in the case of Urban Agglomeration areas, were comparatively limited in the past 30 years (App.3C). However, all figures given in App.1B & 2B have been computed to the present area.

The results derived from the available data can be summarized as follows:

3 The Demographic Dimension

3.1 Urbanization[8]/Metropolization Quota

On the *national* level India (16.68%) and particularly China (12.44% - Tab.2) still rank clearly below the *urbanization quota* of the D.C.s (= 24.1% - Tab.1) as well as most of their Asian neighbours. As mentioned earlier a similar pattern can be derived regarding the *degree of metropolization*: especially the quota of China (5.46%) is still far below the D.C.s average of 14.2% (Tab.1).

Urban Systems in India and China 37

Table 2: Metropolization/Urbanization - Process in China and India 1951/53 - 1989/91 (MQ = Metropolization Quota; UQ = Urbanization Quota)

Size class	Year	CHINA			INDIA			
		No. (000) (%)	Population (1) (000)	MQ/UQ (%)	Year	No.	Population	MQ/UQ
> 1 Mill.	1953	9	17.474	3.00	1951	5	11.997	3.33
> 500.000		16	9.377	1.61		4	2.967	0.82
> 100.000		77	13.046	2.24		65	12.344	3.42
		102	39.897 (4)	6.85		74	27.308	7.57
> 1 Mill.	1981	18	39.035	3.90	1981	12	42.612	6.24
> 500.000		28	20.376	2.04		30	19.834	2.90
> 100.000		134	31.051	3.10		174	31.847	4.66
		180	90.462	9.04		216	94.293	13.80
> 1 Mill.	1989	30	60.710	5.46	1991	23	71.553	8.48 (3)
> 500.000		28	19.170	1.72		30	20.856 (2)	2.49 (2)
> 100.000		272	58.440	5.26		247	47.788 (2)	5.71 (2)
		330	138.320	12.44		300	140.197 (2)	16.68 (2)

(1) Non-Agricultural Population; (2) excludes Jammu & Kashmir; (3) relates to All-India; (4) "urban population" living in "urban places". The total population living in "urban places" of > 100.000 in 1953 amounted to 47.992 (calculated from: Ullman, 1961: 93).
Sources: China - see: APP.1A & 2A; India - see: APP.1B & 2B (author's calculations).

As far as the *regional* level is concerned (Tab.3) the picture, due to the sub-continental character of both countries, is quite different. Generally speaking there is quite a pronounced heterogeneousness regarding the level of metropolization *within* the two countries. In China as well as in India around one third of the provinces and states, respectively, - 8 (1981: 13) out of the 27 provinces[9] in China and 5 (1981: 8) of the 17 major states in India[10] - are still without any metropolitan city and some are even far away from developing one. The latter statement refers particularly to India (Assam, Haryana, Himachal Pradesh, Orissa), whereas in the year 2000 most likely only 4 provinces of China (Guangxi, Tibet, Qinghai & Ningxia) will remain without a metropolitan city.

In particular we can state so far only a very limited number of regions with an already comparatively pronounced metropolization quota of at least two times above the national average: Maharashtra (21.2%) and, close to it, West Bengal (16%) and Gujarat (14.4%) in India; Liaoning (19.7%) and Jilin (11.1%) in China - leaving aside the special cases of Delhi and Beijing, Tianjin and Shanghai, respectively. Thus, the data interpretation on a regional basis discloses a number of concurrences.

Table 3: Metropolization in China and India - The Regional Dimension
(MQ: Metropolitan Quota; LED: Level of Economic Development)

India

STATE/UNION TERRITORY & Metropolis	MQ 1991	MQ 1981	LED[1] 1985	STATE/UNION TERRITORY & Metropolis	MQ 1991	MQ 1981	LED[1] 1985
1	2	3	4	1	2	3	4
ANDHRA PRADESH	8.03	4.75	103	MANIPUR	--	--	19
Hyderabad	6.45	4.75	432	MEGHALAYA	--	--	22
Vishakhapatnam	1.58	--	94°	NAGALAND	--	--	26
ASSAM	--	--	44	MIZORAM	--	--	28
BIHAR	1.27	--	48	ORISSA	--	--	63
Patna	1.27	--	103°	PUNJAB	5.01	--	213
GOA	--	--	307	**Ludhiana**	5.01	--	285°
GUJARAT	14.36	7.48	120	RAJASTHAN	3.45	2.96	62
Ahmedabad	7.97	7.48	301	**Jaipur**	3.45	2.96	118°
Surat	3.68	--	138°	TAMIL NADU	13.65	8.86	133
Vadodara	2.71	--	200°	**Madras**	9.64	8.86	616
HARYANA	--	--	141	**Coimbatore**	2.04	--	192°
HIMACHAL PRADESH	--	--	61	**Madurai**	1.97	--	92°
JAMMU & KASHMIR	--	--	61	TRIPURA	--	--	43
KARNATAKA	9.17	7.87	107	UTTAR PRADESH	3.45	2.39	73
Bangalore	9.17	7.87	256°	**Kanpur**	1.52	1.48	134°
KERALA	3.91	--	105	**Lucknow**	1.20	0.91	209°
Cochin	3.91	--	183°	**Varanasi**	0.73	--	78°
MADHYA PRADESH	3.28	--	68				
Indore	1.67	--	169°	WEST BENGAL	16.00	16.84	128
Bhopal	1.61	--	290	**Calcutta**	16.00	16.84	1.036
MAHARASHTRA	21.19	20.18	119	DELHI	100.0	100.0	893
Bombay	15.97	15.42	1.088	OTHERS [3]	--	--	*
Pune	3.11	2.69	175°				
Nagpur	2.11	2.07	126°	**INDIA**	8.48	6.24	100
Kalyan	+	+	*				

China

PROVINCE & Metropolis	MQ 1990	MQ 1981	LED[2] 1989	PROVINCE & Metropolis	MQ 1990	MQ 1981	LED[2] 1989
1	2	3	4	1	2	3	4
BEIJING	54.87	51.72	313	SHANDONG	4.84	2.74	105
Beijing	54.87	51.72	411	Jinan	1.75	1.37	264
TIANJIN	52.57	50.18	236	Qingdao	1.75	1.37	294
Tianjin	52.57	50.18	354	Zibo	1.34	--	233
HEBEI	3.54	--	91	HENAN	1.37	--	72
Shijiazhuang	1.79	--	273	Zhengzhou	1.37	--	184
Tangshan	1.75	--	227	HUBEI	6.18	5.62	95
SHANXI	5.33	4.94	89	Wuhan	6.18	5.62	250
Taiyuan	5.33	4.94	259	HUNAN	1.81	--	76
NEI MONGOL	--	--	86	Changsha	1.81	--	269
LIAONING	19.74	14.59	169	GUANGDONG	4.78	3.97	155
Shenyang	9.21	8.31	277	Guangzhou	4.78	3.97	474
Dalian	4.39	3.42	365	GUANGXI	--	--	60
Fushun	3.07	2.86	357	HAINAN	--	--	97
Anshan	3.07	--	273	SICHUAN	3.68	3.30	66
JILIN	11.11	5.87	107	Chongqing	2.10	1.91	225
Changchun	6.87	5.87	196	Chengdu	1.58	1.39	170
Jilin	4.24	--	304	GUIZHOU	3.15	--	48
HEILONGJIANG	9.91	6.46	118	Guiyang	3.15	--	224
Harbin	6.89	6.46	236	YUNNAN	3.04	--	62
Qiqihar	3.02	--	152	Kunming	3.04	--	188
SHANGHAI	58.23	52.33	389	TIBET	--	--	72
Shanghai	58.23	52.33	439	SHAANXI	6.05	5.51	76
JIANGSU	3.15	2.83	134	Xi'an	6.05	5.51	195
Nanjing	3.15	2.83	312	GANSU	5.43	5.54	71
ZHEJIANG	2.59	--	134	Lanzhou	5.43	5.54	253
Hangzhou	2.59	--	414	QINGHAI	--	--	98
ANHUI	--	--	75	NINGXIA	--	--	87
FUJIAN	--	--	103	XINJIANG	7.15	--	107
JIANGXI	2.87	--	70	Urumqi	7.15	--	323
Nanchang	2.87	--	209	**CHINA**	**5.46**	**3.90**	**100**

1) CMIE-Index - see note 12;
2) NDP/Capita
3) Arunachal Pradesh, Sikkim, Andaman & Nicobar Islands, Chandigarh, Dadra & Nagar Haveli, Daman & Diu, Lakshadweep, Pondicherry| + included in Bombay;
* no figures avail.; ° metropolitan district (see: Note 12)

Sources: INDIA - Census 1981 & 1991
Centre for Monitoring Indian Economy
(Ed.) (1988): *Index of Levels of Economic Development Around 1985*, Bombay.
CHINA - State Statistical Bureau of the PRC (Ed.) (1981 ff.):
Statistical Yearbook of China 1981-1990.
-"- (1991): China Urban Statistics 1989, Beijing (chin.).
(Author's calculations)

What is more relevant, the *causes* for these *regional imbalances* coincide to a large extent:[11] The regions with a high metropolization quota correspond to the comparatively industrialized parts of both countries, and coincidently, the industrialization started in conjunction with the colonial, i.e. the economic interests of foreign countries mainly along the coastal areas including their hinterland: Calcutta and Bombay (together with its "outposts" Ahmedabad and Surat) in India, the "treaty ports", later the exploitation of former Manchuria, in China. On the other hand, the fact that those regions lacking metropolitan cities are more or less peripherically located, does not necessarily coincide with a generally low level of development and vice versa, at least in India (Haryana versus Bihar, Rajasthan & Madhya Pradesh - see: Tab.3, col.4).[12] In China a pronounced regional east-west incline is still existing mainly as a result of historical factors in combination with the natural constraints and despite a strong counter-balancing governmental policy (see below), whereas in India, due mainly to the different natural preconditions, such a clear-cut regional structure is not that apparent.

3.2 Urbanization/Metropolization Process

Although the 1953 figures regarding China have to be taken with caution,[13] we can state a relatively slow urbanization as well as metropolization process in both countries, especially in China in comparison with the "Third" World Countries as a whole within the last four decades (1950-1990 - figures in %):

	China		India		Total D.C.s	
	1953	1989	1951	1991	1950	1990
UQ*	3.85	6.98	4.24	8.20	4.95	9.91
MQ	3.00	5.46	3.33	8.48	3.40	14.20

*   cities > 100.000 and < 1 mio.   -   compiled from Tab. 1 & 2.

The major reason, apart from a comparatively low population growth (China only), seems to be that the rural-urban migration in both countries is quite below the extent to be observed in many "Third" World Countries. From the compiled data (App.2A & 2B) we can state a number of further concurrences between the two countries: On the one hand we find several cities with a comparative low growth rate (Calcutta, Kanpur, Coimbatore; Shenyang, Fushun, Changcha, Hangzhou); in China additionally two metropolises even below the national average, topped by Shanghai.[14]

On the other hand various metropolises in both countries show remarkable dynamics even in comparison with the fast growing metropolitan cities of other Asian countries like Bangkok, Djakarta, Seoul and Karachi: Delhi, Bangalore,

Surat, Jaipur and Vishakhapatnam in India, and in China the interior cities of Xian, Lanzhou and Qiqihar topped by Urumqi.[15] In general India can claim a faster metropolization rate.

All in all, however, the differences predominate. First of all the growth of the larger metropolises is considerably slower in China than in India (except Calcutta). This is especially relevant with regard to the metropolises along the coastal areas. Surprisingly even the capital of Beijing shows a relatively more moderate growth, especially in comparison with its counterpart Delhi. As indicated by a number of authors[16] this fact manifests that the rapid growth of quite a number of big cities all over China, due mainly to heavy immigration up to 1958, has considerably slowed down in the majority of cities; this means that the official policy was successful in its efforts to contain the growth of the largest cities (Shanghai, Tianjin, Shenyang, Guangzhou, Chongqing and even Beijing) substantially and "to redirect the main focus on urban development to newer cities of the interior."[17]

This unquestionable success of "urban decentralization"[18], however, should not be overinterpreted, because to some extent it seems double-edged. As far as the 'metropolitan decentralization' is concerned a more detailed view reveals, firstly, that half of the 30 Chinese metropolises show a still noticeable increase of 30% and more above the national average (App.2A, col. 15). Secondly, several coastal metropolises have manifested a recovering metropolitan growth since the second half of the seventies. *Shanghai* may serve as an example because the most detailed though not indisputed (App.3A) figures[19] are available here: After an impetuous growth up to the 1960s, the city's growth rate has not only been reduced drastically but decreased by almost one million from 1965 to 1977 (App.3A). However, it increased by 2.744 million from 1977 to 1990 (from 5.470 to 8.214); this was at least partly caused by a net immigration on an average of 138.000 per year for the period of 1978-1980 and a considerable extension of the city area after 1988 (App.3A). Thirdly, this spatial redirection had to be paid for, maybe even dearly, by a pronounced primacy of the rapidly growing metropolitan capitals like Lanzhou etc. causing a remarkable metropolitan-rural development incline within the respective provinces (see: Tab.3, col.4), with which we will deal in the next chapters.

To sum up: Despite some success in limiting the metropolitan growth especially in China, this struggle still remains a major challenge for both countries.

4 The Functional Dimension

4.1 Functional Primacy: The Concept

In our introductory chapter we stressed the functional primacy as the vital component of our concept of metropolization. The *functional primacy* is characterized by two main features:[20]

Table 4: Primacy of Large Metropolitan Cities: Bombay - Shanghai - Paris

No.	Indicator	Year	Bombay GB¹	B.M.R.²	Year	Shanghai Shiqu	Quanshi	Year	Paris A.U.P.³	R.P.⁴
	State/Province		Maharashtra			Jiangsu (+ Shanghai)			France	
	Area (000 qkm)	1981	308		1984	108		1982	547	
	Population (Mill.)	1981	62.8		1984	73.8		1982	54.4	
	I Demographic Primacy									
1	Area (sqkm)	1981	603	4.350	1984	340	6.186	1982	1.000	12.012
2	% of total area	1981	0,2	1,41	1984	0,3	5,73	1982	0,2	2,20
3	Population	1981	8.243	10.724	1984	6.881	12.048	1982	7.156	10.057
4	% of total population	1981	13,1	17,1	1984	9,3	16,3	1982	13,1	18,5
	II Functional Primacy									
5	Net Domestic Product (%)⁵,⁶	1980	33,2	38,7	1984		38,6	1981		26,8
6	NDP/Capita - Metropolis: remaining areas	1980	4,7:1		1984	6,6:1	3,2:1	1981		ca. 3:1
7	Income Tax (%)	1984	7,1					1981		39,37
8	Industry: Employment (%)	1984	88,8	45,8				1981		22,0
9	Industry: Gross Output Value (%)	1983⁸	56,7	58,4	1984	39,3	52,3	1982		ca. 25,0
10	Cargo handled by Ports (%)	1983⁸	47,0		1981 / 1984	17,3⁹	41,3			
11	No. of Telephones (%)	1981 / 1984	21,0	78,7	1984		51,0	1983	-	19,9
12	University & College Students (%)	1982	40,3		1984	43,4	48,4	1974		30,8

Table 4: Primacy of Large Metropolitan Cities: Bombay - Shanghai - Paris (cont.)

13 Hospital beds (%)	1980	32,8	37,3	1984	19,7	29,9	1974	16,7
14 No. of Doctors (%)				1984	31,8	39,4	1982	22,0
15 TV-sets (%)	1980	82,3	91,3				1983	19,6
16 Bed capacities of 3-, 4- & 5-star hotels (%)	1983	87,4	89,2	1985	$>50^{10}$		1984	16,3
17 - de luxe category (5-star) (%)	1983	87,4	87,4	1985	$>70^{10}$		1984	44,1

1) Greater Bombay; 2) Bombay Metropolitan Region; 3) Agglomération urbaine Parisienne; 4) Région Parisienne; 5) See Tab.2 - col.4 & 8; 6) Explanations: see Note 12; 7) Total taxes; 8) Large & Medium Scale Industry only; 9) Export only; 10) Estimated figure.

Sources:
Bombay - Tab.2 & 8 + Government of Maharashtra (Ed.), Statistical Abstract of Maharashtra State for the year 1979-80, Nagpur 1984; MIDC, Bombay (Ed.) Unpublished Records; Indian Posts & Telegraphs Department, Ministry of Communication (Ed.), *Annual Report 1983-84, Delhi 1985*.

Shanghai - Tab.2 & 8.

Paris - INSEE (Ed.), *Tableaux Economique de L'Ile-de-France 1984*, Paris 1984; Conseil Régional d'Ile-de-France (Ed.); *Panorama d'Ile-de-France*, Paris 1984; Pletsch, A. (1981): *Les Cahiers de l'Institut d'Amanagement et d'Urbanisme de la Région d'Ile-de-France*, No.68-Juin 1983, Paris; Service de Tourism Michelin (Ed.), *Michelin France 1984*, Paris.
(author's calculations)

Table 5: Functional Primacy of Metropolitan Cities in China I:
National Level - 1989 (Figures in %)

Nr.	Indicator	Shang-hai	Bei-jing	Tian-jin	Metropolitan Cities (27)	Primacy Index (3-5)	Primacy Index (3-6)	Primacy Ratio (3-5)	Primacy Ratio (6)	Primacy Ratio (3-6)
1	2	3	4	5	6	7	8	9	10	11
I	**POPULATION**									
1	- Population: city proper (shiqu)	0,70	0,62	0,51	5,07	1,83	6,90			
II	**ECONOMY - GENERAL**									
2	- National Income:									
	Total	2,98	2,02	1,78	12,88	6,78	19,66	3,70	2,54	2,85
	-- Agriculture	0,05	0,09	0,68	2,07	0,82	2,89	0,45	0,41	0,42
	-- Industry	4,51	2,93	2,42	18,56	9,86	28,42	5,39	3,66	4,12
	-- Construction	2,92	4,26	1,85	15,10	9,03	24,13	4,93	2,98	3,50
	-- Transportation	5,54	1,61	3,16	20,74	10,31	31,05	5,63	4,09	4,50
	-- Commerce	4,17	2,73	1,77	16,34	8,67	25,01	4,74	3,22	3,62
3	- National Income/Capita (PRC = 100)	424	323	346	253					
4	- Economy: Industry	4,70	2,75	2,46	18,43	9,91	28,34	5,42	3,64	4,11
5	- Economy: Services	3,16	2,73	1,52	14,72	7,41	22,13	4,05	2,90	3,20
III	**TRANSPORTATION & COMMUNICATION**									
6	- Cargo handled at Principal Seaports	29,79	--	4,97	26,33	34,76	61,09	19,00	5,19	8,85
7	- Passenger Traffic: Air	11,73	14,51	0,52	52,84	26,76	79,60	14,62	10,42	11,54
8	- Telephones	4,60	5,88	1,50	19,34	11,98	31,32	6,55	3,81	4,54
IV	**EDUCATION & HEALTH**									
9	- Students enrolled in Institutions of Higher Learning	5,54	6,37	2,54	47,57	14,45	62,02	7,90	9,38	8,99
10	- Hospital Beds	1,62	1,74	1,10	14,81	4,46	19,27	2,44	2,92	2,79
11	- Professional Medical Personal	2,36	2,44	1,53	16,26	6,33	22,59	3,46	3,21	3,27
12	- Doctors	2,59	2,47	1,60	15,63	6,66	22,29	3,64	3,08	3,23
V	**TOURISM**									
13	- Tourists: Foreigners	15,55	18,00	2,62	32,23	36,17	68,40	19,77	6,36	9,91
VI	**INVESTMENT**									
14	- Foreign Investment	12,44	9,39	2,14	13,34	23,97	37,31	13,10	2,63	5,41

Sources: *Zhongguo Chengshi Tongji Nianjian 1990*, Bejing 1991; SSB - PRC (Ed.): *China Statistical Yearbook 1990*, Chicago 1990.
Calculations by the author.

(1) Over-centralization or, more correctly, over-concentration of the main functions - here defined as *primacy indices* (PI) in almost every sphere of life; and - what is of specific importance

(2) the concentration of the population, which is already particularly high (metropolization quota = MQ), is by far surpassed by the figures of the indices for any other sector, i.e. the economic (except, of course, the primary sector), social, cultural, political and administrative sectors. We shall call this relationship between the pertinent primacy index (PI) and the demographic primacy index (MQ) the *primacy ratio* (PR). So PR = PI/MQ. In other words: the axiom PI > MQ or PR > 1 must be considered the crucial attribute of metropolitan primacy.

In order to determine the phenomenon of "metropolization as a development problem" it is of essential importance from the development-policy aspect to note that the over-concentration of every major function of life has occurred - in their vast majority - principally in the metropolises (including the capitals) of "Third" World Countries with strictly centralist governments - just as in the majority of the European nations up to the 20th century.

In this connection we have to argue with an objection often stressed in this discussion: the argument that a substantial number of metropolises within the Western world (e.g. Paris, London) show the same pronounced primacy. As the data compiled in Tab.4 reveal, this view is essentially true only with regard to the demographic aspect, at best to some of the cited functions but never[21] to the same extent and totality as in the "Third" World Countries.

4.2 Functional Primacy in China and India I: Present Situation (Tab.5-9)

Let us start with the present situation in China. As far as the "real" primacy, i.e. the primacy ratio of the metropolitan cities in China is concerned, comparatively detailed information on all cities is included in the data released by the Chinese Government since the mid-eighties. Together with the data published yearly in the *Statistical Yearbook* we can obtain the most comprehensive data set in comparison not only with regard to India but as I think to all countries of the "Third" World. The most relevant primacy indices for the 30 metropolises are compiled in Tab.5. Although not complete, this table contains data of almost all important dimensions: Population (No.I), Economy (II), Transportation and Communication (III), Education and Health (IV), Tourism (V) and Investment (VI). All in all these six dimensions are subdivided into 19 single indicators with regard to the *shiqu*-level figures. The data are proportionally computed according to the *national* level. Their interpretation will be summarized in the following main points:[22]

1. First and foremost the eminent *primacy ratio* in particular with respect to the three large metropolises (Shanghai - Beijing - Tianjin, Tab.5, col.9) and less but still pronounced with regard to the remaining 27 metropolises (col.10) up to the present reveals a strong primacy of these metropolitan cities.

2. The primacy is particularly pronounced in the *industrial and transportation sector*, even outstanding in certain single industrial branches. This is especially relevant for important consumer goods regarding the three major metropolitan cities as indicated in Tab.6.

Table 6: Proportion of Output of Major Industrial Products of Metropolitan Cities* in China - 1984

Product	Shanghai	Beijing	Tianjin	Primacy Index	Primacy Ratio
Sewing machines	31.5	4.8	10.0	46.3	16.3
Bicycles	19.6	0.2	18.3	38.1	13.4
Wrist watches	29.0	3.6	9.8	42.4	14.9
Chemical fibres	24.0	5.8	7.1	36.9	13.0
Cloth	11.1	2.0	3.3	16.4	5.8
Woollen piece goods	18.9	7.9	6.0	32.8	11.5
Leather shoes	9.7	4.7	6.7	21.1	7.4
Washing machines	10.6	8.9	1.8	21.3	7.5
Radio sets	24.2	3.5	1.7	29.4	10.4
TV sets	22.2	5.9	6.1	34.2	12.0
Cameras	35.2	4.2	7.4	46.8	16.5
Motor vehicles	2.9	11.3	3.2	17.4	6.1
Tractors **	21.7	--	20.6	42.3	14.9

* Provincial Level
** 20 horse power and over
Source: *Statistical Yearbook of China - 1985*, p.350 ff. (author's calculations).

3. This far-reaching statement (No.1) is supported by the up to now outstanding primacy of Shanghai compared to all other metropolitan cities. It exceeds the next-ranking metropolis, the capital city of Beijing, in 22 out of the 31 single indicators (Tab.5 & 6). In two cases the primacy index amounts to more than double, in three more than triple and in even eight indicators it surpasses the capital city by more than five times! All in all Shanghai has to be considered as the absolute economic center of the sub-continent: its GNP/capita (of Shanghai Province!) exceeded the national average by 4.2 times in 1988[23] - a high factor when compared to Manila (2.5 : 1), Bangkok (2.9 : 1) and Seoul (1.2 : 1)[24], the three most outstanding primate cities in the Far East.

4. Regarding the capital city of Beijing, however, specific dynamics can be observed concerning quite a number of indicators. This means a noticeable gain on Shanghai. The same is true with Guangzhou compared to Tianjin.- In terms of *international primacy* Beijing has clearly outnumbered Shanghai:

Table 7: International Primacy 1990: Beijing - Shanghai - Tianjin

Indicator	Beijing	Shanghai	Tianjin
Airlines	27	7	1
Foreign Banking & Finance Institutions	84	35	4
Foreign Companies	750	253	35
Hotels 1)	74	53	10

1) international standard.
Source: The China Phone Book Company Pvt. Ltd. (Ed.): *The China Phone Book & Business Directory 1991*, Hong Kong 1991 (author's calculations).

5. As far as the *regional* level is concerned (Tab.8), not only the large metropolitan cities but also the smaller metropolises in the newly developed western half of the country like Taiyuan, Lanzhou and Kunming (and here also the older ones: Xi'an and Wuhan) show a heavy concentration of metropolitan primacy within their region (province). When computing the primacy ratio it even comes close to the "real" primacy of the outstanding primate cities of Shanghai and Beijing in respect of most of the sectors - a certainly remarkable result despite the limitation and also superficiality of such a brief comparison. At the same time this clear-cut primacy discloses a pronounced *metropolitan-rural development incline within the regions*. These results reveal that the governmental policy of deconcentration is to be viewed as only partly successful.

In most aspects these statements find their confirmation when compared to the large Indian metropolitan cities (Tab.9). Like in China we can find a functional division here too: Analogous to Shanghai, Bombay represents the outstanding economic center of the sub-continent (see: esp. Indicators 8, 9, 10, 11 & 13), whereas Delhi's role as the capital is illustrated inter alia by the fast growing number of high-standard hotels (No.12). The same can be observed in respect of Beijing (since 1988).

Table 8: Functional Primacy of Metropolitan Cities in China II: Regional Level - 1989 (Figures in %)

PROVINCE/ Metropolis	I Population (Demographic Primacy) Metropolization Quota (%)	II Economy General National Income (%)	II Economy Industry Gross Output Value of Industry (%)	II Economy Services Total Value of Retail Sales (%)	III Transportation & Communication Passenger Traffic: Air (%)	III Transportation & Communication No. of Telephones (%)	IV Education & Health Stud. of Institut. of Higher Learning (%)	IV Education & Health Hospital Beds (%)	IV Education & Health Medical Technical Personnel (%)	V Tourism Foreign Tourists (%)	IV Investment Foreign Investment
1	2	3	4	5	6	7	8	9	10	11	12
HEBEI											
- Beijing	19,81	47,99	56,94	50,66	98,99	60,15	81,06	45,03	51,90	97,61	96,55
- Tianjin	8,90	22,09	25,53	28,19	94,88	42,35	49,21	21,47	26,58	84,36	76,23
- Shijiazhuang	7,33	19,49	22,89	15,72	3,40	10,80	19,60	13,77	16,72	12,28	17,34
- Tangshan	1,67	3,47	5,05	3,56	0,71	4,36	9,84	4,75	4,83	0,73	0,88
SHANXI	1,91	2,94	3,47	3,19	--	2,64	2,41	5,04	3,77	0,24	2,10
- Taiyuan	6,83	17,25	24,87	18,94	100,00	31,45	60,06	19,67	20,06	37,14	33,79
LIAONING	6,83	17,25	24,87	18,94	100,00	31,45	60,06	19,67	20,06	37,14	33,79
- Shenyang	24,71	46,21	52,39	44,03	96,36	48,17	82,95	41,32	45,19	88,01	87,92
- Dalian	11,62	19,12	21,56	21,55	57,16	23,44	46,66	18,55	21,87	31,05	22,39
- Anshan	6,11	13,58	14,42	12,66	37,25	12,35	28,95	11,66	11,19	49,92	64,29
- Fushun	3,54	7,85	8,77	4,82	1,95	6,03	3,66	6,08	6,68	5,18	1,07
JILIN	3,44	5,66	7,64	5,00	--	6,35	3,68	5,03	5,45	1,86	0,17
- Changchun	13,81	28,66	44,64	28,87	86,04	24,46	84,99	28,28	31,87	94,42	49,85
- Jilin	8,60	14,90	23,92	17,38	86,04	12,01	70,30	17,26	20,70	80,98	11,94
HEILONGJIANG	5,21	13,76	20,72	11,49	--	12,45	14,69	11,02	11,17	13,44	37,91
- Harbin	11,86	18,28	27,32	27,70	82,48	?	70,54	28,18	25,71	45,39	26,28
- Qiqihar	7,97	13,32	20,14	21,25	73,75	?	60,57	19,99	18,76	41,16	26,08
	3,89	4,96	7,18	6,45	8,73	7,84	9,97	8,19	6,95	4,23	0,20

Table 8: Functional Primacy of Metropolitan Cities in China II: Regional Level - 1989 (Figures in %) (cont.)

1	2	3	4	5	6	7	8	9	10	11	12
JIANGSU	13,12	28,85	31,23	32,83	97,53	45,81	67,69	23,51	36,53	79,59	85,41
- Shanghai	9,96	23,90	25,72	26,94	82,51	36,58	42,08	18,05	27,73	70,02	81,43
- Nanjing	3,16	5,25	5,51	5,89	15,02	9,23	25,61	5,46	8,80	9,57	3,98
ZHEJIANG	3,16	8,39	11,67	10,29	84,01	16,17	64,37	11,36	14,78	83,83	35,90
- Hangzhou	3,16	8,39	11,67	10,29	84,01	16,17	64,37	11,36	14,78	83,83	35,90
JIANGXI	3,59	9,26	17,41	11,15	91,07	21,54	55,30	12,42	14,28	52,77	52,47
- Nanchang	3,59	9,26	17,41	11,15	91,07	21,54	55,30	12,42	14,28	52,77	52,47
SHANDONG	8,19	18,36	25,91	19,45	79,95	31,70	52,32	20,22	24,29	66,99	54,63
- Jinan	2,71	5,91	7,63	7,18	3,08	12,93	34,83	8,07	10,62	12,26	3,57
- Qingdao	2,50	6,40	9,63	7,48	76,87	11,46	14,61	5,85	8,09	52,50	44,17
- Zibo	2,98	6,05	8,65	4,79	--	7,31	2,88	6,30	5,58	2,23	6,89
HENAN	2,02	5,13	9,25	6,86	82,72	18,91	42,83	7,99	10,52	28,97	9,02
- Zhengzhou	2,02	5,13	9,25	6,86	82,72	18,91	42,83	7,99	10,52	28,97	9,02
HUBEI	7,05	18,46	26,59	22,08	80,59	32,56	76,12	17,96	21,87	81,08	48,40
- Wuhan	7,05	18,46	26,59	22,08	80,59	32,56	76,12	17,96	21,87	81,08	48,40
HUNAN	2,17	6,65	11,24	9,89	100,00	17,84	52,28	6,94	9,88	33,30	15,62
- Changsha	2,17	6,65	11,24	9,89	100,00	17,84	52,28	6,94	9,88	33,30	15,62
GUANGDONG	5,88	15,41	20,64	17,40	87,11	22,44	67,70	17,47	21,65	55,21	11,60
- Guangzhou	5,88	15,41	20,64	17,40	87,11	22,44	67,70	17,47	21,65	55,21	11,60
SICHUAN	5,35	15,16	30,68	21,48	97,53	36,36	68,71	17,07	18,68	74,33	98,81
- Chengdu	2,59	7,37	13,40	10,11	83,09	21,77	38,87	8,09	9,61	45,48	38,86
- Chongqing	2,76	7,79	17,28	11,37	14,44	14,59	29,84	8,98	9,07	28,85	59,95
YUNNAN	4,13	18,59	34,43	19,40	96,38	28,93	82,69	20,75	20,63	77,48	86,00
- Kunming	4,13	18,59	34,43	19,40	96,38	28,93	82,69	20,75	20,63	77,48	86,00
SHAANXI	8,49	21,41	33,85	31,94	96,74	46,51	83,85	23,43	25,74	77,08	42,81
- Xi'an	8,49	21,41	33,85	31,94	96,74	46,51	83,85	23,43	25,74	77,08	42,81
GANSU	6,82	24,32	43,38	32,89	84,89	45,35	86,94	22,00	23,04	45,48	100,00
- Lanzhou	6,82	24,32	43,38	32,89	84,89	45,35	86,94	22,00	23,04	45,48	100,00
XINJIANG	7,64	21,13	30,55	24,11	73,38	12,44	63,85	15,89	19,64	32,89	k.A.
- Urumqi	7,64	21,13	30,55	24,11	73,38	12,44	63,85	15,89	19,64	32,89	k.A.

Sources: See Tab.5 - author's calculations. k.A. = No figures given.

Geographisches Institut
der Universität Kiel

50 Dirk Bronger

Table 9: Primacy of Large Metropolitan Cities (> 5 Mill.) - India : China

Indicator		Year	Bombay	Delhi	Calcutta	Year	Shanghai	Beijing	Tianjin
I	**Area & Population**								
1	Area (sqkm)	1981	603	1.483	852	1984	340	2.738	4.276
2	Population ('000)	1981	8.243	6.220	9.194	1984	6.881[1]	5.755[1]	5.312[1]
3	Metropolitan Quota (% of total)	1981	1,20	0,91	1,34	1984	0,65[2]	0,48[2]	0,40[2]
II	**Education & Health**								
4	Literacy Rate (%)	1981	68,2	62,7	65,5	1982	91,5	92,6	91,5
5	University & College Students: No. ('000)	1981	134	73	139	1984	81	101	40
	- % of total	1981	4,88	2,65	5,05	1984	5,78	7,21[3]	2,84[3]
6	Hospital Beds: No. ('000)	1984	27,2	13,1	37,7	1984	35,1	30,9	20,3
	-"-	1984	5,41	2,60	7,49	1984	1,62	1,43	0,94
III	**Industry**								
7	No. of Workers: % of total	1982	7,3[4]	1,6[4]	7,2[4]	1981	5,2	2,9	2,6
8	Value of Output: -"-	1982	10,82[4]	1,97[4]	5,51[4]	1985	7,97	3,75	3,49
IV	**Transportation & Communication**								
9	Cargo handled by Ports:								
	- Export (%)[5]	1981	9,0	-		1981	17,31[6]	-	
	- Import (%)[5]	1981	30,0	-			6	-	
	- Total (%)[5]	1981	21,0	-			6	-	
	-"- Total Trade: Total (Mill.t)								
10	International Airport Traffic - Passengers handled:					1984	100,66	-	16.11
	- No. ('000)	1985	7.597	4.867	1.859	1984	620[7]	1.090[7]	10[7]
	- % of total	1985	47,88	30,67	11,72	1984	10,40[7]	18,29[7]	0,17[7]
11	No. of Telephones:								
	- No. ('000)	1985	605	387	284	1984	130	123	49
	- % of total	1985	16,3	10,4	7,6	1984	4,7	4,4	1,8

Table 9: Primacy of Large Metropolitan Cities (> 5 Mill.) - India : China (cont.)

Indicator	Year	Bombay	Delhi	Calcutta	Year	Shanghai	Beijing	Tianjin
V Tourism								
12 Bed Capacities of 3-, 4- & 5-star hotels: No.	1983	7.575	9.811	2.112	1985	5.659		
- Luxury Hotels (5-star) only: No.	1983	3.924	4.403	717	1985	1.241		
VI Economy: General								
13 Income Tax (%)	1984	25,63	8,29	9,55	1984	9,86	2,89	2,61
Revenue (%)								

1) Total *shiqu*.
2) Relates to "Non-agricultural population" (see Tab.2).
3) Students enrolled in "institutions of higher learning".
4) Large & medium scale industry only. Approximate figures (for Calcutta).
5) Foreign trade only.
6) See explanations in: Handke, 1986: 17 f.
7) Including domestic airport traffic.

Sources:
India:
Census of India 1981, Series 1 - India. Primary Census Abstract. General Population, Delhi 1983;
TATA Services Limited, Department of Economics & Statistics (Ed.), *Statistical Outline of India 1986-87*, Bombay 1986;
Government of India, Ministry of Information and Broadcasting (Ed.), *India. A Reference Annual 1982*, New Delhi 1982;
Government of India, Ministry of Planning (Ed.), Annual Survey of Industries 1981-82, New Delhi 1985;
ESCAP, et al. (Ed.), *City Monographs: Bombay*, Yokohama 1982; *Hotel and Restaurant Guide India 1983*, New Delhi 1983;
Central Board of Direct Taxes (Ed.), unpublished records, New Delhi 1986.
China:
State Statistical Bureau, PRC (Ed.), *Statistical Yearbook of China 1985*, Hongkong 1985;
State Statistical Bureau, PRC (Ed.), *China. Urban Statistics 1985*, Hongkong 1985;
Shanghai Tongji Nianjian 1986, Shanghai 1986; Handke, W., *Shanghai. Eine Weltstadt öffnet sich*, Hamburg 1986.

Regarding the latest available data concerning telephone extensions (Tab.10) - here China has recently outnumbered India per capita - the metropolitan-rural development incline is significantly more pronounced in India: Half of all the telephones can be found in 12 metropolitan cities (of 1981) only; more than one third are concentrated in the three mega cities alone. However, also in China we still find a clear-cut urban-rural incline: the share of the (statistically!) 50.4% rural population amounts to only 20.9% (1988).[25]

Table 10:   Metropolitan Primacy China - India: Number of Telephones

Metropolis	No. of Telephones (1986)			Metropolis	No. of Telephones (1988)		
	No.(000)	Share (%) national	regional		No.(000)	Share (%) national	regional
1	2	3	4	1	2	3	4
Bombay	652.3	16.1	77.1[3]	Shanghai shi	396.5	4.2	35.5[6]
Delhi	426.4	10.5	89.0[4]	Beijing shi	669.5	7.1	59.5[7]
Calcutta	299.4	7.4	84.0[5]	Tianjin shi	215.6	2.3	32.0[8]
Total other metropolises[1]	1.378.1 653.0	34.0 16.1		Total other metropolises[2]	1.281.6 1.563.4	13.6 16.6	
Grand Total	2.031.1	50.1		Grand Total	2.845.0	30.2	

1) Number as of 1981;   2) number as of 1985;   3) Maharashtra;
4) Delhi & Haryana;   5) West Bengal;   6) Shanghai & Jiangsu;
7) Beijing & Hebei;   8) Tianjin & Hebei.
Sources: China - see: Tab.3, 4, 5 & 1A; India - see: Tab.4, 5 & 1B
(author's calculations).

4.3 Functional Primacy in China and India II:
Interdependencies between Metropolization and Regional Structures
(Tab.11; Maps 1 & 2)

Although detailed data are not available for India especially on the regional level (Tab.8), the specific spatial-functional structure can be observed here, too. Based on approximate per capita income figures[26] the following compilation gives at least an idea of the striking difference regarding the economic development between the larger metropolitan cities and "their" surrounding region on different spatial levels in China[27] and India - especially in comparison with the metropolitan cities of the United States (Tab.11):

Urban Systems in India and China 53

Table 11: Interdependencies between Metropolitan Primacy and Level of Economic Development - Regional Levels: China - India - USA

Metropolis	Year	Country Name	Country Ratio (4)	State/Province Name	State/Province Ratio	Sub-Province (5) Name	Sub-Province (5) Ratio
1	2	3	4	5	6	7	8
SHANGHAI (1)	1989	China	439	Jiangsu	2,5:1	Huayin	7:1
NANJING (1)	"	"	312	"	1,8:1	"	5:1
GUANGZHOU (1)	"	"	474	Guangdong	3:1	Heyuan	8:1
FOSHAN (1)	"	"	566	"	3,6:1	"	9:1
(SHENZHEN (1))	"	"	1.485	"	10:1	"	24:1
BOMBAY (2)	1985	India	1.088	Maharashtra	9:1	Ratnagiri	31:1
MADRAS (2)	"	"	616	Tamil Nadu	5:1	Pudukkottai	11:1
HYDERABAD (2)	"	"	432	Andhra Pradesh	4:1	Vizianagaram	8:1
BHOPAL (2)	"	"	290	Madhya Pradesh	4:1	Seoni	14:1
NEW YORK (3)	1986	USA	124	New York	1:1	Allegany	1.8:1
LOS ANGELES (3)	"	"	116	California	1:1	Imperial	1.8:1
CHICAGO (3)	"	"	115	Illinois	1.1:1	Johnson	2.1:1

(1) Shi; (2) s. App.1B, col.3 & 4; (3) Metropolitan Statistical Area (MSA);
(4) Country = 100; (5) China: City & Counties, India: District, USA: County.

Sources: China & India - see Tab.3 & note 12. USA - US. Department of Commerce, Bureau of the Census (Ed. - 1988), *County and City Data Book 1988*, Washington (author's calculations).

As far as India is concerned the theorem of a positive correlation between the size of the metropolis and the extent of the (economic) development incline apparently seems to be valid. The ratio between Bombay and the district with the lowest index value amounts to 31 : 1. The respective ratios for Madras, Hyderabad and Bhopal are 11 : 1, 8 : 1 and 14 : 1, respectively. As far as China is concerned comparable complete figures are so far available only for three provinces - Jiangsu, Guangdong and Liaoning - all three above the level of development (Tab.3). At least the four[28] cited metropolitan cities similarly show a degree of economic development far above the national as well as provincial level topped by the special economic zone of Shenzhen.- In contrast to the Indian and Chinese metropolitan cities those of the USA present a completely different picture with an almost equal level of economic development in relation to the respective states (col.6). It seems we can deduce from these results another theorem, e.g. a causal connection between the level of development of a certain country and the dimension of the primacy of the concerned metropolis(es).

Map 1a: Regional Types - India

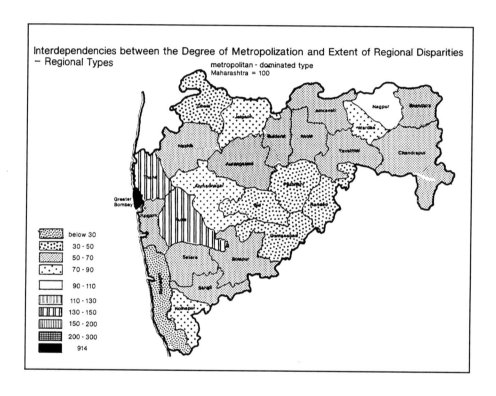

Urban Systems in India and China 55

Map 1b: Regional Types - India

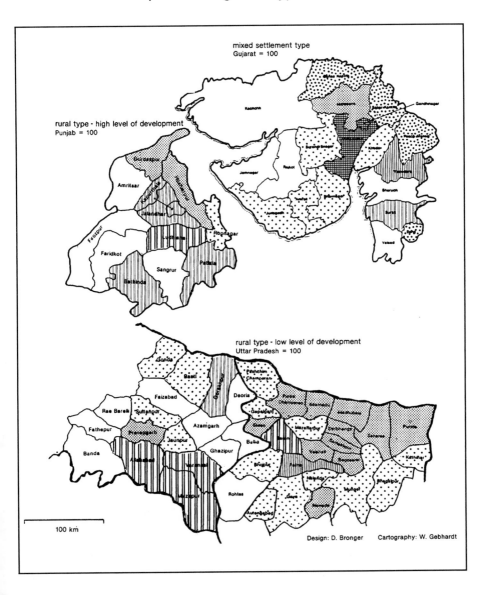

Map 2a: Regional Types - China

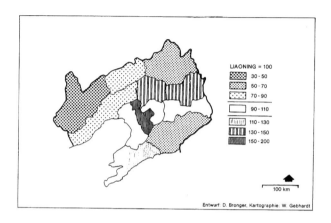

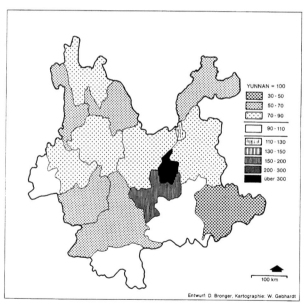

Map 2b: Regional Types - China

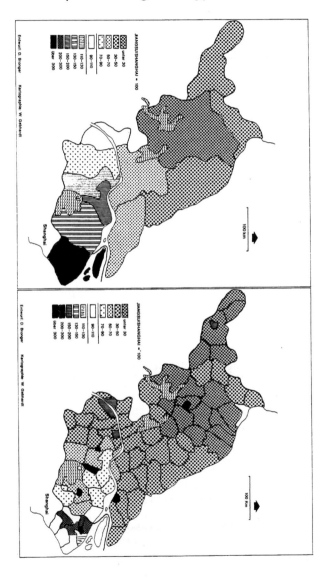

To sum up: Regarding the interdependencies between metropolitan primacy and the level of (economic) development we can deduce the following theorems:

- positive correlation between the extent of regional disparity and the functional primacy of a city/metropolis, which often is to be viewed in correspondence with the size of the metropolitan city (see: Tab.11, col.1: 4, 6, and 8);

- negative correlation between the extent of regional disparity and the metropolitan-distant regions, especially those with a high natural potential;

- interdependence between the extent of functional metropolitan primacy and the dynamics of development of the remaining regions: As a consequence of the exceptional metropolitan dominance in all spheres of life a stagnation of most of the remaining regions can be observed.

From these theorems we can deduce several *regional types* - based on the level of economic development (Maps 1-2):

(1) The *monocentric* regional type dominated by a sole super-metropolis. It is characterized by a pronounced economic development incline between the one metropolis on the one hand and the vast majority of the remaining, predominantly agro-based regions on the other. In the case of Maharashtra/India (Map 1a), with the exception of the two adjoining districts of Thane and Pune, all the remaining 24 districts persist in a deep shadow of (under-)development. The monocentric type can be found in China in quite a number of cases (see also: Tab.8), for example the province of Yunnan with its outstanding metropolis of Kunming (Map 2a).

(2) The *polycentric* regional type we can find in those cases, where several metropolitan or large cities dominate the remaining areas. Regarding India we can find this type inter alia in the State of Gujarat with its three metropolitan cities of Ahmedabad, Vadodara and Surat (Map 1b); in China this type is represented best by the province of Liaoning (Map 2a), where even four metropolises - Shenyang, Dalian, Anshan and Fushun - are located.

(3) Regions without any dominating metropolitan/large city: here a much more equally distributed development can be found; in other words the regional disparities are much less, especially compared to type 1. This structure seems to be independent from the overall level of development. For India this is demonstrated here by Punjab with a high level and the Middle Ganga Valley with a low level of economic development. Their ratio of 2.2 and 2.4 : 1, respectively, is less than one tenth of the large metropolitan cities (Map 1b). Whereas in India this regional type is fairly wide-spread, in China it seems to be not that common; in the case of Jiangsu (Map 2b) this structure can be observed at least partly.

4.4 Functional Primacy in China and India III: Dynamics of Primacy (Tab.12 & 13)

To sum up: The outstanding functional primacy of most of the "Third" World metropolitan cities results in pronounced regional disparities *within* these countries. In view of the overall development of the country/region concerned, a main target of regional planning and development must be to reduce this metropolitan-rural development incline. This conclusion leads to the essential problem - to be answered by the researchers - to investigate the *dynamics* of the demographic and above all the functional *primacy of the metropolitan cities*.

As far as the example of Bombay and the state of Maharashtra is concerned, a deeper investigation reveals the enormous difficulties such regions are faced with: an historically grown outstanding functional primacy of a super-metropolis (see: Tab.4 & 9) in combination with comparatively unfavourable natural as well as infrastructural preconditions of the region itself and - last but not least - financial constraints. Nevertheless the state of Maharashtra has undertaken enormous efforts in developing small-scale industry in so-called "growth centers" to achieve this major goal, i.e. to reduce the pronounced metropolitan primacy and the regional disparities as well.

The all in all limited results of these efforts within the last 30 years summarized in Tab.12[29] and Map 1 cannot be discussed within the context of this paper.[30] They disclose a fundamental dilemma most of the states/regions are faced with: Immediate (short-term) results could be obtained only from the infrastructurally well advanced regions, i.e. the metropolitan regions, first and foremost in Bombay itself. In respect of the limited financial resources its future development therefore seems to make sense and to be advisable. Such a regional policy, however, will not reduce the pronounced rural-metropolitan incline, indispensable for the overall development of Maharashtra as a whole - including its inhabitants.

This fundamental dilemma seems to be valid more or less also in the case of Shanghai: despite serious efforts of the Chinese Government by means of a consequent regional investment policy to reduce the inherited dichotomy coastal areas - western regions[31] and despite some success (Tab.13) the pronounced metropolitan primacy of Shanghai in most of the enumerated dimensions remains almost unchallenged.

Despite a remarkable or at least satisfactory economic development in both countries the policy of a "balanced regional development" could achieve only limited results - or is it more true to say that such a regional strategy could not be held out in either country? This question leads us again to the basic developmental dilemma which can be summarized as the "permanent conflict between growth and justice". It should be a major task of developing country research to provide as many detailed analyses as possible of the complex interplay of the various causal determinants causing these difficulties. Such analyses are an essential precondition for any regional development planning and policy.

Table 12: Dynamics of Metropolitan Primacy: Bombay

INDICATOR	Year	Share: Regional Level (%) Maharashtra			Share: National Level (%) India		
		Greater Bombay		BMR (5)	Greater Bombay		BMR (5)
I POPULATION	1951	(1)	(1)	(1)	0.8	(2), (3)	0.9
	1961	10.5	11.6 (2)	14.0	0.9	1.0 (2)	1.0
	1971	11.8	13.3 (2)	15.5	1.1	1.2 (2)	1.2
	1981	13.1	15.4 (2)	17.1	1.2	1.4 (2)	1.4
	1991	12.6	16.0 (2)	18.7 (4)	1.2	1.5 (2)	1.6
II INDUSTRY							
- Small Scale Industry No. of units	1961	71.4		76.1			
	1971	39.7		42.6			
	1980	22.8		31.9			
	1990	14.5		(3)			
- Medium & Large Scale Industry No. of Workers	1962	66.9		71.9			
	1974	56.6		68.4			
	1980	52.3		63.8			
	1987	43.9		(3)			
III TRANSPORTATION							
- Turnover of Seaports (overseas traffic)	1961				46.7		
	1971				25.1		
	1981				21.0		
	1987				21.0		
IV COMMUNICATION							
- No. of Telephones	1961	81.0					
	1971	76.3					
	1980	76.9					
	1988	73.5					
V EDUCATION							
- No. of university students	1973	30.4					
	1982	40.3					
	1984	46.3					

(1) The State of Maharashtra was founded only in 1960; (2) Bombay U.A. - see Table APP.2B; (3) no data available; (4) estimated figure; (5) Bombay Metropolitan Region.

Sources:
I - see: *Census of India 1951, 1961, 1971, 1981, 1991*.
II - MIDC, Bombay (unpubl. records).
III - *Government of Maharashtra* (Ed.), Statistical Abstract of Maharashtra State (different years); -"-: *Handbook of Basic Statistics of Maharashtra State 1988, Bombay 1989*; Government of India (Ed.), Economic Survey (different years); ESCAP et al. (Ed.), *City Monographs*, Yokohama 1982.
IV - Indian Posts & Telegraphs Department, Ministry of Communication (Ed.), Annual Report (different years)
V - see: III.

(Author's calculations)

Table 13: Dynamics of Metropolitan Primacy: Shanghai

INDICATOR	Year	Share: Regional Level (%) Jiangsu & Shanghai		Share: National Level (%) China	
		Shanghai shi	Shanghai Province	Shanghai shi	Shanghai Province
I POPULATION	1953	11.4	13.2	0.9	1.1
	1957	11.7	13.2	0.9	1.1
	1970	10.5	17.4	0.8	1.4
	1981	8.6	16.2	0.6	1.2
	1989	10.0	16.3	0.7	1.1
II INDUSTRY – Gross value of industrial output	1949				23.8
	1952				19.0
	1957				16.5
	1965				12.6
	1974				15.5
	1981				11.8
	1989				6.9 *
– Per capita output value: Industry & Agriculture (China = 100)	1952				444
	1957				587
	1981				734
	1989				481 *
III TRANSPORTATION – Turnover of Seaports	1952			45.6	
	1965			44.5	
	1978			40.1	
	1989			33.7	
IV COMMUNICATION – No. of Telephones	1981	30.7	51.3	3.2	5.3
	1989	39.3	44.4	4.9	5.6
V EDUCATION – No. of university students (institutions of higher learning)	1981	53.9		7.1	
	1989	46.0		6.1	

* at current prices

Sources:
I - see: APP.1A, 2A, 3A.
II - Field/Lardy/Emerson, 1975: 418; Lardy, 1978: 197; *Statistical Yearbook of China 1981* ff.
III/IV/V - *Statistical Yearbook of China 1981* ff. (author's calculations)

Notes

1) For the following see more in detail: Bronger, 1985 & 1988.
2) The aspect of planning cannot be discussed within the frame of this study. Regarding the example of Bombay see: Bronger, 1986: 48-95.
3) Regarding the determination of metropolitan population figures see: Bronger, 1985a: 71 ff.
4) See inter alia: Aird, 1983; Orleans/Burnham, 1984; Chan/Xu, 1985; Taubmann, 1986; Ma/Cui, 1987.
5) In detail see: Bronger, 1986a: 31-47.
6) See for example the compilation in Ullman, 1961: App.D for the years 1953-1958.
7) Ma/Cui 1987: 388.
8) Living in cities with > 100.000 inhabitants.
9) Excluding the three provincial cities.
10) I.e. those with more than 50.000 sqkm or more than 5 million inhabitants. These 17 states and Delhi comprise 98.5% of India's total population.
11) For the following see: Bronger, 1988: 7 f.
12) As overall economic data like NDP or per capita income do not exist below the state level in India, we have to use an index which gives at least an approximate indicator to characterize the overall level of economic development. For 1985 the Centre for Monitoring Indian Economy, Bombay has worked out a rough proxy indicator again on district level. The nine indicators used and the weight for each of them is given below:

	Indicator	Weight (%) For all districts other than 10 districts indicated in the next column	For 10 districts* with urban population of 72% or more
I	**Agriculture**	**35**	**0**
	1. Per capita value of output of 26 major crops: Average of 1982-83 to 1984-85	25	0
	2. Per capita bank credit for agriculture: June 1983	10	0
II	**Mining and Manufacturing**	**25**	**30**
	3. Number of mining and factory workers per lakh of population: 1984	10	12
	4. Number of household manufacturing workers per lakh of population: 1981	5	6
	5. Per capita bank credit for manufacturing sector: June 1983	10	12
III	**Service Sector**	**40**	**70**
	6. Per capita bank deposit: June 1983	15	26
	7. Per capita bank credit to services: June 1983	15	26
	8. Literacy (%): 1981	4	7
	9. Urbanisation (%): 1981	6	11
Total		100	100

Note: The ten districts are: Greater Bombay, Calcutta, Delhi, Madras, Hyderabad, Ahmedabad, Bhopal, Srinagar, Chandigarh and Yanam in Pondicherry.

13) See the critical assessment by Orleans, 1972: 57 ff.
14) See the explanation in the following chapter.
15) However, the pertinent area of Urumqi in 1953 amounted only to 81.3 sqkm; in 1958 the city area expanded to 640 sqkm (Ullman, 1961: App.D); the 1953 figure of Zibo (in contrast to 1958) seems very doubtful.
16) Fundamentally: Tien, 1973; further: Chen, 1973: 66 ff.; Küchler, 1976: 140 ff.; Chang, 1976: 401 f.; Pannell, 1981: 3 f., 101 f.; Buck, 1981: 116 f.; Kwock, 1981: 148 f.; Fung, 1981: 219 f.
17) Ma, 1981: 112.
18) See inter alia: Buck, 1981: 116; Küchler, 1976: 140 f.
19) In addition see the very detailed compilation in: Bannister, 1977: 259 ff.
20) For the following see: Bronger, 1985: 87 f.
21) This statement is valid for the metropolitan cities of the I.C.s of Western & Northern Europe as well as North America only. Even Tokyo has achieved a similar dominance in Japan in the course of the present century (Schöller, 1976) and this process has actually resulted in "serious disturbances in the equilibrium of the socio-economic structure" (*ibid.*: 97).
22) See also: Bronger, 1988: 19 ff.
23) Calculated from: *Statistical Yearbook of China - 1990*: 36.
24) In the case of Manila and Bangkok this ratio refers also to the metropolitan region; in the case of Seoul the - low - figures relates to the metropolis itself - see: Bronger, 1991: Tab.5.
25) Calculated from *Statistical Yearbook of China - 1989*: 377.
26) For the computation of Indian metropolitan cities - see note 12.
27) The Chinese metropolises are equally computed as in Tab.3 (NDP/capita).
28) Because of their comparatively large area of > 2.000 sqkm (Dalian) or even > 3.400 sqkm (Shenyang - App.1A, col.5) these metropolises have not been considered in this context (Tab.11).
29) The reduction of the small-scale units in the past 30 years (1961-1990) manifested in Tab.12 should not be overestimated, because it refers only to the registered units - and a registration has not been permitted in Bombay since 1980! In reality Bombay's share of the total number of units should come up to 35-40%, apart from the fact that the majority of the metropolitan units are to be counted as progressive, growth-oriented industrial units.
30) More in detail, see: Bronger, 1986 & 1991.
31) In detail see: Taubmann, 1989: 5 f.

Bibliography*

* The statistical references listed at the end of Tab.1-12 are not cited again

Aird, J.S. (1983): "The Preliminary Results of China's 1982 Census", *The China Quarterly*, 96, pp.613-640

Banister, J. (1977): "Mortality, Fertility and Contraceptive Use in Shanghai", *The China Quarterly*, 70, pp.255-295

Breese, G. (1966): *Urbanization in Newly Developing Countries*, Englewood Cliffs

Bronger, D. (1984): "Metropolization in China?", *Geo Journal*, 8.2, pp.137-146

Bronger, D. (1985): "Metropolization as a Development Problem of Third World Countries: A contribution towards a Definition of the Concept", *Applied Geography and Development*, Vol.26, pp.71-97

Bronger, D. (1985a): "How big are the Metropolitan Cities? Metropolization in the Far East: The Demographic Dimension I", *ASIEN*, Nr.14, pp.71-79

Bronger, D. (1985b): "How big were the Metropolitan Cities? Metropolization in the Far East: The Demographic Dimension II", *ASIEN*, Nr.15, pp.94-110

Bronger, D. (1986): "Die 'metropolitane Revolution' als Entwicklungsproblem in den Ländern Süd-, Südost- und Ostasiens. Entstehung - Dynamik - Planung - Ergebnisse. Das Beispiel Bombay", Institut für Auslandsbeziehungen (Ed.), *Umwelt, Kultur und Entwicklung in der Dritten Welt. Zum Problem des Umwelterhaltes und der Umweltzerstörung in Afrika, Asien und Lateinamerika. 7. Tübinger Gespräch zu Entwicklungsfragen*, Stuttgart, pp.48-95 (Materialien zum Internationalen Kulturaustausch, Nr.27)

Bronger, D. (1986a): "Metropolization in India and China - A Comparative Analysis. The Demographic Perspective", Shafi, M./Raza, M. (Eds.), *Spectrum of Modern Geography*, New Delhi, pp.29-62

Bronger, D. (1988): "The Role of Metropolization for the Development Process in India and China. The Demographic and Functional Dimension. A Comparative Analysis", *ASIEN*, Nr.26, 1-33

Bronger, D. (1990): "Die Analyse des regionalen Entwicklungsgefälles als Aufgabe geographischer Entwicklungsländer-Forschung. Erläutert am Beispiel einer vergleichenden Gegenüberstellung von Indien und China", *Zeitschrift für Wirtschaftsgeographie*, Jg.34, H.2, S.101-117

Bronger, D. (1991): "Dynamik der Metropolisierung - Problem der räumlichen Entwicklung in Ländern Asiens", *Internationales Asienforum*, 22.Jg., No.1-2, S.5-41

Buck, D.D. (1981): "Policies Favoring the Growth of Smaller Urban Places in the People's Republic of China, 1949-1979", Ma, L.J.C./Hanten, E.W. (Eds.), *Urban Development in Modern China*, Boulder/ Col., pp.114-146

Chan, K.W./Xu, X. (1985): "Urban Population Growth and Urbanization in China since 1949: Reconstructing a Baseline", *The China Quarterly*, Vol.104, pp.583-613

Chandrasekhar, S. (1960): *China's Population. Census and Vital Statistics*. 2nd ed., Hongkong, 73 pp.

Chang, S.-D. (1965): "Peking: The Growing Metropolis of Communist China", *The Geographical Review*, 55, pp.313-327

Chang, S.-D. (1970): "Some Observations on the Morphology of Chinese Walled Cities", *Annals of the Association of American Geographers*, 60, pp.63-91

Chang, S.-D. (1974): "Peking", *Encyclopaedia Britannica, Macropaedia*, 14, pp. 1-14

Chang, S.-D. (1976): "The Changing System of Chinese Cities", *Annals of the Association of American Geographers*, 66, pp.398-415

Chen, N.-R. (1966): *Chinese Economic Statistics. A Handbook for Mainland China*, Edinburgh

Chen, C.-S. (1973): "Population Growth and Urbanization in China, 1953-1970", *The Geographical Review*, 63, pp.55-72

Cressey, G.B. (1955): *Land of the 500 Million. A Geography of China*, New York, Toronto, London, 387 pp.

Feetham, R. (1931): *Report of the Hon. Mr. Justice Richard Feetham, C.M.G. to the Shanghai Municipal Council*, Vol.I-III, Shanghai

Field, R.M./Lardy, N.R./Emerson, J.P. (1975): "Industrial Output by Province in China", *The China Quarterly*, pp.406-431

Fung, K.I. (1981): "Urban Sprawl in China: Some Causative Factors", Ma, L.J.C./Hanten, E.W. (Eds.), *Urban Development in Modern China*, Boulder/Col., pp.194-221

Handke, W. (1986): *Shanghai. Eine Weltstadt öffnet sich*, Hamburg (Mitteilungen des Instituts für Asienkunde Hamburg, 154)

Küchler, J. (1976): "Stadterneuerung in der VR China", Küchler, J./Müller, M./Tömmel, I., *Stadtentwicklungsprozeß - Stadtentwicklungschancen: Planung in Berlin, Bologna und in der VR China*, Göttingen, pp.137-218 (Geographische Hochschulmanuskripte, 3)

Kwok, R.Y.-W. (1981): "Trends in Urban Planning and Development", Ma, L.J.C./Hanten, E.W. (Eds.), *Urban Development in Modern China*, Boulder/Col., pp.147-193

Lardy, N.R. (1978): *Economic Growth and Distribution in China*, Cambridge, London, New York, Melbourne, 244 pp.

Lo, C.-P./Pannell, C.W./Welch, R. (1977): "Land Use Changes and City Planning in Shenyang and Canton", *The Geographical Review*, 67, pp.268-283

Lo, C.-P./Welch, R. (1977): "Chinese Urban Population Estimates", *Annals of the Association of American Geographers*, Vol.67, No.2, pp.246-253

Ma, L.J.C. (1981): "Introduction: The City in Modern China", Ma, L.J.C./Hanten, E.W. (Eds.), *Urban Development in Modern China*, Boulder/Col., pp.1-18

Ma, L.J.C./Cui, G. (1987): "Administrative Changes and Urban Population in China", *Annals of the Association of American Geographers*, Vol.77, No.3, pp.373-395

Machetzki, R. (1982): "Natürlicher Wirtschaftsraum und Regionalwirtschaften der VR China", *CHINA aktuell*, pp.642-653

Murphey, R. (1953): *Shanghai: Key to Modern China*, Cambridge, Mass.
Murphey, R. (1980): *The Fading of the Maoist Vision: City and Country in China's Development*, New York, London, Toronto
Orleans, L.A. (1972): *Every Fifth Child: The Population of China*, London
Orleans, L.A./Burnham, L. (1984): "The Enigma of China's Urban Population", *Asian Review*, pp.788-804
Pannell, Cl.W. (1981): "Recent Growth and Change in China's Urban System", Ma, L.J.C./Hanten, E.W. (Eds.), *Urban Development in Modern China*, Boulder/Col., pp.91-113
Schier, P. (1989): "Verwaltung und politische Führung von Shanghai", Institut für Asienkunde (Ed.), *Shanghai. Chinas Tor zur Welt*, Hamburg, pp.52-72
Schinz, A. (1983): "Fengtian - Mukden - Shenyang. Wandlung einer chinesischen Großstadt seit der Forschungsreise F. v. Richthofens 1869", *Geowissenschaften in unserer Zeit*, 1983, 1/6, S.198-209
Schöller, P. (1976): "Tokyo: Entwicklung und Probleme wachsender Hauptstadt-Konzentration", Leupold, W./Rutz, W. (Eds.), *Der Staat und sein Territorium. Beiträge zur raumwirksamen Tätigkeit des Staates*, Wiesbaden, pp.86-105
Shiger, A.G. (1957): *Administrativno - territorial'noe delenie zarubezhnuikh stran: spravochnik. Vtoroe, ispravlennoe izdanie* (The Administrative-territorial Divisions of Foreign Countries. Second revised edition), Moskva
Taubmann, W. (1986): "Stadtentwicklung in der Volksrepublik China", *Geographische Rundschau*, Jg.38, H.3, S.114-123
Taubmann, W. (1989): "Wirtschaftsgeographische Gliederung, natürliche Ressourcen, Raum- und Stadtplanung", Louven, E. (Hrsg.), *Chinas Wirtschaft zu Beginn der 90er Jahre*, Hamburg, pp.3-28
Tien, H.Yuan (1973): *China's Population Struggle. Demographic Decisions of the People's Republic, 1949-1969*
Trewartha, G.T. (1951): "Chinese Cities: Number and Distribution", *Annals of the Association of American Geographers*, 41, pp.331-347
Ullman, M.B. (1961): "Cities of Mainland China: 1953 and 1958", Washington, D.C. (International Population Reports, Series P-95, No.59). Reprint in: Breese, G. (Ed.), *The City in Newly Developing Countries: Readings on Urbanism and Urbanization*, Englewood Cliffs, N.J. 1969, pp.81-103
Zhao, Zukang (1982): Local Authorities and Human Settlements Development in Shanghai. An Outline of the Development of Shanghai Human Settlements, Shanghai (mimeogr.)

Appendix 1A: Area and Population of Metropolitan Cities in China - 1990

No. Metropolis (1)	diqu (3)		shiqu			Density (per sqkm) col.7:5
	Area (sqkm)	Population (000)	Area (sqkm)	Population Total	(000) NAP	
1 2	3	4	5	6	7	8
1. Shanghai (2)	6.341	13.342	749	8.214	7.774	10.379
2. Beijing	16.808	11.035	1.370	6.570	5.390	3.934
3. Tianjin	11.305	9.663	4.276	5.746	4.556	1.065
4. Shenyang	8.515	5.645	3.495	4.540	3.600	1.030
5. Wuhan	8.393	6.533	1.627	3.750	3.284	2.019
6. Guangzhou	7.434	5.854	1.444	3.580	2.914	2.018
7. Harbin	6.929	4.024	1.637	2.830	2.443	1.492
8. Chongqing	23.114	14.711	1.534	2.984	2.270	1.480
9. Nanjing	6.516	4.961	947	2.500	2.090	2.207
10. Xi'an	9.983	5.974	1.100	2.757	1.954	1.833
11. Dalian	12.574	5.134	2.415	2.400	1.723	714
12. Chengdu	12.390	9.086	1.382	2.810	1.710	1.237
13. Changchun	18.881	6.266	1.116	2.110	1.680	1.505
14. Taiyuan	6.988	2.537	1.460	1.960	1.530	1.048
15. Jinan	5.818	4.040	2.119	2.323	1.480	698
16. Qingdao	10.654	6.572	1.103	2.060	1.460	1.327
17. Anshan	4.744	2.743	622	1.390	1.200	1.929
18. Fushun	10.816	2.203	675	1.350	1.200	1.778
19. Lanzhou	13.086	2.467	1.632	1.510	1.190	729
20. Zhengzhou	7.446	5.214	1.010	1.710	1.160	1.149
21. Zibo	3.471	2.900	2.961	2.460	1.140	385
22. Kunming	15.561	3.510	2.081	1.520	1.130	543
23. Changsha	11.818	5.445	367	1.330	1.110	3.020
24. Hangzhou	16.596	5.710	430	1.340	1.100	2.558
25. Nanchang	7.402	3.630	617	1.350	1.090	1.767
26. Qiqihar	52.633	5.836	4.365	1.380	1.070	245
27. Shijiazhuang	3.255	2.750	307	1.320	1.070	3.485
28. Urumqi	11.444	1.269	835	1.160	1.050	1.257
29. Tangshan	13.472	6.442	1.090	1.500	1.040	954
30. Jilin	27.120	4.052	1.213	1.270	1.040	857
31. Guiyang			2.436	1.530	1.020	419
TOTAL 1-31 Metropolization Quota (%)	371.507	167.088	49.587	79.254 5.46	62.468	1.256

(1) > 1 Mill. non-agricultural population; (2) Census 1990; (3) 1989

Sources:
- Shanghai: 1990 Census figures.
- Beijing: Statistical Bureau, *Beijing Statistical Yearbook 1991* (chin.).
- Tianjin: Statistical Bureau, *Tianjin Statistical Yearbook 1991* (chin.).
- other metropolitan cities: SSB - PRC: *China Statistical Yearbook 1991*, p.584.

Appendix 1B: Area and Population of Metropolitan Cities in India - 1991

No.	Metropolis	Area (sqkm)	Population (000)	Density (per sqkm)
1	2	3	4	5
1.	Greater Bombay M.C.	603	9.909	16.433
1a.	Greater Bombay U.A.	1.132 *	12.572	11.106
2.	Calcutta U.A.	852	10.916	12.812
3.	Delhi U.T.	1.483	9.370	6.318
4.	Madras U.A.	572	5.361	9.372
5.	Hyderabad U.A.	378	4.280	11.322
6.	Bangalore U.A.	366	4.087	11.167
7.	Ahmedabad U.A.	222	3.298	14.856
8.	Pune U.A.	344	2.485	7.224
9.	Kanpur U.A.	299	2.111	7.060
10.	Nagpur U.A.	237	1.661	7.008
11.	Lucknow U.A.	146	1.642	11.247
12.	Surat U.A.	95 *	1.517	15.968
13.	Jaipur U.A.	210	1.514	7.210
14.	Cochin U.A.	189	1.140	6.032
15.	Coimbatore U.A.	291	1.136	3.904
16.	Vadodera U.A.	114	1.115	9.781
17.	Indore U.A.	114	1.104	9.684
18.	Patna U.A.	109	1.099	10.083
19.	Madurai U.A.	112	1.094	9.768
20.	Bhopal M.C.	285	1.064	3.733
21.	Vishakhapatnam U.A.	97	1.052	10.845
22.	Varanasi U.A.	104	1.026	9.865
(23.	Kalyan M.C. included in 1a		1.014	)
24.	Ludhiana M.C.	110	1.012	9.200
	TOTAL 1-23	7.861 *	71.656	9.115
	Metropolization Quota (%)		8,56 **	
			8.49 +*	

* Approx. figure;
** excluding Jammu & Kashmir;
+* relating to All-India
U.A. = Urban Agglomeration; U.T. = Union Territory; M.C. = Municipal Corporation

Sources:
col.3 - calculated from: *Census of India 1981*, Series-1: India, Part-II-A (iii) *Standard Urban Areas*, New Delhi 1988;
col.4 - *Census of India 1991*, Series-1: *India*, New Delhi 1991;
author's calculations.

Appendix 1C: Area and Population of Large Cities in China - 1990

No. Large City (1) (>0.5 Mill.)	diqu		shiqu			Density (per sqk)
	Area (sqkm)	Population (000)	Area (sqkm)	Population(000) Total	NAP	col.7:5
1 2	3	4	5	6	7	8
1. Baotou	9.991	1.721	2.153	1.200	980	455
2. Fuzhou	11.968	5.192	1.043	1.290	870	834
3. Handan	2.791	2.010	457	1.110	840	1.838
4. Wuxi	4.650	4.121	397	930	830	2.091
5. Xuzhou	11.258	7.618	172	910	810	4.709
6. Yichun	26.907	933	20.169	870	800	40
7. Datong	2.080	1.092	2.080	1.110	800	385
8. Benxi	8.420	1.511	1.308	920	770	589
9. Luoyang	15.208	5.514	544	1.190	760	1.397
10. Hefei	7.266	3.714	458	1.000	730	1.594
11. Nanning	10.029	2.484	1.384	1.070	720	393
12. Huhehaote (Hohhot)	6.079	1.361	2.054	890	650	316
13. Suzhou	8.488	5.566	178	840	710	3.989
14. Huainan	2.121	1.748	1.091	1.200	700	642
15. Jixi	5.402	1.121	2.300	860	680	296
16. Daqing	5.500	918	5.107	940	660	120
17. Fuxin	8.938	1.815	448	730	640	1.429
18. Liuzhou	5.279	1.548	651	740	610	937
19. Shantou	8.935	8.355	246	860	580	2.358
20. Jinzhou	10.301	2.903	804	720	570	709
21. Mudanjiang	49.888	2.777	1.351	710	570	422
22. Xining	3.456	1.017	350	650	550	1.571
23. Ningbo	9.365	5.076	1.033	1.090	550	532
24. Zhangjiakou	2.964	987	710	670	530	914
25. Changzhou	4.375	3.217	187	670	530	2.834
26. Dandong	19.176	2.793	526	650	520	989
27. Hegang	17.479	1.027	4.551	650	520	114
28. Kaifeng			359	692	508	
TOTAL 1-28	280.750	79.627	51.752	25.162	18.988	367
Urbanization Quota (%)					1,66	

1) > 0.5 Mill. non-agriultural population.

Sources: See App.1A, page 67.

Appendix 1D: See page 72.

Appendix 2A: Population Growth of Metropolitan Cities in China 1900-1990

No.	Metropolis	1900	1920	1930	1938	1948	1953
1.	Shanghai	950	1.539	3.122	3.595	5.020	5.354
2.	Beijing	728 (1)	1.181	1.369 (5)	1.574	1.672 (11)	2.768
3.	Tianjin	100	839	1.392	1.223	1.708 (11)	2.694
4.	Shenyang		250 (2)	527 (6)	772	1.121	2.300
5.	Wuhan		750 (2)	1.584 (7)	1.242	1.062	1.427
6.	Guangzhou		*	830 (5)	1.022	1.413	1.599
7.	Harbin		200 (2)	320 (5)	468	760 (12)	1.163
8.	Chongqing		351 (3)	298 (8)	528	1.003 (11)	1.773
9.	Nanjing		300 (2)	522 (5)	440	1.137	1.092
10.	Xi'an		*	188 (9)	218	503	787
11.	Dalian		237 (4)	586 (6)	504	723 (11)	892
12.	Chengdu		423 (3)	441 (8)	458	727	857
13.	Changchun		70 (2)	*	360	630	855
14.	Taiyuan		80 (2)	139 (8)	177	252	721
15.	Jinan		300 (2)	437 (9)	472	591 (11)	680
16.	Qingdao		131	318 (10)	592	788	917
17.	Anshan		*	*	120	166	549
18.	Fushun		181	118 (6)	215	513	679
19.	Lanzhou		110 (2)	103 (8)	122	204	397
20.	Zhengzhou		35 (2)	80 (13)	197	150	595
21.	Zibo		*	*	*	*	184
22.	Kunming		*	170 (5)	184	300	699
23.	Changsha		180 (2)	312 (5)	464	396	651
24.	Hangzhou		*	468 (5)	575	570	697
25.	Nanchang		*	206 (5)	275	267	398
26.	Qiqihar		43	76 (6)	97	175	345
27.	Shijiazhuang		*	*	194	198	373
28.	Urumqi		*	*	45	88	141
29.	Tangshan		76	100 (5)	146	137	693
30.	Jilin		230	143 (6)	132	247	435
31.	Guiyang		*	117 (9)	145	263 (11)	271

* = no figure available.
1) 1913; 2) 1922; 3) "*xian* administrative area"; 4) 1926: Dairen only; 5) 1929; 6) 1936; 7) 1927; 8) 1934; 9) 1935; 10) 1928; 11) 1946; 12) 1947; 13) 1922; 14) 1931; 15) 1907; 16) related to the present area of 749 sqkm (s. App.1A) the figure will amount to 79.

Urban Systems in India and China

1958	1970	1981		1990		Growth Rate China = 100		
		Σ	NAP	Σ	NAP	1953-1990 Σ	1981-1990 Σ	NAP
5.781	5.802	6.134	6.086	7.830	7.500	75 (16)	112	108
4.148	5.000	5.430	4.665	7.000	5.770	130	113	108
3.278	3.600	5.023	3.829	5.770	4.570	110	101	105
2.423	2.800	3.918	2.937	4.540	3.600	102	101	107
2.226	2.560	3.157	2.662	3.750	3.284	135	104	108
1.867	2.500	3.077	2.338	3.580	2.914	115	102	109
1.595	1.670	2.460	2.094	2.830	2.443	125	101	102
2.165	2.400	2.597	1.900	2.984	2.270	86	100	105
1.455	1.750	2.087	1.702	2.500	2.090	118	105	108
1.368	1.600	2.145	1.580	2.757	1.954	180	113	109
1.590	1.650	1.452	1.208	2.400	1.723	138	145	125
1.135	1.250	2.428	1.376	2.810	1.710	169	101	109
988	1.200	1.696	1.309	2.110	1.680	127	109	112
1.053	1.350	1.702	1.239	1.960	1.530	140	101	108
882	1.100	1.290	1.010	2.323	1.480	175	157	128
1.144	1.300	1.153	1.013	2.060	1.460	116	156	126
833	1.050	1.177	996	1.390	1.200	130	103	106
1.019	1.080	1.163	1.012	1.350	1.200	102	102	104
732	1.450	1.381	1.075	1.510	1.190	196	96	97
785	1.050	1.381	859	1.710	1.160	148	108	118
875	850	2.192	623	2.460	1.140	688	98	160
900	1.100	1.399	997	1.520	1.130	112	95	99
709	825	1.047	835	1.330	1.110	105	111	116
794	960	1.156	905	1.340	1.100	99	101	106
520	675	1.033	815	1.350	1.090	174	114	117
704	760	1.193	899	1.380	1.070	206	101	104
623	800	1.031	809	1.320	1.070	182	112	116
320	*	942	880	1.160	1.050	423	108	105
812	950	1.293	865	1.500	1.040	111	102	105
583	720	1.049	815	1.270	1.040	150	106	112
504	660	1.296	827	1.530	1.020	290	103	108

Sources:
1900 - Murphey, 1953 (Shanghai); Chang, 1965 (Beijing);
1920 - *Chinese Yearbook 1923*; Trewartha, 1951;
1930 - *Chinese Yearbook 1943*; Trewartha, 1951;
1938 - Ullmann 1961;
1948 - Ullman, 1961; Trewartha, 1951;
1953 - Shiger, 1953; Ullman, 1961;
1958 - Ullman, 1961; Chen, 1966;
1970 - Chen, 1973;
1981 - *Statistical Yearbook of China - 1981*;
1990 - *Statistical Yearbook of China - 1991*.

Appendix 1D: Area and Population of Large Cities[2] in India - 1991

No.	Large City (>0.5 Mill.)	Area (sqkm)	Population (000)	Density (per sqkm)
1	2	3	4	5
1.	Agra U.A.	82	903	11.012
2.	Jabalpur U.A.	231	887	3.840
3.	Allahabad U.A.	82	842	10.268
4.	Vijayawada U.A.	83	839	10.108
5.	Jamshedpur U.A.	147	835	5.680
6.	Meerut U.A.	81	833	10.284
7.	Trivandrum U.A.	94	825	8.777
8.	Dhanbad U.A.	204	818	4.010
9.	Kozhikode (Calicut) U.A.	138	801	5.804
10.	Asansol U.A.	153	764	4.993
11.	Nasik U.A.	145	724	4.993
12.	Gwalior U.A.	303	720	2.376
13.	Tiruchirapalli U.A.	145	711	4.903
14.	Amritsar M.C.	115	709	6.165
15.	Durg-Bhilainagar U.A.	120	689	5.742
16.	Mysore U.A.	82	652	7.951
17.	Rajkot U.A.	69	651	9.435
18.	Jodhpur M.C.	79	649	8.215
19.	Hubli-Dharwar M.C.	191	648	3.393
20.	Solapur U.A.	25	621	24.840
21.	Ranchi U.A.	182	614	3.374
22.	Faridabad Complex	178	614	3.449
23.	Bareilly U.A.	59	612	10.373
24.	Aurangabad U.A.	50	592	11.840
25.	Gawarhati	45 (1)	578	12.844
26.	Chandigarh U.A.	59	575	9.746
27.	Salem U.A.	98	574	5.857
28.	Kota M.C.	221	536	2.425
29.	Ghaziabad U.A.	77	520	6.753
30.	Jalandhar M.C.	95	520	5.474
	Total 1-30	3.633 (1)	20.856	5.741
	Urbanization Quota (%)		2,49 (2)	

1), 2): See App. 1B.
Sources: See App. 1B.

Urban Systems in India and China 73

Appendix 2B: Population Growth of Metropolitan Cities in India 1901-1991

No.	Metropolis	1901	1911	1921	1931	1941	1951	1961	1971	1981	1991	Growth 1901-1991 India=100	Growth 1951-1991 India=100	Growth 1981-1991 India=100
1.	Bombay *	928	1,139	1,380	1,391	1,801	2,994	4,152	5,971	8,243	9,909	301	142	97
1a.	Bombay **							4,600	6,721	9,683	12,570			105
2.	Calcutta **	1,488	1,718	1,851	2,106	3,578	4,589	5,737	7,031	9,194	10,860	206	101	96
3.	Delhi +	406	414	488	636	918	1,744	2,659	4,066	6,220	9,370	651	230	122
4.	Madras **	594	604	628	775	930	1,542	1,945	3,170	4,289	5,361	255	149	101
5.	Hyderabad **	448	502	406	467	739	1,128	1,249	1,796	2,546	4,273	269	162	136
6.	Bangalore **	159	189	237	306	407	779	1,200	1,654	2,922	4,108	729	226	114
7.	Ahmedabad **	186	217	274	314	595	877	1,206	1,742	2,548	3,280	497	160	104
8.	Pune **	164	173	199	250	324	606	791	1,135	1,686	2,444	420	172	117
9.	Kanpur **	203	179	216	244	487	705	971	1,275	1,639	2,103	292	128	104
10.	Lucknow **	256	252	241	275	387	497	656	826	1,008	1,669	184	144	134
11.	Nagpur **	167	119	165	242	329	485	690	930	1,302	1,657	280	146	103
12.	Surat **	130	125	127	111	186	237	318	493	914	1,517	329	274	134
13.	Jaipur **	160	137	120	144	176	291	410	637	1,015	1,514	267	223	121
14.	Coimbatore **	53	47	75	108	190	287	448	736	920	1,136	604	169	100
15.	Cochin **	61	70	73	110	139	177	292	505	686	1,135	525	274	134
16.	Vadodera **	104	99	95	113	153	211	310	467	745	1,115	302	226	121
17.	Indore **	98	54	105	143	204	311	395	561	829	1,104	318	152	108
18.	Patna **	172	171	151	194	236	326	415	551	919	1,099	180	144	97
19.	Madurai **	106	134	144	188	245	371	491	712	908	1,094	291	126	98
20.	Bhopal **	77	56	45	61	75	102	223	385	671	1,064	390	446	128
21.	Vishakhapatnam**	41	43	45	57	70	128	211	363	604	1,050	722	351	141
22.	Varanasi **	226	217	211	220	279	370	506	635	797	1,018	127	118	103
23.	Kalyan **	11	13	18	26	31	169	247	396	649	1,014	2,600	257	100
24.	Ludhiana ***	49	44	52	69	112	154	244	401	607	1,012	582	281	135

* Greater Bombay; ** Urban Agglomeration; + Union Territory; *** Municipal Corporation.

Source: *Census of India 1901-1991.*

Appendix 3A: Area and Population Development - Shanghai 1928-1990

	"built-up area"	city only (shiqu)		city & counties (shiqu & xian)		
	sqkm	Area (sqkm)	Population (000)	Area (sqkm)	Population Σ (000)	Net Immigration
1928		893 (1)	3.122 (2)			
since 1928		829 (3)				
ca.1935		528				
ca.1935 a		861				
1945 a		893				
1945 b		636	3.660			
1949	80					
1949 a		82	4.189	636	5.029	
1949 b		893	5.020			
1953 a		82	5.353	636	6.152	
1953 b		893	6.204			
1953 c		700				
1953 d		861				
1957	116					
1957 a		117	6.098	654	6.897	
1957 b		893	6.890			
17.1.1958			1.756	1.750	6.977	
12.12.1958			5.910	5.910	10.280	
since 1958		853				
-.-		932				
1965 a		141	6.431	5.909	10.938	
1965 b		141	6.430	6.185	10.937	-44.8
1970 a+b		141	5.802	6.185	10.725	-312.4
1975 a+b		141	5.570	6.184	10.767	-5.1
1976 a+b		141	5.519	6.186	10.813	-1.9
1977 a+b		141	5.470	6.187	10.864	7.9
1978 a+b		159	5.573	6.184	10.892	67.0
1979 a+b		159	5.914	6.186	11.321	264.9
1980 a+b		159	6.012	6.184	11.462	82.7
1981 a		223	6.134	6.185	11.628	
1982 a		230	6.268	6.187	11.805	
1983 a		230	6.391	6.187	11.940	
1984 a		349	6.881	6.185	12.048	
1985 a	184	351	6.983	6.186	12.167	
1986 a		375 (4)	7.101	6.341 (4)	12.323	
1987						
1988	247	353.5	7.327		12.620	
1989	248		7.780		12.760	
1990		748.7	8.214	6.341	13.342 (5)	

Appendix 3A: Area and Population Development - Shanghai 1928-1990 (cont.)

---

1) "Greater Shanghai"; 2) 1930; 3) "Municipality of Greater Shanghai";
4) including water area; 5) including temporary residents.

Sources:
1928	-	Feetham-Report, 1931: 17.
since 1928	-	Murphey, 1953: 17, 49, 163.
ca. 1935	-	*Chinese Yearbook 1943* (calculated by the author).
ca. 1935a	-	*China-Handbuch*, 1974: 1204.
1949 & 1957	-	Fung, 1981: 272, 289.
1953 ff.a	-	*Renmin Shouce 1950* ff.; *Shanghai Tongji Nianjian 1983* ff.; Fung, 1989: 269 ff., quoted in: Schier, 1989: 61.
1945a	-	Cressey, 1950: 18.
1945 ff.b	-	Zhao, 1982: 1-5; Ma, 1981: 224, 253 (area for 1977 & 1980).
1953c	-	Chandrasekhar, 1960: 41.
1953d	-	see: 1935a.
17. 1.1958		
12.12.1958	-	Fung, 1981: 272 f.
since 1958	-	Tien, 1973: 328.
-.-	-	*China Handbuch*, 1974: 1204.
1990	-	Census 1990 figures.

Appendix 3B: Area and Population Development - Shenyang 1900-1988

Year	"built-up area" Area (sqkm)	"built-up area" Population (000)	1 Area (sqkm)	1 Population (000)	1 + 2 Area (sqkm)	1 + 2 Population (000)	1 + 2 + 3 Area (sqkm)	1 + 2 + 3 Population (000)
1900 (1)	11.0	100	11.0	100				
1917 (2)	15.9	250+						
1930 (5)	15.3	245++						
1936 (1)	31.5	527	63.0	527				
1945 (2)			121.7	1.465				
1948 (1)	78.6	1.021	262.2	1.021				
1950 (4)					3.099	1.551		
1953 (7)						2.300		
1958 (1)	124.5	1.923	249.0	1.923	3.099	2.423		
1972 (3)	106.0	2.800						
1973 (2)	156.5	2.867						
1974 (6)							8.000	4.200+++
1981 (8)			164.0	2.940	3.495	3.918	8.515	5.029
1982 (9)			173.0 (10)	2.905	3.495	4.020	8.515	5.140
1985 (11)	164.0				3.495	4.201	8.515	5.327
1988 (12)	164.0				3.495	4.441		

+ = 1922 (Trewartha, 1951: 344); + + = 1928 (ibid.); + + + = 1975 (MA, 1981: 224). 1 - *shiqu*; 1+2 - *shiqu* & *jiaoqu*; 1+2+3 *shiqu* & *jiaoqu* & *xian*.

Sources:
1) Schinz, 1983: 208; 2) Lo/Pannell/Welch, 1977: 275; 3) Lo/Welch, 1977: 250; 4) Cressey, 1955: 38; 5) Chang, 1970: 70; 6) Küchler, 1976: 144; 7) Ullman, 1961; 8) *Statistical Yearbook of China - 1981*: 39; 9) *Statistical Yearbook of China - 1983*: 59; 10) China Official Annual Report 1982/83: 30; 11) China Urban Statistics 1986: 218 ff.; 12) *Statistical Yearbook of China - 1989*: 665.

Appendix 3C: Territorial Development of Metropolitan Cities in India: 1951-81

	1951 M.C.	1951 U.A.	1961 M.C.	1961 U.A.	1971 M.C.	1971 U.A.	1981 M.C.	1981 U.A.
1. Calcutta	84		103	518	104	569	104	852
2. Bombay	69 (1)	235 (2)	69	438	69	603	69	603
3. Delhi	102 (3)		327	1.485 (4)	446 (5)	1.485	541	1.485
4. Madras	127		127	226	128	531	170	572
5. Bangalore	67		134	464 (6)	175	499	228	366
6. Hyderabad	135		187	220	169	299	171	375 (8)
7. Ahmedabad	52		93	124	93	124	98	222 (8)
8. Kanpur	45		262	297	270	299	262	299
9. Pune	129		130 (7)	282	139	325	139	344
10. Nagpur	53		218	239	218	239	218	237
11. Lucknow	47		104	135	96	128	104	146
12. Jaipur	65		65	104	206	259	181	210

1) City of Bombay; 2) Greater Bombay; 3) Delhi and New Delhi; 4) Union Territory; 5) U.A.; 6) according to the same census: 501.21 km² ('Bangalore Metropolitan Town Group'); 7) "Poona Town Group": 170.03 km²; 8) estimated figures.

Source: Census of India 1951-1981.

Rural-Urban Migration in China

by Thomas Scharping

For decades China has been a closed country, closed to the outside world, but also closed and compartmentalized in her internal set-up. Regional mobility was much reduced and largely confined to organized forms of resettlement, peasants were effectively tied to the countryside and prevented from migrating to the cities. This has helped China to avoid the problems of rapid urbanization, rural exodus and rampant unemployment which have plagued so many other Third World countries. However, with the advent of economic reforms the positive aspects of past policy have given place to a growing awareness of the costs involved. These include human costs in terms of learning, creativity and motivation foregone. They also include the social costs of conservatism, nepotism and festering conflicts which can make work in many institutions and enterprises so galling. The conflicts accrue because the lack of mobility in Chinese society perpetuates long-time dependency relationships and effectively closes a way out of many unresolved issues in the daily life of enterprises and organizations. And, finally, these costs translate into an economic bill being footed: low productivity, slow growth and reduced income.

It is in recognition of these facts that migration has become liberalized to a certain degree in the 1980s. With the rising number of migrants a concomitantly rising number of migration studies has been published, some of them throwing light on the hitherto neglected history of past population movement, some of them discussing the age-old problems of migration that now come to the fore again. This paper is heavily indebted to the survey work of many Chinese colleagues and repeated discussions with them. Above all, it draws on the national sample survey of migration in 74 cities and towns that was conducted in 1986 under the leadership of the Academy of Social Sciences.[1] Whenever possible, data from that survey are analyzed with reference to the rural-urban migration component only. In this way, numbers can be compared with the work of other authors who base their conclusions mostly on total migration including urban-urban mobility.[2] The 1986 national survey is complemented by smaller regional samples of both permanent and temporary migration emanating from Peking[3], Shanghai[4], Wuhan[5] and Henan[6]. Finally, annual registration data[7] as well as results of the 1987 micro-census[8] and preliminary results of the 1990 population census[9] are used.

Overall Dimensions

Unless stated otherwise, migration here is defined as a change of permanent residence or move to a temporary domicile for more than one year involving movement across county or city borders. Its rural-urban component in China has been certainly reduced if compared to migration rates prevalent in other developing nations. Nevertheless, the once widely held picture of a frozen urbanization process does not hold true. Quite the contrary, the 1986 sample survey shows a sizable movement from the villages to the towns and cities that took place over the years. This, of course, is mostly due to the large-scale influx of the 1950s and accelerated urban growth in the 1980s. But even during the 1960s and 1970s rural-urban migration never really ceased.

The total number of rural-urban in-migrants between 1949 and 1985 has been variously estimated to between 60 Mio. and 79 Mio. averaging between 1.67 Mio. and 2.20 Mio. per year.[10] These are approximations only as changing classification rules for urban places, the balancing of gross and net migration and questions of data validity continue to present puzzles. But by and large it can be accepted that about one third of urban growth during that period of time was due to net rural-urban migration, another third to reclassification of places and redrawing of city boundaries, the last third to natural increase.[11]

In the 1980s the pace of migration certainly has increased. The 1987 microcensus yielded a figure of 13.50 Mio. rural-urban migrations during 1982-1987, of which 42% were directed to cities, 58% to towns.[12] Preliminary census results for the period 1985-1990 show that the last five-year total has meanwhile increased to 16.45 Mio.[13] When comparing these figures, it should be noted, however, that in contrast to the censuses of 1982 and 1990 with their one-year-limit, the 1987 microcensus defined migration as a move to another domicile for more than six months. Numbers therefore are not strictly comparable.

The 1986 migration survey substantiates the prominent role of rural-urban influx and allows a differentiation according to city size. It shows that in all size-classes migration from rural areas has supplied the largest share of total urban in-migration with towns being in the forefront, metropolitan areas close to the average and intermediate cities trailing behind. A metropolis is defined here as having more than 1 Mio. inhabitants, a large city as having 0,5 to 1 Mio., a medium city as having 0,2 to 0,5 Mio. and a small city as having up to 0,2 Mio. inhabitants. The towns are limited to chartered towns with a separate administration.

Trends in time

Whereas Table 1 sums up results of migration in the first 36 years of the PRC, Table 2 offers a closer look at the dynamics involved. It demonstrates an highly uneven course of development and corroborates the well-known fact that campaigns and political factors have played an overriding role in migration patterns. The first five years of the PRC are marked by a high migration intensity directed at the large metropolitan areas. This is an era of normalization after the civil war in which refugees, displaced rural inhabitants and a new revolutionary elite all

Table 1: Percentage of urban in-migration by place of origin, 1949-1986

	Metropolis	Large city	Medium city	Small city	Town	Average
total	100.0	100.0	100.0	100.0	100.0	100.0
city	36.7	36.8	34.7	33.3	15.4	31.5
town	16.0	22.6	24.2	24.7	25.8	21.1
village	44.5	38.7	39.4	40.9	56.9	45.2
other	2.8	2.0	1.7	1.1	2.0	2.2

Source: Ma Xia and Wang Weizhi 1988, p.7.

converge on the political and economic centers of the nation. First attempts at registration are made in the cities but there is no anti-urban policy in effect.

During the heyday of the first five-year plan and at the start of the Great Leap Forward rural-urban migration surges ahead. As shown in the Table it continues to be metropolitan-oriented. This is the result of the pull exercised by ambitious industrialization and modernization projects with the concomitant progress in urban consumption and job opportunities.

Altogether 8 Mio. rural migrants enter the cities during 1953-57 and this number swells to a huge wave of 20 Mio. rural in-migrants in 1958 and 1959 alone. At the same time juvenile unemployment starts to develop into a major urban problem and the rectification campaign of 1957/58 takes its toll. Therefore we witness first migration checks and forced reverse migrations in 1955 and 1957.

Rural-urban migration enters a trough in the early 60s when 20 Mio. new urbanites are being sent back to their native villages and a rustification movement for urban youth commences. This is also the time when the strict immigration, employment and rationing controls are effected which until now serve as the major break on spontaneous mobility.

During the Cultural Revolution political factors complicate the picture even further: Starting in 1968 the forced movement of urban youth, cadres and socially discriminated groups to the countryside develops into a massive campaign involving over the years some 17 Mio. youth and an unknown number of urban adults. However, Table 2 substantiates the surprising fact that at the same time masses of new rural in-migrants flock to the supposedly emptied cities, 14 Mio. people according to some sources.[14] Indications are that this is intimately connected to the prominent role of the army in the early Cultural Revolution period: Relatives of army personnel are granted urban residential permits and demobilized soldiers are offered the incentive of much desired urban job placements. Apparently the majority of such placements involve large and medium cities as the percentage for the metropolitan areas in Table 2 stays conspicuously low.

Table 2: Percentage of rural-urban migrants by years of migration

Years	Metropolis	Large city	Medium city	Small city	Town
1949-86	100.0	100.0	100.0	100.0	100.0
1949-50	5.0	1.0	1.5	2.1	1.0
1951-52	5.0	1.1	2.4	2.4	1.5
1953-54	4.6	1.2	3.4	3.0	1.9
1955-56	5.4	3.8	4.0	3.7	2.7
1957-58	7.5	6.2	5.6	4.0	3.2
1959-60	4.3	4.9	4.9	4.1	2.0
1961-62	1.1	2.4	2.9	1.6	1.8
1963-64	1.7	2.8	2.6	2.1	1.7
1965-66	1.6	7.1	2.7	2.4	3.7
1967-68	1.5	2.8	2.5	2.8	2.0
1969-70	2.7	11.8	6.5	4.5	4.1
1971-72	5.0	10.5	6.1	5.8	4.9
1973-74	3.9	5.0	3.1	5.8	4.5
1975-76	6.2	6.8	6.8	6.3	5.6
1977-78	9.2	4.8	6.8	6.8	5.7
1979-80	15.7	8.2	12.7	11.4	13.9
1981-82	6.7	6.3	9.4	9.0	9.7
1983-84	6.5	6.7	9.5	11.3	9.6
1985-86	6.4	6.6	6.4	11.0	18.3

Source: Calculated from sample in *CQQDZZ* 1988, pp.137-139.

With the fall of Lin Biao and the anti-Confucius campaign of 1973/74 rural-urban migration is reduced once more, only to recover again with the ascendancy of Deng Xiaoping and the beginning of the return of sent-down population. The all-time record is recorded in the period from late 1978 to 1980 when about 8 Mio. sent-down youth return to the cities and a large number of former banishments for cadres, intellectuals and political offenders are revoked.[15]

The figures for the early 1980s show an end of this abnormal situation in 1981. But they also point to the fact that the migration volume generally rises with the advance of economic reform. A noted watershed is the year 1984 when the government permits peasants to settle in small cities and towns provided they care for work, food rations and housing themselves. This is reflected in the sudden jump of the migration percentage for towns in 1985-86. Absolute numbers for 1985 alone amount to 6 Mio. peasants taking advantage of this opportunity.[16]

When analyzed in conjunction with comparable figures for total migration[17] the figures of Table 2 convey a much clearer story: With the exception of towns, the percentages for rural-urban migration to cities in the early 50s are always higher by 1-3 percentage points - another proof of the concentration process taking place at that time. During 1975-80 the same phenomenon can be observed for metropolitan areas. Apparently, migration was biased in favor of big agglomerations again. The opposite holds true for the 1960s: Whereas urban-urban migration continued on a low level, rural-urban migration can only be termed depressed. Strikingly lower than for total migration are also the percentages of rural-city migration in the 1980s. They serve notice of the fact that new liberalization measures are foremost directed at migration within the urban sector. An exception is only the migration to towns. Here the percentage for rural-urban movement surpasses that of total mobility.

Structure of rural-urban migration

Stressing the heavy political content of migration patterns does not mean denying the fact that personal factors enter the picture, too. As a matter of fact, lobbying for preferred schooling places and job assignments, demands for the reunion of families separated by the strict migration checks and private calculations in military recruitment, work recruitment and job transfer all play important roles. Finally, some very basic facts of life exercise an influence: Movement of residence is involuntary and not work-connected during childhood, it usually peaks when young people enter higher institutions of learning, take up work or marry and it levels off during later periods of life again.

A variant of this world-wide observable pattern can be studied in Table 3. It shows the mentioned peak in the age-groups of 15-29 years. Larger cities tend to raise the demands on educational standards and work capacity. Therefore a higher percentage for migrants between 20 and 29 years of age can be seen. At the same time big cities are much more restrictive in issuing residential permits for adult peasants or allowing rural relatives to permanently move to their urban kinsfolk. Accordingly, the percentage of migrants above the age of 40 is lower as in the case of small cities and towns.

If reckoned by sex, the composition of rural-urban migrants is noticeably different from that of the total migrant population. Whereas in the latter group men are dominating in all age-specific cohorts much bigger female shares can be detected in the sample used here. This has been interpreted as a sign of the importance of marriage- and family-induced migration among rural-urban migrants - a hypothesis born out by some other regional data.[18]

The marital status of in-migrants can be gleened from Table 4. Unsurprisingly, it shows the low divorce rates typical for the Chinese population at large and a relatively high percentage of singles connected with the young age-structure of

Table 3: Percentage of rural-urban migrants by age-groups, 1949-1986

Age	Metropolis	Large city	Medium city	Small city	Town
0-99	100.0	100.0	100.0	100.0	100.0
0- 4	4.4	5.0	5.1	7.4	6.3
5- 9	5.0	5.3	6.5	6.6	7.3
10-14	5.0	5.8	5.4	6.7	7.6
15-19	18.0	20.2	20.0	18.6	18.8
20-24	30.7	33.2	29.6	25.3	22.8
25-29	18.2	15.9	13.5	13.3	12.0
30-34	7.1	5.7	6.3	6.6	7.3
35-39	3.6	3.3	4.3	5.0	4.6
40-	8.0	5.5	9.4	10.5	13.2

Source: Calculated from sample in *CQQDZZ* 1988, pp.114-116.

migrants. Under closer scrutiny there is also the familiar predominance of unmarried men which among migrants is even more pronounced than among the ordinary population. The percentage of married migrants in small cities and towns is higher than in larger cities, as it is easier to obtain the necessary residential permits for spouses here.

Table 4: Percentage of rural-urban migrants by marital status, 1949-1986

Status	Metropolis	Large city	Medium city	Small city	Town
Total	100.0	100.0	100.0	100.0	100.0
unclear	0.1	1.0	0.3	0.1	0.1
single	56.2	43.4	47.3	38.8	43.2
married	40.7	53.5	49.3	58.1	53.4
widowed	2.5	1.9	2.7	2.8	2.8
divorced	0.3	0.0	0.4	0.1	0.5
other	0.2	0.3	0.2	0.1	0.1

Source: Calculated from sample in *CQQDZZ* 1988, p.152.

Rural-urban migration in China clearly favors persons with above-average educational attainments. This is demonstrated in Table 5 which allows three observations: First, there is an obvious link between city size and length of schooling. Larger cities claim the better educated migrants. Second, all percentages for advanced schooling are higher than the comparable figures for total population. This corroborates the thesis mentioned above. Third, the standards of rural-urban migrants are significantly lower than those of their urban-urban counterparts[19] - a reflection of the limited educational opportunities in villages and towns.

Table 5: Percentage of rural-urban migrants by educational standard, 1949-1986

Age	Metropolis	Large city	Medium city	Small city	Town
Total	100.0	100.0	100.0	100.0	100.0
unclear	0.2	0.2	0.3	0.4	0.5
Coll.grad.	1.7	1.2	1.1	1.3	2.0
Coll.student	0.2	0.1	0.3	0.1	0.4
senior high	19.3	12.2	13.1	14.2	17.5
junior high	34.4	30.5	30.5	28.7	31.9
elementary	26.0	40.1	34.0	31.2	30.1
illiterate	18.2	15.7	20.7	24.4	17.4

Source: Calculated from sample in *CQQDZZ* 1988, pp. 153-154.

Turning to the occupation of rural-urban migrants at migration time we find an expected majority of peasants. The category worker refers to employees of rural industry which serves as a spring-board for change to an urban post. Cadres, military and students as particularly mobile groups claim a larger percentage of migrants than is typical of their share of total population. In a rural environment their numbers nevertheless do not reach the proportions typical for urban-urban migrants. Notoriously low is the percentage of specialists and practitioners of service trades among rural-urban migrants. In sum, the occupational composition of migrants from rural areas shows the slow progress in the division of labor that has been made in the Chinese countryside until now.

Causes and effects of migration

Figures for causes and effects of rural-urban migrations are weak. They must be deduced from the larger sample of total urban in-migration or from fragmentary data referring to different universes. So the conclusions reached from Table 7 should be treated with a degree of caution.

They indicate that despite heavy political censorship social and personal causes such as co-migration, marriage-induced migration, family relationships, study and retirement dominate. Altogether these causes add up to some 45% in the 1986 survey. However, the wide margins to comparable data from the other studies strike a skeptical note. Data pertaining to study and training obviously are highly dependent on the educational endowment of the place under scrutiny. Work recruitment, school enrolment and assignment of graduates is known to have varied widely during different periods of time. And the mutual exclusiveness of the categories used is not sure. For instance, returned youth from the countryside could be enumerated under work recruitment, transfer of work, study and training as well as return of resettled youth.

Table 6: Percentage of rural-urban migrants by occupation, 1949-1986

Age	Metropolis	Large city	Medium city	Small city	Town
Total	100.0	100.0	100.0	100.0	100.0
unclear	0.1	0.0	0.0	0.2	0.0
worker	17.6	15.0	11.7	10.9	18.5
peasant	45.2	54.0	52.7	47.1	30.7
cadre	3.1	2.4	3.6	4.3	9.7
off.personnel	1.0	0.6	1.1	0.6	2.7
specialist	1.4	1.5	1.9	1.0	3.8
service trade	1.3	0.6	0.7	1.2	2.2
military	3.6	2.8	3.5	2.0	1.3
other employm.	3.6	3.0	2.5	4.7	3.1
retired	0.5	0.2	0.4	0.3	0.5
student	7.2	5.2	7.0	6.7	8.7
unempl. youth	3.3	3.7	3.9	3.8	3.4
housework	9.0	8.3	7.5	14.0	11.7
other unempl.	3.1	2.8	3.5	3.2	3.6

Source: Calculated from sample in *CQQDZZ* 1988, pp. 155-157.

Table 7: Causes of urban in-migration in %

Cause	cities and towns 1949-86	cities 1951-86	Peking 1981	Shanghai 1981
Co-migration with family members	23.3	17.6	13.8	4.4
Transfer of work	19.0	23.2	19.4	9.4
work recruitment	9.6	23.4[a]	5.3	28.5
migration after marriage	9.0			
moving to live with relatives	8.6			6.9
assignment for graduates	7.4	6.8	1.1	
demobilization of soldiers	5.7	8.8		
return of resettled youth	4.0			3.2
study and training	3.1	20.2	14.3	6.7
job hunting	1.7			
political reasons	1.6			
retirement	0.9			5.6
other	5.6			35.3

a) Including retirement and political reasons.
Sources: Ma Xia and Wang Weizhi 1988, p.9; Ren Suhua 1988, pp.20-21; Hu Huanyong 1984, p.349.

Underlying this somehow elusive causal structure are powerful economic forces at work: Over two thirds of all migrants report an improvement of income, work and living conditions after having moved to towns and cities. Income levels are also positively related to educational standard and city size. As expected, migrants with better schooling have been rewarded with a significantly higher share of cadre or specialist positions. They have also occupied relatively more positions in privileged state enterprises as opposed to urban collectives or private firms. And comparisons of their performance with that of non-migrants tell a decidedly positive story of initiative honored.[20]

The rewards of migration are there, to be sure. But they are distributed and channelled by a vast bureaucracy. One striking feature of Table 7 catches the eye: Job hunting (*wu gong jing shang*) seems to be the only spontaneous activity free from administrative interference - at least in recent years. All other causal factors are subject to either outright political fiat or to some sort of bureaucratic quota handling: Co-migration, living with relatives and marriage-induced moving - yes, after consent has been given; work recruitment in state and collective enterprises - yes, after the labor plan has been consulted; assignment or study - sure, after the Educational Commission, provincial authorities and other agencies have reached agreement; return from the countryside and various remedial policies - well, upper echelons are still debating the case ...

But some innocent 1.7% of all rural-urban migrants, job hunters from the villages who turn up in the cities, have been turned loose on society. Since this is a percentage from a longitudinal survey the number is small. It mirrors the degree of ossification Chinese society has reached during the last decades. Yet, in the 1980s numbers have certainly been growing. After 1988, however, the situation seems to be volatile, as ideological verdicts against private business and the vicissitudes of economic reform have caused a certain stagnation.

Table 8 tries to catch the picture from the urban employment side. It shows the job opportunities available to rural-urban migrants during the reform decade. These are aggregate numbers encompassing both state, collective and private employment. A representative cross-tabulation of employment of rural labor in the various urban ownership sectors is not available, but indications are that more and more rural migrants are working in the urban private or collective sector with the state sector still being powerful but slowly losing ground.[21]

This is also the message conveyed by a Peking survey of private commercial and industrial enterprises operating in the city districts. In 1987 they employed more than 15.000 employees, the majority being temporary rural migrants from outside Peking Municipality. Especially noteworthy was the large number of migrants in tailoring, repairing and restaurant service. The majority of these people did not enjoy permanent resident status in Peking but rather worked there under temporary residential permits. In 1987 this category of floating population in Peking had grown to 1.15 Mio. people. At the same time, the number of in-migrants with completed formalities for permanent resident status had only amounted to gross 0.095 Mio., net 0.051 Mio.[22]

Table 8: Newly employed rural labor force in cities and towns, 1978-89

Year	Mio.	as % of total new urban employment
1978	1.48	27.3
1980	1.27	14.2
1982	0.66	9.9
1984	1.23	17.0
1985	1.50	18.5
1986	1.67	21.0
1987	1.67	20.9
1988	1.60	18.9
1989	1.20	19.4

Sources: ZRTN 1989, p.197; ZTN 1990, p.130.

"Temporary" urban-rural migration

By general consent "floating population" (*liudong renkou*) does not include commuters between place of work and place of residence who return home on the same day. But as far as the extension of stay is concerned the definition of "floating population" gets blurred. Regulations require newly arrived people in urban areas to fill out a registration card in hotels and guesthouses or - if living in a private household - to register with the local public security station after three days of stay. If this registration is effected the person is granted a temporary residential status (*zanzhu hukou*) for three months which may be renewable on application.[23]

However, because of inconvenience or fear of refusal many people eschew registration and stay in the cities without permit. There is no way to know precise numbers but surveys offer some hints: In 1982 some 4.8 Mio. people, 13% of the national total for floating population, were not in possession of any household registration.[24] Two years later in Shanghai 46% of the floating population living in households had not acquired a temporary residential permit. This amounted to 0,271 Mio. people - approximately 4% of the Shanghai city population at that time.[25]

Therefore, numbers for temporary residential permits do not reflect the real situation. They are even more problematic because many holders of temporary residential status tend to prolongue their stay indefinitely. Whereas in 1982 there were 6.4 Mio. holders of *zanzhu hukou* staying away from their permanent domicile for more than one year, this number has climbed to between 19.8 and 21 Mio. in 1990 - a steep rise both in absolute and relative terms. Especially affected are boom regions like Peking, Shanghai, Guangdong and Hainan where percentages are well above the national average. Another prominent group are border

Rural-Urban Migration 87

areas like Heilongjiang, Inner Mongolia, Tibet, Qinghai and Xinjiang, where preferential treatment for much-needed specialists and technical personnel nowadays often includes the right to keep the permanent residence at the place of origin.[26]

In such a way, the floating population with extended stays in urban areas has been continuously on the rise. According to Shanghai surveys, the percentage of people with one to five years stay has climbed from 15.9% to 31.9% of the total floating population by 1988.[27] Under these conditions the difference between permanent and temporary status of residence becomes highly theoretical. For all purposes, it boils down to a different administrative handling of housing, employment, food rationing and schooling questions. Economically, however, an ever-growing part of the floating population in urban areas is there to stay. Both as producers and consumers they participate in the daily life of cities. An increasing number of studies therefore includes this segment of the population under the bracket of permanent residents or migrants.[28]

Obviously, the large influx of floating population is above all an urban phenomenon involving both rural-urban and urban-urban movements. Judging from Peking and Shanghai data, the percentage of unregistered peasants there has fluctuated between 25% and 68%.[29]

Table 9: Floating population, absolute numbers in Mio., 1978-1990

Year	China	Peking	Shanghai	Tianjin	Kanton	Shenzhen
1978		0.30				
1982	30.00					
1983						
1984		0.70	0.75			
1985	40.00	0.80	1.10			
1986		1.10	1.80			
1987		1.15				
1988	50.00	1.31	1.25	1.13	1.10	
1989				0.80		0.93
1990	70.00					

Sources: Xinhua, 21/9/1988; Zhang Qingwu 1986, p.3; Fudan daxue 1986, pp.1-2; *Beijing Ribao*, 14/11/1984; *Wenhui Bao*, 27/10/1984; *RMRB*, 26/2/1989; *ZRB*, 21/12/1990; *ZRN* 1988, pp.71, 110; *ZRN* 1989, pp.92, 94, 113; *ZRN* 1990, pp.142-194.

Numbers have generally been rising although in this realm, too, a certain slackening has been noticeable during the last two years. It is much harder to secure data for temporary urban residents than for regular in-migrants. Table 10 gives some results of the 1986 migration survey of 74 cities and towns in 16 provinces of China which has also been the most extensive survey of temporary migrants to date. The sample is arranged by age-groups using the same brackets as for permanent migrants in Table 3.

In contrast to the data in Table 3, the age-structure of temporary migrants is much more even. The critical cohort of people aged 15 to 24 years sticks out again. The percentages are, however, significantly lower than those for permanent migrants. As the duration of urban stay for members of the floating population is far from being clear and living conditions are highly unstable, children are rarely taken along with. The larger number of older people among the floating population is conspicuous and so is the clear prevalence of male migrants: No family reunions and rural sweet-hearts here but rather business with a traditional division of labor between outside tasks for men and inside chores for women.

Table 10: Percentage of temporary urban residents from rural areas by age-groups, 1986

Age	Metropolis	Large city	Medium city	Small city	Town
0-99	100.0	100.0	100.0	100.0	100.0
0- 4	2.9	2.8	2.7	5.1	2.0
5- 9	2.3	0.6	1.3	2.6	2.2
10-14	2.0	1.1	3.7	6.8	5.6
15-19	16.5	14.7	15.2	22.2	18.7
20-24	19.8	19.2	23.3	23.1	14.7
25-29	7.3	4.0	9.4	6.0	4.6
30-34	7.1	7.3	11.0	1.7	6.7
35-39	5.4	2.8	4.8	4.3	5.2
40-	36.8	47.5	28.6	28.2	40.5

Source: Calculated from sample in CQQDZZ 1988, pp.240-242.

Table 11 confirms this impression: Visiting relatives and job hunting are the most important reasons for temporary migrations. They indicate strong economic motives as "visiting relatives" often disguises the desire for a long-term stay. Alternatively, it can serve to entrust children to grandparents, thereby freeing a couple to pursue an income maximizing work strategy. The sample under discussion is confined to temporary migrants staying in private homes. Once floating population in hotels and guesthouses is considered, causes like official business, schooling and tourism occupy a far more important position.[30]

But these are purposes of stay that mainly concern city visitors from other urban places. Many studies show that for most peasants temporary urban residence means buying and selling, transporting goods and looking for all kinds of gainful

Table 11: Causes of temporary urban in-migration to households in %, 1986

Age	Metropolis	Large city	Medium city	Small city	Town
Total	100.0	100.0	100.0	100.0	100.0
off.business	4.4	0.3	1.4	1.8	1.8
schooling	2.0	2.6	0.6	2.2	3.9
visit relatives	68.6	72.1	63.0	75.7	76.8
job hunting	9.6	6.6	24.6	6.9	4.1
medical treatment	3.3	2.3	0.9	1.1	2.2
tourism	2.3	0.7	1.3	0.4	0.7
other	9.7	15.4	8.1	12.0	10.5

Source: Calculated from sample in *CQQDZZ* 1988, pp.242-243.

self-employment: Preferred jobs are hawkers and peddlars, refuse collectors, nannies, and odd repairmen. A big group are rural construction gangs which are hired in cities. Their number has risen from 3.35 Mio. in 1978 to 8.55 Mio. in 1988, a figure equal to 45% of all Chinese construction workers.[31]

Table 12 provides a good look at the rural side of the picture. It illustrates the causes of temporary out-migration as surveyed by a large sample of Henan peasants. While on leave from the home village, over 80% of these peasants worked in urban places, with big cities in a clear first place before small towns. 57% of these floating migrants were self-employed or worked in private business, the state sector absorbed 23% of them, urban collectives gave work to 19%. In

Table 12: Causes of temporary rural out-migration in Henan, 1989

Cause	Percentage
job hunting	62.4
trading	9.5
transport activities	6.2
repairing	5.4
business contacts	4.4
refuse collection	3.7
visiting relatives	3.6
medical treatment	2.1
working as nanny	1.2
schooling	0.8
tourism	0.3

Source: Sample survey in: *RYJ*, No.3/91, pp.42-46.

the vast majority of cases (over 80%) the jobs being taken up were sought out privately or recommended by friends, local work-gang leaders organized 12%. The village administration handled a meagre 2% of all cases. The average length of work outside of the village was 166 days and average income amounted to 970 Yuan per head. Remittances from migrants to their home families averaged 686 Yuan per head.

Henan peasants make up some 6% of the 50 Mio. odd people from the countryside who have roamed through China since the mid-1980s.[32] They are a harbinger of things to come, as 100 Mio. more are expected to quit agriculture in the coming decade. Their arrival will be greeted by some, but others are starting to shiver right now.

Conclusions

The above analysis has been mainly descriptive. Size and composition, historical development and motivational structure of rural-urban migration has been assessed. Because in recent years much attention has been paid to small rural towns, the discussion focused more on the big cities. What remains weak in both cases is the study of economic consequences. Sure, all available reports point out the income gains for the migrating rural labor force involved. But the overall balance of social costs and benefits is far from clear. It may well be that gains are privatized while costs are socialized. More systematic work on the direction, volume and use of remittances, on the consequences for land use and yields as well as on the externalities of migration would serve to clarify some of these issues.

Classical theory would have it that labor flows to high wage regions while capital moves in the reverse direction until at some point equilibration takes place. While the span of time ever since the economic reforms is still too short to reach firm conclusions, indications are that in China only the first part of the formula is at work: Rural excess labor moves to urban high consumption areas, but capital and investment stays in the cities. How to combat this situation would be a further subject deserving study.

Finally, the perennial issues of rural industrialization versus urban concentration are as pressing as they always have been. Of course, in a constantly changing environment they will never be solved satisfactorily. But this report contains some disturbing signs that the small town strategy does not work to the extent Chinese planners would like to see.

Notes

1) CRQQDZ 1988.
2) Ma Xia and Wang Weizhi 1988; Sha Jicai and Chen Guangbi 1988; Sha Jicai 1990; Xiong Yu 1988; Wang Xiangming 1988.
3) Luo Maochu et al. 1986; *LW*, 8.12.1986, 15.12.1986, 22.12.1986; *RYJ*, No.2/1988, pp.25-27.
4) Fudan daxue 1986, 1988; Zhang Kaimin et al. 1990.
5) *ZRN* 1988, pp.378-388.
6) *RYJ*, No.3/1991, pp.42-46.
7) Ren Suhua 1988; *Beijing shi renkou tongji ziliao huibian 1949-1987*; ZRTN 1989.
8) *ZRTN* 1989; *Zhongguo 1987 nian 1% renkou chouyang diaocha ziliao, quanguo fence*, 1988.
9) *RPZS* 1991.
10) Ma Xia 1987; Wang Xiangming 1988.
11) Cf. Wang Xiangming 1988, pp.19-20; *New China's Population*, p.81.
12) *ZRTN* 1989, p.573.
13) *RMRB*, 21/5/1991.
14) Feng Lanrui 1982, pp.115-116.
15) Scharping 1981, pp.67-82, 136-168, 342-359, 451-462; Chan Kam Wing 1985, pp.596-613.
16) *ZRN* 1985, p.90; Ma Xia 1987, p.7.
17) Ma Xia and Wang Weizhi 1988, p.6.
18) Ma Xia and Wang Weizhi 1988, p.7. Cf. also Wuhan data in *ZRN* 1988, pp.378-388.
19) Xiong Yu 1988, p.23.
20) Ma Xia and Wangweizhi 1988, pp.9-10; Sha Jicai and Chen Guangbi 1988; Sha Jicai 1990.
21) Taubmann 1991, p.15.
22) *RYJ*, No.2/1988, pp.25-27; *Beijing renkou tongji ziliao huibian 1949-1987*, p.370. For private enterprises and self-employed people cf. also Heberer 1989.
23) *ZRN* 1985, p.90.
24) Zhang Qingwu 1986, p.3; Wei Jinsheng 1984, p.35.
25) Fudan daxue 1985, pp.28-30.
26) *RPZS* 1991, pp.10-11; *ZRB*, 21/12/1990. Cf. also Cao Liqun 1985.
27) *ZRN* 1990, pp.121-127.
28) This has been the practice of the 1986 national migration survey and other studies ever since. Cf. also the different position of public security authors who stress the crucial criterion of permanent residence status: Zhang Qingwu 1986; Zhang Qingwu 1988; Ren Suhua 1988.
29) Luo Maochu et al. 1986, p.3; Fudan daxue 1986, p.3; *ZRN* 1988, p.71.
30) Compare the regional figures from Peking and Shanghai surveys: Fudan daxue 1986, p.3; *ZRN* 1988, p.71; Luo Maochu et al. 1986, p.4.
31) *ZRTN* 1989, p.198.
32) *ZRN* 1990, p.121.

Sources and Abbreviations

Beijing shi renkou tongji ziliao huibian 1949-1987, Peking 1988
BR: *Beijing Ribao*, Peking
Cao Liqun (1985): Cao Liqun, "Woguo jingji tizhi gaige guocheng zhong de renkou qianyi wenti", in: *RX*, No.2/1985, pp.8-12
Chan Kam Wing (1985): Chan Kam Wing and Xu Xueqiang 1985, "Urban Population Growth and Urbanization in China Since 1949: Reconstructing a Baseline", in: *China Quarterly*, No.104, pp.583-613
"Chengshi liudong renkou guanli di xin wenti", in: *RYJ*, No.2/1988, pp.25-27
CRQQDZ (1988): *Zhongguo 1986 nian 74 chengzhen renkou qianyi chouyang diaocha ziliao*, Peking 1988
Feng Lanrui (1982): Feng Lanrui, *Laodong baochou yu laodong jiuye*, Peking 1982
Fudan daxue (1985): Fudan daxue liudong renkou diaochazu, "Chengshi jingji gaige zhong di yi xiang zhongyao renkou wenti - liudong renkou", in: *RK*, No.2/1985, pp.28-30
Fudan daxue (1986): Fudan daxue liudong renkou diaochazu, "1985 nian yu 1984 nian Shanghai shiqu liudong renkou de bijiao fenxi", in: *RK*, No.2/1986, pp.1-4
"Guanyu nongcun renkou waichu liudong qingkuang de diaocha", in: *RYJ*, No.3/1991, pp.42-46
"Guowuyuan guanyu nongye jinru jizhen luohu wenti de tongzhi", in: *ZRN* 1985, p.90
Heberer (1989): Heberer, Thomas, *Die Rolle des Individualsektors für Arbeitsmarkt und Stadtwirtschaft in der Volksrepublik China*, Bremen 1989
Hu Huanyong (1984): Hu Huanyong, *Zhongguo renkou dili*, Vol.I, Shanghai 1984
LW: *Liaowang*, Peking
Luo Maochu et al. (1986): Luo Maochu et al., "Quanmian renshi renkou liudong xianxiang, shenshen xuanze duice", in: *RY*, No.3/1986, pp.2-7, 19
Ma Xia (1987): Ma Xia, "Sanshi nian lai woguo de guonei renkou qianyi ji jinhou de zhanwang", in: *RY*, No.2/1987, pp.3-9
Ma Xia and Wang Weizhi (1988): Ma Xia and Wang Weizhi, "Zhongguo 74 chengzhen renkou qianyi diaocha yanjiu baogao", in: *CQQDZZ 1988*, pp.2-14
New China's Population, New York 1988
Qin Pinduan (1986): Qin Pinduan, "Jingji tizhi gaige yu renkou liudong", in: *RYJ*, No.3/1986, pp.6-11, 57
Ren Suhua (1988): Ren Suhua, "Woguo chengshi renkou qianyi qingkuang jianxi", in: *RY*, No.3/1988, pp.19-23
RK: *Renkou*, Shanghai
RMRB: *Renmin Ribao*, Peking
RPZ (1982): *Zhongguo 1982 nian renkou pucha ziliao*, Peking 1985
RPZS (1991): *Zhongguo disi ci renkou pucha de zhuyao shuju*, Peking 1991
RX: *Renkou Xuekan*, Changchun
RY: *Renkou Yanjiu*, Peking
RYJ: *Renkou yu Jingji*, Peking

Scharping (1981): Scharping, Thomas, *Umsiedlungsprogramme für Chinas Jugend 1955-1981*, Hamburg 1981

Sha Jicai (1990): Sha Jicai, "Guanyu Zhongguo chengzhen yimin de wenhua chengdu yu jingji shouru de xiangguan fenxi", in: *RY*, No.1/1990, pp.8-13

Sha Jicai and Chen Guangbi (1988): Sha Jicai and Chen Guangbi, "Guanyu yimin de wenhua chengdu yu jingji shouru de fenxi", in: *RYJ*, No.2/1988, pp.35-40

Taubmann (1991): Taubmann, Wolfgang, 'Rural Urbanization' in the hinterland of bog agglomerations in the PR of China, Paper for the Second European Conference on Agricultural and Rural Development in China, Leiden 1991

Wang Sijun (1990): Wang Sijun, "Bashi niandai Zhongguo renkou chengzhenhua gaiguan", in: *ZRN* 1990, pp.121-127

Wang Xiangming (1988): Wang Xiangming, "Renkou qianyi he liudong dui renkou chengzhenhua jincheng de yingxiang", in: *RYJ*, No.2/1988, pp.19-24, 51

Wei Jinsheng (1984): Wei Jinsheng, "Guonei renkou qianyi he liudong yanjiu de jige jiben wenti", in: *RYJ*, No.4/1984, pp.32-37, 50

Xiong Yu (1988): Xiong Yu, "Woguo renkou de chabie qianyi", in: *RY*, No.4/1988, pp.20-24

Zhang Kaimin et al. (1990): Zhang Kaimin et. al., "Jiefang hou de Shanghai renkou qianyi", in: *RYJ*, No.6/1990, pp.29-32, 22

Zhang Qingwu (1986): Zhang Qingwu, "Dui woguo liudong renkou de chubu tanxi", in: *RYJ*, No.3/1986, pp.3-5

Zhang Qingwu (1988): Zhang Qingwu, "Guanyu renkou qianyi yu liudong renkou gainian wenti", in: *RY*, No.3/1988, pp.17-18

Zhang Shanyu (1990): Zhang Shanyu, "Woguo shengji renkou qianyi moshi de zhongda bianhua", in: *RY*, No.1/1990, pp.2-8

Zhongguo 1987 nian 1% renkou chouyang diaocha ziliao, quanguo fence, Peking 1988

ZRB: Zhongguo Renkou Bao, Peking
ZRN: Zhongguo Renkou Nianjian, Peking
ZRTN: Zhongguo Renkou Tongji Nianjian, Peking
ZTN: Zhongguo Tongji Nianjian, Peking

Rural Urbanization in the People's Republic of China

by Wolfgang Taubmann

1 Introduction

In almost all countries of the Third World a close connection can be observed between modernization, industrialization, a growing spatial division of labour, a high migration rate and increasing urbanization.

The term "urbanization" stands for a complex process and is difficult to grasp. A simple statistical-demographic criterion to measure the level of urbanization is the percentage of the urban population out of the total population. In the case of the PRC, however, already this definition causes problems.

Urbanization also includes:

- intensifying exchange processes between linked production and distribution,
- increasing professional differentiation dominated by industrial and tertiary occupation,
- urban life-styles regarding social interaction, consumption, and leisure,
- and urban infrastructure, public utilities and service industries.[1]

The level of urbanization in China - regarding the urban population as a percentage of the national total population - is discussed differently by various authors.[2]

Taking the total urban population as a measure, in 1988 China had the highest level of urbanization (49.6%) of all countries with low income.[3] Taken the non-agricultural urban population as a criterion - as suggested by Ma (1987) - the level of urbanization would only be 18.5%. From my point of view both data are incorrect. Taking the first datum, the level of urbanization is far too high, taking the latter, it is too low. In the meantime many inhabitants in suburban districts with agricultural *hukou* (household) have a non-agricultural occupation and thus are de-facto urban inhabitants. Therefore the result of the census of 1990 seems to be realistic: an urban population of 26.15%; 18.63% living in cities and 7.52% in towns.[4]

Independent of whether the statistical data show a high or low level of urbanization, the capacity of the cities, specially of the big cities, to absorb new inhabitants, is nearly exhausted. That is no new situation. All administrative regulations introduced since the middle of the 50s to limit migration into cities are still valid. Erecting barriers between city and county around 1955 is understandable, as the growth of cities - not regarding administrative designations of new cities -

between 1949 and 1957 was primarily caused by migration (54%).[5] The strict control of migration can be proved: Between 1958 and 1988 the share of migration, causing the growth of those cities already in existence in 1949, was 32.9%.

As barriers between city and countryside continue to exist, the processes of modernization and development largely have to take place *within* the rural areas. If we want to use the term "rural urbanization", those elements which are considered as urban have to spread into the countryside.

The following criteria could be regarded as a measure for rural urbanization:

- Growing employment opportunities outside agriculture, not only in rural enterprises, but also in commerce and public services, in connection with different forms of ownership.

- A growing professional and social differentiation of an originally almost homogenous group of peasants or agricultural workers, resulting in different forms of educational participation, cultural interests, life styles and forms of migration.

- The development of rural central places at the base of the settlement system that are closely related to their rural surrounding area, functioning as supply-, education- and service centres, at the same time as locations of the producing sector. These rural central places can also absorb a considerable number of surplus rural working force.

2 Rural-urban barriers

Because of their separation in the last forty years, city and countryside have developed a more or less different system of economy, ownership and administration.

Of great importance is still the household registration (*hukou*) system, which divides the Chinese population into a privileged urban or non-agricultural and a rural-agricultural segment without privileges. Especially noncash welfare and the "quality of life" opportunities constitute the decisive rural-urban differences.[6] The rural agricultural families at the bottom of the hierarchy of residential status as a rule are not legally allowed to move into cities or towns and to change their permanent residence.[7]

Of course, every year there is a certain quota of *hukou* changes. There are different reasons: e.g. work assignment frequently passed on to young people that inherit the workplace of their parents or to peasants who have given their land to urban factories or institutions; attendance of a school or an university education or family reunions.[8]

Most rural migrants, however, stay only for a short time in cities as temporary inhabitants or as floating population (*liudong renkou*). As temporary or contract workers (*linshi* or *hetong gong*) the rural migrants are underprivileged compared to urban workers. They receive lower wages and less social benefits.

The *hukou* system also leads to segmented labour markets. In fact, a rural *hukou* prohibits a permanent employment in state-owned factories. One reason are the overstaffed urban enterprises. Probably 20 to 30 million workers in urban areas are underemployed.[9] This can be explained by the government's preference to capital-intensive heavy industries for decades with only a limited growth of employment opportunities.

As the state-owned industry is primarily concentrated in the cities, the hierarchical structure of the different forms of ownership - state-owned versus collectively or privately owned - establishes a barrier between city and countryside. The administrative systems, too, are very different. Rural inhabitants under the administration of a township or an administrative village receive e.g. an economic or a certain welfare support by the villagers' committee or the team.[10] Such organiztions have often replaced former clan groups.[11] Urban inhabitants are confronted with a street bureau as the lowest state institution, and as a rule they receive social benefits via their work unit (*danwei*).

3 Characteristics of rural urbanization in China

Frequently the number of towns and their inhabitants are taken as a criterion of rural urbanization. Though this criterion is not convincing, statistical data related to the socio-economic structure of the *zhen* (township) inhabitants at least give some hints concerning the level of urbanization of rural areas.

According to the results of the population census in 1982 there was nearly no difference in the structure of trades and occupations of the employed population in cities and towns.[12] If one takes, however, the results of the 1% Population Sample Survey of 1987, there are clearly marked differences in the economic structure between city and town.

This can be explained by the considerably increased number of designated *zhen* between 1982 and 1987, having grown almost four times: 1982 2,660 towns, 1987 9,121.[13] The share of the smaller *zhen*, that have retained a number of agrarian features, has been greatly increased. Obviously this trend has continued. According to the results of the census of 1990 there were 9,321 towns under the jurisdiction of counties and 2,614 towns under the administration of a city.

Table 1: Trades of employed population in cities and towns 1982 and 1987 in percent

	Cities		Towns	
Trade	1982	1987	1982	1987
Agriculture	24.5	28.9	20.9	58.6
Industry	42.3	38.5	37.3	21.1
Construction	6.9	4.8	5.3	2.4
Transportation	5.7	4.7	6.8	2.6
Commerce	7.2	8.2	12.1	6.8
Service trades	1.8	3.0	1.6	1.1
Science, education, health	7.0	6.9	7.8	4.0
Finance	0.4	0.5	0.9	0.4
Government administration	3.9	4.5	7.2	1.7
Other	0.3	0.2	0.1	0.1
Total	100.0	100.0	100.0	100.0
Abs. in mio.	81.74	108.5	32.58	107.4

1982 Population Census of China; *1% Population Sample Survey 1987*.

Though already in 1984 a great number of towns was not able to fulfill the officially necessary criteria of upgrading, they have nevertheless got *zhen* status. Own computations of the *zhen* statistics in 1984 show that out of the 2,777 towns with a total population above 20.000, more than one fourth (26.5%) had less than 10% non-agricultural residents. In 27.7% of all 6,211 designated towns lived less than 2000 non-agricultural inhabitants.[14] While many underqualified settlements are offcially designated towns and thus a part of the formal urban sector, many small market places meet the official criteria without possessing the administrative status of a town and are included in the rural sector.[15]

An additional reason for the low percentage of agricultural inhabitants was the introduction of the "town administering village" (*zhen guan cun*) system which enlarged the administrative boundaries of a designated town to include its surrounding villages.[16]

According to the results of the 1% Population Sample Survey of 1987 the *zhen* population has an intermediate position right between that of the *shi* cities and that of the rural areas. In the analysis of trades as well as of the structure of occupation, *zhen* have a lower amount of people working in factories, in construction and in all service industries (Fig.1.). On the other hand, towns are very different from rural counties that in 1987 were still strictly dominated by employment in agriculture (Fig.2).

The level of education as well as the number of illiterates, too, clearly show the intermediary position of the *zhen* population between city and county. In the hierarchy from the *shi* to the *zhen* and further to the *xian* (county) population the disparity of chances of the male and female population with regard to education and employment opportunities is also growing. The female population in the counties is always to be found at the very bottom (Fig.3).

Though the data of 1982 and 1987, because of the greatly increased number of the *zhen*, do not show an increasing differentiation of employment as a criterion of rural urbanization but almost the contrary, there is no doubt that the non-agrarian employment opportunities have conspicuously grown in the last ten years.

4 Employment opportunities in non-farm economic activities

The non-farm possibilities of employment are very difficult to estimate correctly, especially since the State Statistical Bureau and the Ministry of Agriculture work on the basis of different data material. According to the *Statistical Yearbook of China* the total non-agricultural rural labour force in 1989 was 84.98 million, i.e. 20.8% of the total rural labour force, whereas the percentage in 1978 was only 10.3 (see Tab.2).

The figures released by the Ministry of Agriculture indicate that in 1989 93.67 million persons were occupied in all kinds of rural enterprises (*xiangzhen qiye*) - almost the same number as in state-owned enterprises, that means nearly 9 million more than the figure of the total non-agricultural rural working force published by the State Statistical Bureau (Fig.4). Besides the enterprises run by townships/towns (*xiangban qiye*) and villages (*cunban qiye*) with ca. 50% of all employed persons, the individual households and private enterprises (*siying qiye*) have to offer jobs outside agriculture (ca. 20-30%). About 80% of the 13.7 million individual households (*geti gongshan hu*) with ca. 21.6 million people and of the ca. 115,000 private enterprises with about 1.85 million employees are located in rural areas.[17] The rest of the employed persons are working in 110,000 semi-private joint or cooperative enterprises (*hezuo jingyin zuzhi, jiti qiye*) with about 1.8 million employees.[18]

Table 2: Rural labour force in million persons

Year	Total	Agri-cultur.	Non-agr.	Educ./Cult./Health	Rural enter-prises	Townsh. vill.-run
1978	306.38	274.88	31.50	10.54	-	*28.78
1979	310.25	278.35	31.90	10.76	-	*29.09
1980	318.38	283.34	35.02	11.20	-	*29.99
1981	326.72	289.80	36.92	12.38	-	*29.70
1982	338.67	300.62	38.05	11.55	-	*31.13
1983	346.90	303.50	43.40	13.91	-	*32.35
1984	359.68	300.80	58.88	19.12	52.08	+38.48
1985	370.65	303.51	69.14	19.46	69.69	+41.52
1986	379.90	304.68	75.22	20.36	79.37	+43.92
1987	390.00	308.70	81.30	22.32	87.76	+47.03
1988	400.67	314.56	86.11	24.08	95.45	+48.94
1989	409.39	324.41	84.98	24.74	93.66	+47.20

* brigade-run enterprises, + town/township- and village-run enterprises

Sources: ZTN 1990; Agriculture Yearbooks; China Rural Statistics; Furusawa 1990.

The difference between both data sets can apparently be explained by the fact, that the State Statistical Bureau (SSB) classifies labour force by the *main* activity, i.e. agricultural workers who perform non-agricultural work in a rural enterprise as a sideline, are *not* included.[19] In contrast, the Ministry of Agricuture *does* include the peasant industrial workers, engaged in rural enterprises. Since 1985 the number of employees in rural enterprises for the first time has been higher than that published by the SSB on the total rural non-agricultural employment. This indicates that on the one hand the number of peasant-workers and on the other the number of private and individual enterprises (mainly industry, construction, and transport) has increased considerably. From 1984 to 1989 the employees in the township/town- and village-run enterprises have only grown by 22.7%, whereas in all other rural enterprises they have increased by 241.6% (including the peasant-workers there).

If one tries to evaluate all rural occupation outside agriculture by combining both data sets, there is to be found a number of roughly 118 to 119 million persons: about 94 million workers in the rural enterprises and about 25 million in sectors not related to township/town and village enterprises, such as cultural and educational jobs, medical and public health jobs, banking, post, telecommunication etc.[20]

Since 1988 all data have shown a stagnation or even a regress in non-agricultural occupation in rural areas. Since 1988 the number of employees in rural enterprises as well as the total non-agricultural employment has decreased, primarily as a result of the belt-tightening measures (tightened credits) by the government and the cutbacks in the capital construction investment.[21] In 1988/89, for the first time over a long period, the number of agricultural workers has grown by 10 million persons, whereas the average increase in the decade before was only 5 million per year. This is a heavy burden for the agricultural labour market since, according to several evaluations, at least 150 - 200 million agricultural workers have to find jobs outside the farm sector within the coming decade. This is about 50% of the agricultural labour force in 1989.[22] Hidden unemployment or latent underemployment in agriculture also prevents gains in productivity, because the marginal productive force of labour is tending towards zero.[23]

The question arises whether the present situation is just a general economic slowdown or whether it shows the structural weakness of the economy in rural areas. More and more people are of the opinion that the rural industry - and consequently its labour absorbing capacity - is running down, because the initial stimulating macro-economic conditions have been abolished by the politics of readjustment (*zhengbei zhengdun*).[24]

5 Rural enterprises - development and structural problems

In many cases rural enterprises have been founded by urban enterprises as affiliated companies thus being able to use cultivated land for construction or to produce outside the plan.[25]

However, the development of rural enterprises dominates on the basis of "self-accumulated capital" raised by townships, villages or peasants themselves. Until 1988 the growth rates of rural industry - measured by the gross industrial output value - were extremely high. Between 1985 and 1988 they amounted to 30 to 40% each year! Because of the higher comparative profits the rural inhabitants and institutions permanently transferred money from agriculture into rural enterprises. This comparative advantage of rural industry has reduced the willingness of peasants to till the land and to grow grain.[26]

Already in the middle of the 80s many rural enterprises mainly in the richer coastal regions have exceeded their accumulation capacity by too fast an expansion and thus have run into a debt overload.[27]

The fast growth has for some time covered the fact that limited capital and limited plant size have remained a general characteristic of rural enterprises, having even become more severe.[28] Between 1984 and 1989 the average number of employees per enterprise has diminished from 8.6 to 5.0.[29] Advantages of scale economy as a rule are non-existent, the technological standard in general is old-fashioned and consequently low.[30] The results are low productivity and limited profits.

A further problem seems to be that because of the distorted price structure in favour of industrial products the manufacturing industry in rural areas dominates with about 60% of all employees in rural enterprises, whereas trade and the service industry are growing too slowly.[31] Whether the pocessing industry possesses a similar pattern of production as the urban industry is controversially discussed. Huang Shouhong et al. are of the opinion that only 15% of the rural manufacturing industries are in active competition with the big urban enterprises, especially the small cotton spinning plants.[32] It can be observed that agricultural products up to 80% are reprocessed in cities. The urban enterprises as a rule are better equipped and have a skilled labour force, thus being more appropriate for reprocessing agricultural products than rural enterprises.

Rural enterprises competing with urban industry have a great disadvantage with regard to raw material, especially agrarian products such as cotton, sheep's wool, as well as energy and the sales markets.[33] They have to buy energy and raw materials principally on the market at negotiated prices, whereas state-owned enterprises buy at so-called parity prices. Finished products, too, have to be sold by the producers themselves to 70 or even 80%. In the countryside there are no independent trading organizations that could take over the sale.[34]

Inspite of their low productivity, inspite of the waste of resources and their low product quality, collective and private rural enterprises possess an obvious value, as they offer almost the only possibility to reduce the problems of the rural labour market. As for the rural working force the urban labour market is nearly unattainable, there is always the tendency that the town/township-run enterprises are overstaffed.[35] This is problematic as the competitiveness of the rural industry depends on cheap labour. However, the opportunity costs for the rural industry have first of all to be seen in comparison to the underemployed agricultural workforce.

6 Relationship between *zhen* or township development and rural enterprises

There is a close connection between the development of the rural settlement structure or infrastructure and the rural industry.

Transport and communication systems, town and township construction, rural social and medical welfare, and the rural educational system to a great extent are dependent on the transfer of profits and taxes of the rural industry. The rural collective enterprises pay e.g. at least three different kinds of taxes for urban construction to the towns: product tax, value added tax, and business tax. The percentage that township/town governments are allowed to keep varies between 5% and 12% of the taxes.[36] The taxation of private enterprises is differently regulated. They pay a certain amount of their turnover to the local tax office. Frequently, however, the private enterprises have to pay extra fees such as presents, donations, banquets etc. Many private enterprises seem to be run as collective enterprises either because they can thus be more easily controlled by the local government or because they want to gain a similar preferential treatment as the collective enterprises.[37]

In addition to taxes fees are raised. According to research work in the province of Jiangsu the average profit rate is about 10%. Out of this rate many social and other fees have to be paid to the community, rising up to 45% of the profit. Out of the depreciation funds sometimes more than ten different kinds of withdrawals are paid over.[38] Frequently too much money is taken off, therefore the accumulation of capital becomes very difficult, sometimes the capital stock is completely used up.[39]

The relations between the township/town and village-run enterprises and the township and town administration can be described by two characteristics:

1) On the one hand, local governments try to direct all resources into their own enterprises and to support them as long as possible. Even marginal producers that should leave the market might be kept. Local egoism tries to maximize the welfare of the members of their own community. Though it happens that township-or village-run enterprises take their location not in their own community but in a more favourable place in the neighbouring township, this does not normally happen.

2) On the other hand, local governments constantly try to direct the operations of township enterprises and to raise as many non-tax fees and levies as possible. This can be explained by the fact that the township/town governments possess a double function as owners of the enterprises' fixed assets and as local administration and that the connections between enterprises and administrative offices are not formally regulated. The town/township governments e.g. have no tax sources of their own. Transfer of tax money by higher administrative units does not seem to exist.[40] Though fomally designated towns are "entitled to a share of the county's industrial and infrastructure investment funds",[41] they actually do not eceive financial transfer because of the limited county level resources.

Standardized and regularized upper limits for local fees and an allocation of a certain amount of money to the local governments by higher state units would reduce the direct dependence of the town/township governments on their own enterprises. So far the rural enterprises take charge of, properly speaking, state tasks for their own community, as e.g. investment in agriculture, expenses in finding employment for rural labourforce, expenditures for rural welfare services, education or administration, for bridges, roadbuilding, power stations, and irrigation canals.[42]

The too close connections between rural enterprises and the townships and towns can also be explained by the mesh of interests regarding party, administration and local entrepreneurs.

7 Social and occupational differentiation of the rural workforce

The diversification of the rural economy and new job opportunities creates many forms and stages of transition from agricultural to non-agricultural activities, in many cases combined with migration.

On the household level there are different ways to combine agricultural and non-agricultural incomes. At the present moment it is also difficult to take these different forms as a gradual transition from agricultural to non-agricultural activities. As the development is instable, the rural employees fluctuate between different ways of income or they combine shifting sources of income. The increase of non-agrarian occupation is closely connected with the influence of big cities and the coastal regions with a favourable economic development.

The following socio-economic groups can be distinguished:[43]

1) A big number of peasants has no possibility to work outside agriculture or in some kind of sideline production. This group either remains on the level of subsistence or it belongs to the 58 million impoverished peasant households with less than 200 RMB yearly income per person. They live either in the so-called rural poverty areas of the Southwest or Northwest of China under unfavourable natural conditions, or they have no family members being able to work and thus are dependent on the support of the village collective.[44]

2) The spezialised peasant households or those that have moved from cultivation to animal husbandry or to sideline production do not only fulfill the state requisition procurement quota but they produce also for the market. They are dependent on the purchasing power of nearby urban sales markets.

3) People changing their economic activities from cultivation to processing jobs in village level collective or private enterprises.[45] Work and living place remain in the village. About 23.4 million rural workers are occupied in village-run and 4-5 million hired workers in private enterprises.[46]

4) The peasant-industrial workers or workers are commuting daily (*baidong renkou*) from their village to a nearby town or township seat. The place of living remains in the village, i.e. their household registration and their families.[47] Farming is done in their spare time or during the factory holidays in the busy season. The majority of the workforce in rural enterprises belongs to the groups of peasant-industrial workers under 3) and 4).

This most common form of combining different income sources may include different steps of transition from agricultural to non-agricultural occupations.

5) At least one - often a male - member of a peasant family has changed to non-farm activities and has migrated to a nearby town. As a temporary resident he/she is living there and is returning home to the family for holidays or sporadically. Cultivation, sideline production or animal husbandry in the village often is done by a female family member. Among former farmers, living now in towns, there is a rather large group of those who have received a permanent *zhen* household registration though they have to provide for their own grain (*zi li kouliang de changzhu jumin*). According to official statistics 7.6% of all non-agricultural residents in the towns belong to this group.[48]

6) Long-term migration from the village to a town or to a city inside or outside the county or even the province seems to be limited, though we do not have precise data about that group. It seems, however, that the group of rural inhabitants, being part of the so-called floating population (*liudong renkou*) is relatively big. According to Lu Xueyi and Zhang Houyi (1990) about 30 million peasants belong to that group, 9 million of them living outside their home province. They work either as seasonal or temporary workers in urban factories and do most of the dirty, tiring or dangerous work, do business as selfemployed or farm the land in the suburbs.

7) Private entrepreneurs and so-called individual households are of greater importance in rural areas than in the cities. About 1987 there were at least 0.2 - 0.3 million private enterprises. Moreover, there were about 1 million specialized individual labourers (e.g. carpenters, bricklayers, tailors, plasterers etc.) and about 13.7 million individual households.[49]

Besides the above mentioned groups that represent the bulk of rural employees the following strata should be mentioned in rural areas:[50] cadres in the government and party administrtion, administrative leaders or managers of town/township- or village-run enterprises, staff members in education, culture, health, social welfare etc.

A rough estimation of the size of the mentioned groups is given in the following table:

Table 3: Socio-economic differentiation of the rural work force

Agricultural workers, peasants	ca. 55 - 57 %
Peasant-industrial workers	24 %
Rural administrators	6 %
Town/township-run enterprise managers/administrators	3 %
Individual workers/households	5 %
Private enterprise owners	0.1 - 0.2 %
Private employees	4 %
(Peasant) intellectuals	1.5 - 2 %

Source: Lu Xueyi/Zhang Houyi 1990.

Though the data in themselves only give a rough idea of the importance of the individual groups, in any case it has become clear that an originally mostly homogeneous group of farmers with almost the same level of income inside collective agriculture has changed into a relatively differentiated rural society characterized by many urban traits.

8 Rural urbanization and spatial mobility

An increasing professional and social diversity in rural areas implies a higher spatial mobility - above all migration and commuting.

There exist only disparate data concerning the effect of migration on towns as places of destination and the countryside as areas of origin. Table 4 - calculated on the basis of the 1987 1% Population Sample Survey - show the net-migration between rural counties (*xian*), towns (*zhen*) and cities (*shi*) from 1982 to 1987:

During this period 20.76 million people left the rural area.[51] One third of the migrants from rural counties moved into cities (*shi*), 41% into towns (*zhen*) and 25.5% into other places of the rural area. During the same period there were only 7.21 million in-migrants into the rural counties, so there is a net rural-urban migration of 13.54 million people. The biggest part among the in-migrants into villages are interrural migrants (73.5%). Only 15.8% originated from towns and 10.7% from cities, as shown in Figure 6. The left semi-circle represents the out-migrants, the right half the in-migrants. The circle sectors are proportional to the percentage of migrants to or from cities, towns, and rural counties.

Table 4: Migration between cities, towns, and rural counties, July 1982 to June 1987

from into		City (shi)	Town (zhen)	County (xian)	Total
City (shi)	abs. % %	32,923 29.4 59.9	10,097 9.0 23.6	69,046 61.6 33.3	112,066 100.0 36.7
Town (zhen)		14,313 11.8 26.1	21,317 17.6 49.8	85,473 70.6 41.2	121,103 100.0 39.7
County (xian)		7,704 10.7 14.0	11,371 15.8 26.6	53,083 73.5 25.5	72,158 100.0 23.6
Total		54,940 18.0 100.0	42,785 14,0 100.0	207,602 68,0 100.0	305,327 100.0

Calculated according to the *Tabulations of China 1% Population Survey 1987*, National Volume, 1988, pp.677-723.

In comparison with the cities and the rural areas the real winners in migration are the towns with a net-migration of 7.8 million people. 12.1 million people in-migrated, 70.6% of them from rural areas, and only 4.28 million left, most of them migrating from town to town. Cities, too, had a positive net-migration with 5.7 million people, however, below that of the towns. The main reason presumably was that government has made it easier to move into *zhen* since 1984. Former peasants were allowed to settle permanently in towns (except county seats) under certain conditions. They could obtain - as mentioned above - a non-agricultural registration, but they had to provide their own grain. This may explain why in the 1% Sample Survey this type of settlement had the greatest number of in-migrants, because already in 1988 4.59 million residents of this status had been registered.[52] It is most likely, however, that the migration into towns inspite of all kinds of promotion does not come up to official expectations.

Taking into consideration the sample of migrants, as defined above, the question arises whether 30.5 million migrants in five years, i.e. 6.11 million each year, represent the proper migration rate. If the number of about 60 million "floating people" is correct, only one tenth of the mobile population would have been included. All those mobile people who have changed their residence or are on business trips or just visiting relatives, and whose household registration (*hukou*) still remains in their former or permanent residence, are called "floating population" (*liudong renkou*). Different mobile groups as long-term and short-term migrants, floating people and even commuters, can only be distinguished by regarding local and regional examples. It becomes more and more difficult to discern between these various forms of rural mobility.

By taking the market towns in the counties around Shanghai, the importance of *zhen* (designated towns) and *jizhen* (market towns) may be shown for those groups that left agriculture and found a non-agricultural occupation. In 1986 there were 190 market towns in the 10 counties. From 1980 to 1986 the permanent population of these towns had grown from 704.000 to 858.000. During the same time the number of inhabitants having a temporary permission of residence (*linshi hukou*) grew almost three times, i.e. from 22.000 to 65.000, whereas the so-called floating population increased from about 555.000 to 931.000.[53] It is very likely that the floating population includes many traders, construction workers and farmer-labourers that either for a shorter or longer period stay in market towns or commute daily or weekly from their home villages into the market towns. The number of labourers in the towns in 1986 of about 947.000 was higher than that of the permanent residents.

Not only the extent of migration is important, but also the age, sex, and education of the migrants. One frequently mentioned thesis is that the most active and best qualified workers move from agriculture into non-agrarian activities. Thus the qualification of the agrarian workforce is permanently deteriorating.

The thesis of selective migration, anyway, holds true, when the 1% Population Sample Survey of 1987 is analyzed. The age structure of town residents is quite different from that of the migrants into *zhen* (Fig.5). As a matter of fact, the age groups between 20 and 25 years dominate migration into towns. The migrants into *zhen* are standing inbetween those moving into cities and the intrarural migrants. Among the intrarural migrants females between 20 and 25 years represent 40% of all migrants, whereas young men are the foremost group of the rural-urban migrants. The migrants into towns show a balanced distribution between young males and females (Fig.6).

If the age structure of the migrants and the reasons for migration are seen together, it becomes obvious, that long-term intrarural migration is primarily explained by marriage, i.e. about two thirds of all migration movements are caused by marriage, whereas rural-urban migrants first of all look for a job. The migration into *zhen* is explained by three equally important reasons: work, marriage and family reunion (Fig.7). Since the 1% Population Sample Survey only includes long-term migration, the reasons of migration certainly are biased. It is to be supposed that especially the short-term migrants and the floating people first of all are looking for a job.

A comparison of the occupational structure of the in-migrants into towns and of the resident employed population shows an interesting feature: both the male and female in-migrants have a more urban profile of occupation than the resident *zhen* workforce, i.e. a higher percentage of technicians, government administrators, commercial and production workers, but a lower share of agricultural workers. We do not have informations about the migrants' place of origin, in any case the long-term inmigrants improve the urban character of the town labour force (Fig.8).

An extended sample survey of the Academy of Social Sciences carried out in 222 villages in 10 provinces in 1986 informs us about the occupational and areal mobility of village employees.[54]

Of altogether 189.006 interviewed employees in 1986 37.1% had either temporarily (21.2%) or permanently (15.9%) left agriculture. In 1986 still 64.9% of all employees were agrarian inhabitants,[55] whereas in 1978 they came up to 92.%. The increase of non-agrarian job opportunities in rural areas is well documented by this sample.

In this context employees that had left their home village in 1986 are of interest: 38.4% of all those that had left agriculture, or 14.3% of all employees working in the village.

If peasants that have left agriculture and have migrated are compared to those that no longer are working on the land but have stayed in the village, some differences regarding occupation can be seen. Former peasants staying in their home village, work in village-level or lower enterprises, while the migrants firstly work in construction and secondly in many other branches.

It is a striking fact that specially seasonal migrants have a significantly lower educational level (39.6% illiterates, 38.3 % primary school) than those having left for a longer period (14.9% illiterates, 33.0% primary school) and those working in the village (27.6% illiterates, 38.3% primary school). Most of those working outside agriculture only for some months per year, are illiterate. As village-run enterprises generally expect some kind of education of their employees, illiterates have almost no other chance earning some extra money than by working in construction, in transport or as pedlars. Without any doubt, there is a close correlation between the level of education and the length of absence from farming.

There is another sample survey, in general coming to the same results as the above-mentioned, that explains why people leave farming and look for a new job.[56] The most important reason is "low income from farming, higher income from industrial and commercial work" (59.3% of all interviewed persons), secondly "insufficient farm land and surplus labour power" (13.9%), thirdly "the unwillingness to do farming as it is too tiring" (9.9%). Most likely these reasons can be generalized, i.e. non-agrarian employment compared to farming seems to be preferable, whereas in former years no one had any choice at all since nearly everyone was tilling the land.

Table 5: Seasonal or long-term migration of rural labour force (1986)

Migrants	Total	Long-term	Seasonal
Organized migration	36.2	29.3	37.5
Voluntary/spontaneous m.	63.8	70.7	62.5
Total	100.0	100.0	100.0
Destination of migration			
Other villages within county	20.8	14.2	22.5
Other villages within prov.	24.1	14.7	26.6
Other villages outside prov.	3.9	6.2	3.3
Market towns (jizhen)	5.3	5.8	5.1
Towns/county seats	12.1	15.3	11.2
Small/medium-sized cities	29.4	28.7	29.7
Large cities	3.8	12.1	1.6
Abroad	0.6	3.0	--
Total	100.0	100.0	100.0
Educational level			
University/College	--	0.3	--
Trade school	--	0.2	--
Upper sec. school	7.0	16.8	4.4
Lower sec. school	21.2	34.7	17.7
Primary school	37.2	33.0	38.3
Illiterate	34.5	14.9	39.6
Total	100.0	100.0	100.0
Absolute numbers	26,993	5,596	21,397

Source: Geng De-cheng (ed.) 1989, Tab.3.

In general the survey shows: those with the most comprehensive education have the best chance to find work outside agriculture and away from their own village.

Of course there are great regional differences, if one takes the destinations of migrants or the employment opportunities of the migrated rural labor force. Therefore it is not possible to point out only *one* clearly marked pattern, as the following table shows:

Table 6: Destination of rural migrants in different provinces 1986

Province	JS	ZJ	FJ	HEB	SX	HL	GX	QH
Destination								
Other villages	59.0	10.1	20.4	38.6	52.5	18.7	35.7	78.3
Market towns	2.3	14.5	4.7	9.6	19.5	3.1	6.2	3.4
Towns/Country seats	15.9	26.0	5.6	25.8	17.6	63.0	12.1	10.5
Small and medium -sized cities	13.3	31.3	63.8	18.0	7.7	13.8	35.4	6.8
Large cities	9.5	18.1	3.6	8.0	2.7	1.4	10.6	-
Abroad	-	-	1.9	-	-	-	-	-
Total	100.0	100.0	100.0	100.0	100.0	100.0	100.0	100.0

JS: Jiangsu, ZJ: Zhejiang, FJ: Fujian, HEB: Hebei, SX: Shanxi,
HL: Heilongjiang, GX: Guangxi, QH: Qinghai.
Source: Geng De-cheng (ed.) 1989.

Whereas e.g. in the provinces of Jiangsu, Shanxi, and Qinghai intrarural migration is dominating, in Heilongjiang towns and county seats are preferred by migrants or in Fujian the small and medium-sized cities.

The transition from agriculture to non-farm activities often connected with the described selective migration may result in a deterioration of the agricultural labour force's qualification and in an agriculture sometimes just run by old people or women. In some cases peasant-workers even let their fields lie fallow for a season. Many peasant-industrial workers or people who have left agriculture are in a dilemma: on the one hand the land becomes a burden to those peasants who have been transferred to non-agricultural acitivities, on the other hand they want to keep it as a kind of reinsurance because of the uncertain political situation.[57]

Because of the general uncertainty and because of the permanently diminishing appreciation of income opportunity by farming, many peasants do no longer invest in farming but in building a house or in increased consumption.[58]

Inspite of these drawbacks, the positive effects might be of greater importance specially for the home regions of the migrants. The migrants and floating people often send part of their income to their family members back home and thus cause a money transfer into economically weak regions.

Last not least they transport a permanent stream of informations and ideas from the cities and towns to the rural regions. They learn about new ways of life, new work techniques, new markets or materials - knowledge and abilities they pass on by contacts with their places of origin.

9 Possible development strategies

Strategies for the development of rural economy and small towns are possible on two levels:

A) Macroeconomic level

1) On the macroeconomic level the price gap, after having been closed in the middle of the 1980s for some years, has widened again. Consequently the price relations between agricultural and industrial products would have to change again in favour of agriculture.

2) During the last years subsidies have been constantly changed in favour of urban inhabitants, whereas subsidies for the input for farm production have been lowered. Thus it would be necessary to change again the relation between agrarian and consumptive subsidies.[59]

3) In 1978 10.6% of all public construction investment was put into agriculture and forestry, in 1988 it was just 3.0%. During the same decade the investments of collectives and individual peasants have gone down as well. Thus the general economic setting of rural production has deteriorated.[60]

As long as the general economic setting does not decisively favour rural areas, the relations between city and countryside, inspite of ten years of reform, will not be changed.

B) Regional and local level

Rural industrialization needs some kind of economy of scale. It is also dependent on conditions such as transport systems, markets, knowledge of marketing, and the quality of the labour force.[61] Easy contact between purchasers and producers is one of the most significant preconditions for non-farm activities of the rural labour force. Regarding these activities there is a considerable variation within China.[62] Taking the PRC as a whole the best chances of development are to be found in the economically prosperous regions such as in the Beijing-Tianjin-Tangshan Area, the Changjiang Delta or the Pearl River Delta. While in 1989 the national average percentage of non-farm activities among rural economic activities was 21%, the respective share in the counties under the administration of Shanghai Municipality was 70%, in the counties of Beijing 55% and in the counties of Tianjin 48%; the figure in Jiangsu was 39%, in Zhejiang 35%, but e.g. in Yunnan only 9% and in Sichuan 13%.[63] On the provincial basis there is a strong correlation between the percentage of township-run enterprise employment figures and the percentage of non-farm activities of the rural labour force (r = 0.909).

Rural industry and specially village-run enterprises, being developed regionally in an indiscriminate way, in the long run will only lead to a waste of cultivated land by incoordinate settlement and extension as well as a waste of raw material, and it will destroy the still intact rural environment. Regional planning should take the conditions of growth very seriously and not just enforce economic growth by all means, especially where there are no suitable conditions.[64]

Rural urbanization and industrialization must not imply that almost each village has its own factories. Just because of the scattered locations, environmental pollution and the waste of cultivated land by many village-level enterprises cannot be controlled.[65] On the contrary a "decentralized centralization" according to the position of a town within a settlement hierarchy should be regarded as an aim in regional-economic planning.

The settlement system in transition between the urban and rural sphere may be characterized by the two following types of hierarchy that on the one hand can be defined by the administrative system, and on the other by the size or retailing and service functions. Obviously there is a close correlation between the administrative position and the order of central place functions of the towns:

Designated towns under the county administration and township seats constitute the official threshold between urban and rural status. Within a central place hierarchy all towns between a county town proper - or even a county-level city - and a rural market (*cunzhen*) are arranged according to the importance of their market function. Guo Huacheng and Lin Shenghe are calling all these settlements market towns, the two highest-level towns together with the county-level cities are classified as small cities/towns (*xiao chengzhen*).[66]

On a meso- or micro-scale, rural industry as a rule will find comparatively suitable locations in such towns, which have a certain level of infrastructure and limited agglomeration advantages (scale economy),[67] i.e. only in the prosperous regions or in the peri-urban areas lower-level towns are suitable for development, in poorer or peripheral regions the development should be concentrated on higher-level towns.

Administrative Hierarchy		Settlement Hierarchy
		(County-level city) (xianjishi)
Seat of county administration (xianzhengfu suozaidi)		County town proper (chenguan zhen)
Designated county adm. town (xian xia zhen)		Designated town (jianzhi zhen)
Township seat (xiangzhengfu suozaidi)	jizhen	Township market town (xiangzhen)
Administrative village (xingzhengcun)		Rural market (village) (cunzhen)
		Hamlet (cunzhuang)

In some cases the extension of settlements should include small as well as medium-sized towns, if regional economic conditions make this necessary. Such a strategy would make it easier to find suitable industrial zones as well as areas for residential houses and service institutions. As the rural urbanization process generally lags behind the speed of industrialization, modernized and expanded rural town facilities such as roads, markets, warehouses and storage, cultural, educational and service institutions have to be linked with those industrial zones. At the same time it would be desirable that there were a stricter control of spending funds and a better coordination among the different regional and sectoral projects.

Notes

1) Schöller 1983, pp.25 f; Johnston 1983, p.363.
2) Ma/Cui 1987, pp.373-395 or Chan/Xu 1985, pp.583-613.
3) *World Development Report 1990*, ZTN 1990, Ministry of Urban Construction.
4) Because of a stricter use of the concept "urban area" the number is considerably below the hitherto "total urban population", however higher than that of the non-agricultural urban population. In the census 1990 the population living in rural areas of urban districts is not taken into consideration just as the population of villages that are under the jurisdiction of a town. See *Major Figures of the Fourth National Population Census of China*, 1991.
5) Taking only into consideration the population growth of the 98 cities already existing in 1949, the share of the natural population growth is calculated to 46% out of the total population increase. The base of calculation is the respective excess of birth of all cities. Source: *China. The Fourty Years of Urban Development 1990*.
6) Yan Xiaofeng et al. 1990, pp121 f.
7) Zuo Xuejin 1989, p.21.
8) See *Zhongguo renkou, Shandong fence 1989*. Between 1966 and 1986 only about 24 million rural labourers have been transferred into cities by receiving an urban *hukou* (Christiansen 1990, pp.102 f).
9) Li Yuzhu 1990, pp60 f.
10) Christiansen, ibid.
11) Yan Xiaofeng et al. 1990, pp121 f.
12) Cf. *1982 Population Census of China 1985*, tab. 58 and 59. See Ma Rong 1990, pp.131 f.
13) 1982 Population Census, tab. 23; Ministry of Construction.
14) Own computation of the data published in the *Manual of Town Population*, ed. by the Ministry of Public Security 1985. The criteria for a designated *zhen* town in 1984 were at least 2,000 non-agricultural inhabitants in a township with a total population of less than 20,000. In a township with more than 20,000 inhabitants the percentage of the non-agricultural population should exceed 10%.
15) Lee 1989, p.772/3; Taubmann 1987, p.76.
16) See Lee 1989, p.784.
17) The figures are from 1987. Liang Chuan-yun 1990.
18) See *Zhongguo Tongji Nianjian 1990*, p.394; *China Agriculture Yearbook 1987*, p.244; for definition see Odgaard 1990/91, pp.29 f.; Byrd/Lin (Eds.), 1990, p.XII.
19) See Surplus Labour Utilization Study Group..., 1990 p.3.
20) Ibidem.
21) Furusawa 1990, p.10.
22) Jiang Xiaohua 1988, p.10; Liu Zheng-peng 1987, p.22; some authors - e.g. Du Runsheng 1988 - are writing about a figure of 200 million released workers.

23) Huang Shouhong et al. 1990, pp.39-46.
24) E.g. Yang Jianjun 1990.
25) Christiansen 1990, p.98.
26) Bao Youti 1990, pp.62-64.
27) Yu Guoyao/Li Yandong 1989, pp.22-27.
28) Wang De 1990.
29) Furusawa 1990, table 1.
30) Ding Jiaxin 1990, pp.64 f., Yang Jianjun 1990.
31) In 1985 the number of employees in commerce and restaurants was larger than in 1988 (16.9 million versus 14.2 million).
32) Huang Shouhong et al. 1990, pp.39-46.
33) Bao Youti, 1990, pp.62-64.
34) Chen Jiyan et al. 1989, pp.17-26.
35) Cf. also Zhang Jianguang 1990; Song 1990.
36) Cities retain at least 7%. Cf. Deng Zhu 1990. See *CNA*, No.1414, 1990; Byrd/Gelb 1990, p.358.
37) Ren Dakai 1990, p.3.
38) Yu Guoyao/Li Yandong 1989, pp.22-27.
39) Byrd/Gelb, ibid.
40) Cf. also Chen Jiyan 1989.
41) Lee 1989, p.781.
42) Huang Shouhong et al. 1990, pp.39-46, Song 1990.
43) Lu Xueyi/Zhang Houyi 1990, pp.16-21.
44) Cf. also Küchler 1990, pp.124-138.
45) Fei Xiatong 1989/90, p.51.
46) Lu Xueyi/Zhang Houyi 1990, pp.16-21.
47) Ma Rong 1990, pp.131 ff.
48) According to the Ministry of Construction 1988: 4.6 million persons.
49) Liang Chuan-yun et al. 1990.
50) According to Lu Xueyi/Zhang Houyi 1990, pp.16-21.
51) According to the survey, migrants are defined as persons that either have changed their *hukou* or that have left their residence of permanent registration already half a year before the survey.
52) Oral communication by the Ministry of Construction, Fieldwork 1989; Central Committee, Circular on Rural Work, Manual of Administration 1986, Appendix.
53) *Shanghai Jizhen 1980-1986*, Shanghai 1988.
54) Geng De-Chang (ed.) 1989.
55) There is a slight difference between the data. Obviously some former peasants are still registered as agricultural workforce.
56) Wu Huailian/Xia Zekuan 1990. The sample was conducted in 24 villages among 985 families in August 1988.
57) Sa Ren 1990, p.3.
58) See Wu Huailian/Xia Zekuan 1990, p.75.

59) Ding Jiaxin 1990, pp.64 f.
60) *China Statistics Abstracts 1990*, p.62; Ding Jiaxin, *ibid.*
61) Wang De 1990.
62) Blank/Parish 1987.
63) *Zhongguo Tongji Nianjian 1990*, p.330.
64) See also Deng Zhu 1990.
65) *Zhongguo Nongcun Jingji*, 5, 1990, pp.3-14.
66) Guo/Lin 1991, p.4.
67) See Kwok 1987.

References

Agricultural Publishing House (Ed.): *China Agriculture Yearbook 1987*, Beijing 1988
Bao Youti: "A Symposium Summary - Views on Township Enterprises in the Eighth Five-Year Plan in the 10-Year Development Plan", in: *Zhongguo Nongcun Jingji*, No.8, 20 Aug. 1990, pp.62-64 (JPRS-CAR-90-090 v. 7 Dec. 1990)
Bian Yanjie: *Work-unit Structure and Status Attainment: A Study of Work-Unit Status in Urban China*, Ph. D.-Thesis, State University of New York at Albany, 1990
Blank, G./ W.L. Parish: Rural Industry and Nonfarm Employment: Chinese and Comparative Perspectives, Conference on Chinese Cities in Asian Context, Hong Kong, June 1987
Bureau of Administration: Manual of Administration of the People's Republic of China (*Zhonghua renmin gungheguo xingzheng qu hua shouce*), Beijing 1986
Byrd, W.A./Lin Qingsong (Eds.): *China's Rural Industry. Structure, Development, and Reform*, Oxford u.a.: OUP 1990
Byrd/Gelb: "Why Industrialize? The Incentives for Rural Community Governments", pp.358 ff.; in: Byrd, W.A./Lin Qingsong (Eds.): *China's Rural Industry. Structure, Development, and Reform*, Oxford u.a.: OUP 1990
Chen Jiyan et al.: "Problems Faced in the Development and Reform of China's Rural Economy and Ideas for Countermeasures", in: *Jingji Yanjiu* (Economic Research), No.10, 20. Oct. 89, pp.17-26 (JPRS-CAR-90-013, 21 Febr. 1990)
Chen Yaobang: "The Strategic Significance Behind Developing Township Enterprises in China", in: *Zhongguo Keji Luntan*, No.2, 18.3.1990, pp.1-4 (JPRS-CAR-90-049, 11 July 1990)
Christiansen, F.: "The Ambiguities of Labour and Market in Periurban Communities in China During the Reform Decade", in: J. Delman, C. Stubbe Östergaard and F. Christiansen (Eds.): *Remaking Peasant China*, Aarhus: Aarhus University Press, 1990, S.94-105
Deng Zhu: Reflection on the Way of China's Urbanization of Last Decade, Paper presented to the International Geographical Union (IGU) Regional Conference Beijing 1990

Department of Population Statistics, State Statistical Bureau: *Tabulation of China 1% Sample Survey in 1987*, National Volume, Beijing 1988
Ding Jiaxin: "A Study of the Rationalization of Economic Relations between Cities and Rural Areas", in: *Jingji Yanjiu*, No.3, 20 March 1990, pp.64-67 (JPRS-CAR-90-047, p.26 f)
Delman, J., C. Stubbe Østergaard and F. Christiansen (Eds.): *Remaking Peasant China*, Aarhus: Aarhus University Press, 1990
Du Rensheng: "Rural employment in China: The choices", in: *International Labour Review*, Vol.127, No.3, 1988, pp.371-380
Fei Xiatong: "Small Towns: Reexploration", in: *Chinese Sociology and Anthropology*, Fall 1989/90, vol.22, no.1, pp.42 f.
Furusawa Kenji: "Rural Enterprises under Reevaluation", in: *China Newsletter No.88*, Sept.-Oct. 1990, pp.10-15
Geng De-chang (Ed.): Statistical Data on the Situation of the workforce in more than 100 villages (1978-1986) (*Chuanguo baicun laoding li qinkuang diaoche ziliaoji*), Beijing: Statistical Publishing House 1989
Guo Huan-Cheng/Lu Qi: The Development of Rural Enterprises in China and the Countermeasures, Paper presented to the IGU Regional Conference, Beijing 1990
Guo Huan-Cheng/Lin Sheng-he: *Geographical research on zhen development*, Department of Geography, Peking University 1991
Howard, P.: "Rice Bowls and Job Security: The Urban Contract Labour System", in: *The Australian Journal of Chinese Affairs*, Issue 25, January 1991, pp.93-114
Huang Shouhong et al.: "Town and Township enterprises as a Motive force in the Development of National Economy", in: *Jingji Yanjiu*, No.5, 20 May 1990, pp.39-46 (JPRS-CAR-90-066, 29 Aug. 1990)
Jiang Xiaohua: "Massive Transfer of the Rural Surplus Labor", in: *Liaowang*, Overseas Edition, 2/1988, No.7, S.10-11 (JPRS-CAR-88-018)
Johnston, R. et al. (Eds.): *The Dictionary of Human Geography*, Oxford 1983, p.363
Küchler, J.: "On the Establishment of a Poverty-Oriented Rural Development Policy in China", in: J. Delman, C. Stubbe Østergaard and F. Christiansen (Eds.): *Remaking Peasant China*, Aarhus: Aarhus University Press, 1990, pp.124-138
Kwok R. Yin-Wang: Rural Urbanization: Strategy of Rural Town Development, Conference on Chinese Cities in Asian Context, Hong Kong, June 1987
Lee, Yok-shiu F.: "Small Towns and China's Urbanization Level", in: *The China Quarterly*, Issue 120, pp.771-786
Li Yuzhu: "Countermeasures against unemployment", in: *Jingji Yanjiu*, No.8, 20 Aug. 1990, pp.60-66, 80 (JPRS-CAR-90-090, 7 Dec 1990)
Liang Chuan-yun: Manual for the economy and management of privat enterprises in China (*Zhongguo siying qiye jingying guanli zhinan*), Beijing 1990
Liu Zheng-Peng: "A method to estimate the surplus agricultural labour-force", in: *Nongye jishu jingji*, 1/1987, p.22

Lu Xueyi/Zhang Houyi: "Peasant Diversification, Problems, Remedies", in: *Nongye Jingji Wenti*, No.1, 1990, pp.16-21 (JPRS-Car-90-040, 29 May 1990)
Ma J.C./Gonghao Cui: "Administrative Changes and Urban Population in China", in: *Annals of the American Association of Geographers* (AA) (3), 1987, pp.373-395
Ma Rong, "Development of Small Cities and Towns, and China's Modernization", in: *Zhongguo Shehui Kexue*, No.4, 1990, pp.131-146 (JPRS-CAR-90-069, 7 Sept. 1990, pp.25-37)
Ministry of Public Security, China. Manual of Town Population, Beijing 1985 (Gongan Bu - San Ju, *Zhongguo. Chengzhen Renkou Ziliao Shouce*)
Odgaard, O.: "Inadequate and Inaccurate Chinese Statistics: The Case of Private Rural Enterprises", in: *China Information*, Vol.V, No.3 (Winter 1990 -1991), pp.29-38
Ren Dakai: "Law Contemplated on the Phenomenon of Village Enterprises Falsely Claiming To Be Collectives", in: *Jingji Ribao*, 24 May 1990, S.3 (JPRS-CAR-90-057, vom 31.July 1990)
Rural Economy Unit, State Council Research Office, and Rural Development Research Institute, CASS: "Development of China's Township and Town Enterprises and Their Macrocoordination With the National Economy", in: *Zhongguo Nongcun Jingji*, No.5 and 6, 20 May and 20 June 1990, No.5, 20 May 1990, pp.3-14
Sa Ren: "Population, Employment, Urbanization - A Summary of Viewpoints From the International Scientific Symposium on the Development of Village Communal Regions and the Population Shift", in: *Zhongguo Xiangzhen Qiye Bao*, p.3, 5 Jan. 90 (JPRS-CAR-90-020, 14 March 1990)
Schöller, P.: "Zur Urbanisierung der Erde", in: *Deutscher Geographentag*, Tagungsbericht und wissenschaftliche Abhandlungen, 43. Deutscher Geographentag Mannheim 1981, Wiesbaden 1983, S.25-34
Song Boqin: "Guided relocation: A new approach to resolving the problem of surplus agricultural population", in: *Jingji Cankao*, 23 July 1990, p.4 (JPRS-CAR-90-079, 25 Oct. 1990)
State Statistical Bureau (Ed.), *China Statistical Yearbook*, various years
State Statistical Bureau, Urban Social and Economic Survey Organization (Comp.): *China - The Forty Years of Urban Development*, Beijing 1990
Surplus Labor Utilization Study Group of the Chinese Academy of Social Sciences' Rural Development Institute: "The Surplus Agricultural Labor Shift - A 10-Year Assessment", in: *Zhongguo Xiangzhen Qiye Bao*, 30 March 1990, p.3 (JPRS-CAR-90-040, 29 May 1990)
Taubmann, W.: "The Role of Small Cities and Towns in the Process of Modernization of The People's Republic of China", in: *Applied Geography and Development*, Vol.29, 1987, pp.73-92
Wang De: Rural Urbanization - A Case Study of the Developed Area, Wuxi and Jiangyin Counties. Paper presented to the IGU Regional Conference Beijing, August 1990

Wei Jinsheng: "Some Basic Problems in the Study of Internal Population Migration and Movement", in: *Renkou yu jingji*, 25 Aug. 1984, pp.32-37 (JPRS-CPS-84-081, 4 Dec. 1984)

Wu Huailian/Xia Zekuan: "The Investigation of the Situation of the Outflowing Peasants in 24 Villages", in: *China City Planning Review*, Vol.6, No.4, 1990, pp.60-76

Yan Xiaofeng et al.: "'Social Differentiation' Problem Groups: Differentiation and Integration of China's Social Structure at the Present Stage", in: *Zhongguo Shehui Kexue*, No.4, 1990, pp.121-130 (JPRS-CAR-90-069, 7 Sept. 1990)

Yang Jianjun: An Analysis of the Current Condition of Urbanization of the Rural Population in China, Paper presented to the IGU Regional Conference, Beijing 1990

Yu Guoyao/Li Yandong: "The Difficulties and Problems Facing Township and Town Enterprises", in: *Nongye Jingji Wenti*, No.10, 23 Oct. 1989, pp.22-27 (JPRS-CAR-90-011, 12 Febr. 1990)

Zhang Jianguang: Economic Dilemma and Development of Rural Areas in Metropolis: An Example of Chongqing City, Paper presented to the IGU Regional Conference Beijing 1990

Zheng Chong: "A Brief Discussion of Farm Labor in Our Country", in: *Jingji Ribao*, 9 Dec. 1989, p.2

Zuo Xuejin: *Population Paradoxes in China - Population Viewed as Producers and Consumers*, Ph.D. Thesis, University of Pittsburgh 1989

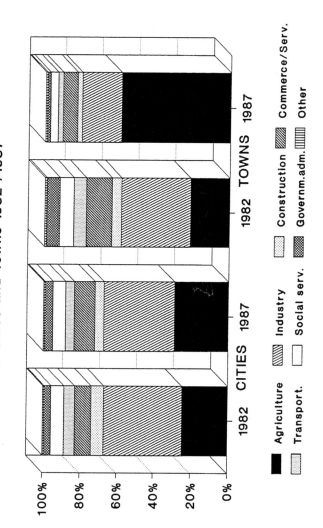

Figure 1: Trades of Employed Population in Cities and Towns 1982/1987

1982 Population Census of China;
1 % Population Sample Survey 1987

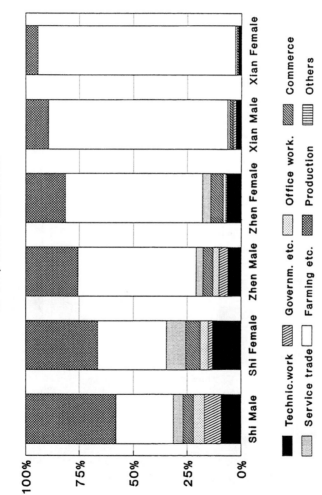

Figure 2: Employees by Occupation in Shi, Zhen and Xian

1% Population Sample Survey 1987

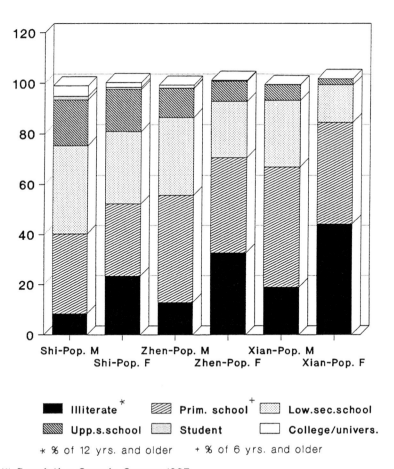

Figure 3: Educational Level and Illiteracy
Resident Pop. of Shi, Zhen and Xian

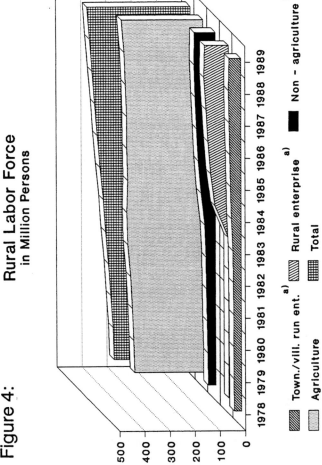

Figure 4: Rural Labor Force in Million Persons

Sources: a) Agriculture Yearbooks;
b) ZTN 1990; China Rural Statistics;
Furusawa 1990

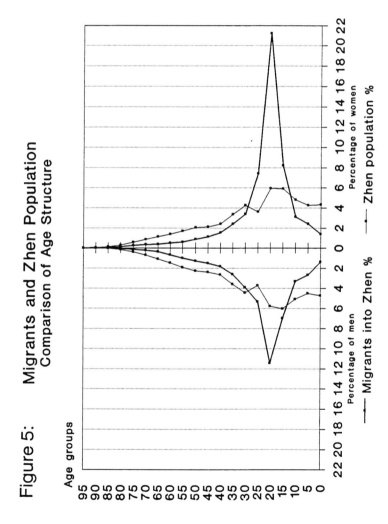

Figure 5: Migrants and Zhen Population
Comparison of Age Structure

Rural Urbanization

Figure 6: Age Structure of Migrants into Shi, Zhen and Xian

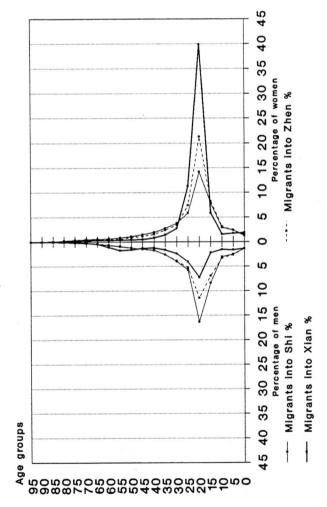

1% Population Sample Survey 1987

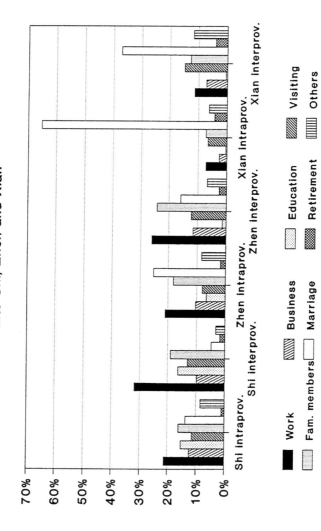

Figure 7: Reasons of Migration into Shi, Zhen and Xian

1% Population Sample Survey 1987

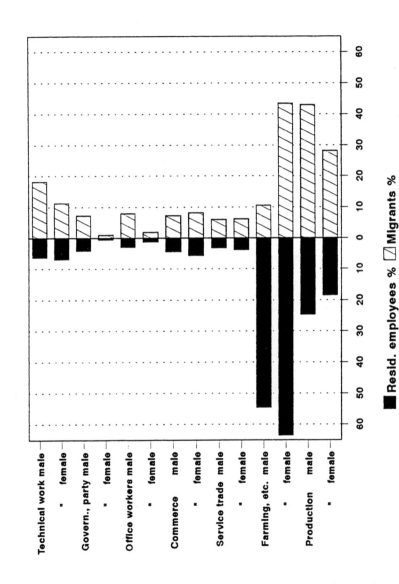

Figure 8: Zhen-Employees and Migrants into Zhen
Comparison of Employment Structure

Changing Rural-Urban Relations in China

by Kok Chiang Tan

1 Introduction

Since the late 1970s, China has undertaken a series of major socio-economic reforms. These reforms have been classified either as rural or urban, and many of them have been carried out within these two realms as if they were unrelated. But after the publication of several studies on small towns in China (Tan 1986a, b, 1990a, 1991), this author is of the opinion that, because they are premised upon the construction of a commodity exchange economy, rural reforms have not only contributed to the revitalization of many small towns but also caused the development of a socio-economic force from below, which will ultimately lead to the creation of a whole new set of rural-urban relations. Given the current conditions of imperfect market operations, to ensure continued integration and improved functioning of the urban system, the developing rural-urban relations must be given certain administrative guidance and direction.

2 Pre-Reform Rural-Urban Relations

In the late 1970s, there were few socio-economic ties between the countryside and the urban centres. As a result of the preoccupation to destroy the pro-1949 rural-urban relations, and of three decades of deliberate rural-urban segregation aimed at a rapid development of heavy industries in the cities, the countryside was virtually cut off from the city (Ding 1990). Even in those rural areas which were included within urban jurisdiction, such as the suburban counties of Beijing and Shanghai, integration was not supposed to exist, as the boundary which divided these rural areas from the central city districts was treated as a clear socio-economic barrier. Rural-urban segregation was exemplified by a household registration system which aimed at restricting rural-urban migration. Rural-urban transfer was possible only under official sanction, and when socio-economic conditions in the urban centres declined, even those rural migrants who had been permitted to enter the cities would be repatriated (Ma 1990).

Rural-urban exchange was carried out through a state procurement and distribution system which completely by-passed the old private trading establishments. State-run commerce operated through such organizations as the Supply and Marketing Cooperatives, which collected the agricultural products to supply the urban population and industries, and distributed the industrial goods to the rural population. When urban industries were decentralized into smaller urban places, there was also a limited involvement of either the peasants or the rural economy, as these industries often brought with them their own employees from the city as well as maintaining their former suppliers and customers. Even where industries were created ostensibly to serve agriculture, they might not use local resources and peasant labour.

The division between the city and the countryside could be seen in terms of two entirely different socio-economic worlds across which little unofficial and spontaneous penetration was possible. This division was symbolized by the fact that of all types of income gaps, the rural-urban one was the most glaring (Ding 1990).

Monopolized by the state-owned sector, the city performed the functions of manufacturing und processing of virtually all primary products. With direct grants from the state, the state-owned enterprises guaranteed their employees a standard of living and a "cradle to grave" welfare system which were beyond the dreams of the rural folks. The privileges enjoyed by urban residents included state-subsidized foodgrains, subsidiary food, cotton fabric, fuel and other essentials, as well as housing, transportation, education, health care and social welfare.

This is not to say that the Chinese cities had been completely transformed from the dilapidation left over by the Japanese invasion and the civil war. Indeed, the subsidies enjoyed by the urban residents were precisely due to the poor conditions of the cities. The emphasis placed on heavy industrialization did not leave much to finance the construction of urban infrastructure, especially in the older sections of the city. The predominance of the state-owned enterprises, which were responsible only to higher-level state ministries, also hindered municipal planning. These urban problems were in turn used to argue for the continuation of control of rural-urban mobility.

But as the producer of cheap food and primary products, the countryside was decidedly the disadvantaged side in this dualism. Collectivization and the practice of self-reliance meant that rural communities could not expect much direct state assistance but had to depend primarily on their own resources during good and bad years. In fact, they often had to shoulder every conceivable kind of levy to meet local administrative and social needs. Even when rural projects were organized as parts of the national plan, the peasants were expected to supply free labour and other inputs. In addition, the countryside continued to be regarded as possessing an unlimited ability to sustain the city and employ its surplus labour, despite mounting rural unemployment and underemployment (Deng 1989). Accounting for four-fifths of the country's population, and with a growth rate much faster than the urban centres, and because the labour absorption potential of traditional agriculture had been used up after three decades of continuous development, the rural areas were increasingly burdened with an expanding surplus labour force. Yet the policy of self-sufficiency which, on the one hand, allowed the rural economy to be dominated by foodgrain production, and on the other, discouraged even the traditional household sideline production for exchange, deprived the countryside of its comparative advantage and took away from the peasant household an important opportunity to employ its spare labour (Li, Xiangzhang 1989).

Although rural industries were set up, they were not geared towards the commercial processing of primary products, the development of cottage industries, or entering into production association with urban industries. Organized along the concept of "small and complete", their role was to support self-sufficiency, and they were thus restricted to the "three locals" (using local capital and material inputs, and serving the local market). Even in areas with favourable conditions, rural industries were only expected to support agricultural intensification by providing inputs to agriculture such as fertilizers, cement and electrical power, and repairing agricultural tools.

Under such conditions, small towns which used to serve as a link between the city and the countryside could not sustain their age-old role as the socio-economic centre of the surrounding countryside. Since peasants had very few goods to sell in the town markets, the small towns stagnated; some of them virtually lost their economic basis as the collecting and distributing centres of the peasants' farm and sideline products. No economic stimuli could be returned to the countryside. A downward spiral in the economy of the countryside took place, and rural-urban segregation deepened.

3 Recent Reforms

The recent reforms in rural China have been aimed at raising peasant incentive, productivity and income, and at facilitating the growth of a commodity economy. The people's commune was abolished and communal farming was replaced by individual household operation under a responsibility system. Basic rural and agricultural decision-making power was taken from the administrators and bureaucrats and turned over to the actual operators. Individual households entered into contractual arrangements with their production teams to operate an amount of village land the allocation of which was based on, among a number of factors, the amount of labour force or the actual size of the household. This allocation will remain basically stable over a generation, but is subject to occasional minor size adjustments as the amount of labour force or the actual size of the household changes. The link to household size arises from the fact that the contracted responsibility includes first and foremost the responsibility to produce the household's necessary foodgrains. The responsibility also includes producing a surplus beyond self-sufficiency to contribute to the production team's collective fund and state procurement quota. The level of contribution is usually set so that it can be achieved and some products are left for private disposal by the peasants onto the free rural market for cash income.

Other measures to raise incentives included a significant increase in the state procurement prices for agricultural products, a narrowing of the list of agricultural products subject to state procurement, and the official sanctioning and support of rural markets.

With the demise of the people's commune, the problem of surplus labour was exposed. Rural communities have been reported to have between one-third and one-half of their labour force redundant. No longer able to benefit from community make-work projects and having the responsibility of improving the economic well-being of their own household entrusted to them, the peasants began eagerly to scrounge for alternative employment. In response, the state adopted the following policies to provide a relaxation to the household registration system and allow a limited degree of rural-urban mobility: (1) the temporary acceptance of rural migrants into cities as domestic servants and contract workers on construction sites; and (2) the encouragement of peasants, as a group not entitled to the special privileges reserved for the *bona fide* urban residents, to set up trading and service enterprises in towns.

To strengthen the foundation of a commodity economy in the countryside, the state also provided laws for the creation of a series of urban-oriented regions. These included: (1) lowering the qualifying standards for officially designated towns, thus all centres that were designated as towns during the early 1950s were redesignated as such, and many settlement nodes that had grown since then, such as commune headquarters, were also given the official designation; (2) expansion of the boundary of the designated towns beyond their built-up area so that they could provide leadership to the smaller undesignated towns within their jurisdiction, thus giving administrative recognition to the centrality of the designated town and defining its hinterland; and (3) extension of the form of territorial organization of the major cities to most prefectural centres and some county seats, by designating them as cities and by extending their municipal jurisdiction to cover the whole prefecture/county unit, so that they could provide planning guidance and coordination to their administratively subordinating counties/townships (Tan 1989).

While many peasants have taken advantage of the above-mentioned relaxation of the household registration system by temporarily "leaving the soil *and* the village", many more have been attracted by the new incentives for a commodity economy to carry out manufacturing activities within township and village enterprises, producing for rural and urban markets far and near.

Rural non-farm acitivites have been undertaken by a trinity of mutual dependence between the rural enterprises which operate the activities, the rural community which usually owns the enterprises and in which the enterprises are located, and the local government which administers the rules and regulations affecting the enterprises. The rapid growth of rural non-farm activities in small towns, both designated and undesignated, has contributed to the revitalization of the rural economy and rejuvenation of small towns as central places (Tan 1990b).

This rise of rural enterprises has led to a situation where the rural non-farm economy constitutes a new third sector beside the existing rural agricultural and urban industrial sectors. Encouraged by its sudden thrust into the rural economy, some observers hold the view that this new sector "symbolizes the direct participation of China's peasantry in the process of industrialization" (Li, Keqiang 1991). Others hope that as it grows, this new sector would lead to the ultimate breakdown of the rural-urban dichotomy, and bring about national economic integration (Zhang, Gengsheng 1988). They expect rural-urban links, in the first instance within the framework of the newly established urban-oriented regions, to develop and become solidified. As the nuclei of these urban-oriented regions are regional medium-sized cities which are in turn tied to the major cities, national integration could follow. It is further argued that the process of national economic integration is made inevitable especially because the numerous small towns are scattered throughout the country.

4 Nature of Rural Development

However, it is important to point out that rural industrialization of the type that has taken place in the Chinese countryside since the late 1970s, is preconditioned upon the influence radiating from a well-developed urban economy, where markets and skills are easily available, and sources of information are wide-ranging. Only areas along the more developed east coast and those forming the hinterland of major cities, past and present, possess these conditions. Large areas in the central and western parts of the country, which account for more than four-fifths of the national territory and three-fifths of the total population, are without these necessary conditions. Thus, despite the wide distribution of small towns, the above-mentioned development has been very localized. Beginning in the Southern Jiangsu region of Suzhou-Wuxi-Changzhou, rural industrialization has engulfed the whole of the Changjiang River Delta, and spread along the coast to the Shandong and Liaodong Peninsulas in the north, and in the south to Ningbo and Wenzhou in Zhejiang, Southern Fujian, and the Zhujiang River Delta in Guangdong. It then leapfrogs across vast territories to involve the suburban counties of major interior cities such as Wuhan, Xi'an, Chongqing, and Chengdu.

Wherever they are, to a considerable degree, the peasants are still faced with the continued existence of the basic tenets of rural-urban dualism. The assigned role of the countryside continues to be that of the producer of cheap food and agricultural raw materials to support the population and industries in the city. Rural enterprises have little opportunity to become involved in the processing of major agricultural products, because these are still procured by the state and turned to urban state-owned industries. Rural enterprises have therefore been forced to operate as urban industries, producing finished goods from raw materials obtained elsewhere. While the state has tolerated this breach in the existing rural-urban division of labour, as units outside the state-owned sector, rural enterprises are still excluded from the state production plan, and therefore have to obtain their supplies and dispose of their products on the free but still very imperfect market. Chinese scholars have themselves admitted that rural enterprises have risen from the cleavage of the rural-urban dichotomy (Liu 1988).

The household registration system controling rural-urban migration is still in effect. Although some peasants have been temporarily permitted into the towns and cities, they are still regarded by urban administrations as peasants and not as *bona fide* urban residents. As during the days of strict rural-urban segregation, when the economic conditions in the cities show signs of decline, these people will be returned to the countryside. During the economic downturn in the late 1980s, about 18 million former peasants were repatriated (Li, Keqiang 1991).

Indeed, it is the state's policy to continue transferring redundant labour out of agriculture into the rural secondary and tertiary sectors, but without physical relocation. The state's model is the Southern Jiangsu region of Suzhou-Wuxi-Changzhou, the pioneer of rural industrialization. Here large numbers of community-owned industrial enterprises are located in many small towns, and peasants are drawn from practically every househould to work as industrial workers in these enterprises. But the economically transferred labour force continues to reside in the village homes nearby, commuting to work on bicycles. To the community, this unique pattern of local redeployment of rural labour, referred to as "leaving the soil but not the village, entering the factory but not the town", is attractive as it reduces the demand for urban infrastructure and permits maximum resources to be allocated to industrialization, while at the same time it allows the industrial worker to continue to play a role in agriculture. For the state, the redeployed labourer's continuation as rural resident who still maintains a close tie to agriculture and the rural economy is an important consideration, especially from the perspective of the diffusion of modern ideas. But more important is the fact that, as members of rural households, the redeployed labourers can go on obtaining food supplies directly from their responsibility plots, thus saving the state from having to supply them with subsidized foodgrains and subsidiary foodstuffs. "Leaving the soil but not the village, entering the factory but not the town", characterized by some as rural urbanization (Cai 1985), therefore, avoids a further weakening of the concept of urban population on which rural-urban segregation has been built.

The pressure to solve the surplus labour problem locally, along with the trinity of mutual dependence which has fostered the immediate interests of the rural community, the enterprises and the local government, is one important factor behind the unending spiral of spontaneous development of rural enterprises in every rural community that possesses the conditions to do so. This process is also helped by the absence of macro-level economic planning guidance, because rural enterprises are excluded from the state production plan (Fan and Zhu 1989). Even in communities that do not possess these conditions, because the development of rural enterprises has become an end in itself, local governments often force themselves to adopt this as a major strategy of rural development.

The Tan study (1990b) on recent developments in the rural non-farm sector shows that this parochialism of industrial development, whereby rural enterprises are closely tied to their administrative regions in terms of location, and are fully dependent on consanguinity in terms of personnel, is forcing rural enterprises into a rut as their management is constantly met with political interference, their performance adversely affected by backward technology and a redundant labour force, and their corporate interests sacrificed for social ends. As the massive closure of rural enterprises in the late 1980s which forced the return of 5% of the rural industrial labour force to agricultural pursuits (Xu, Boyuan 1991) testifies, they may in fact have worked themselves into a dead alley.

In addition, some observers have felt that the type of rural industrialization which has been carried out has brought to the countryside a number of long-term consequences which may be characterized als "rural ills" (Gu et al 1989). Parochialism of industrial development which sees the development of a scattered pattern of competing centres, also leads to the proliferation of industrializing small towns in the rural landscape. Rural industrialization in the form of a high density of small towns, resulting from the spontaneous and haphazard growth, has caused unnecessary duplication, as well as an uneconomic use of facilities and amenities. Despite the belief that rural urbanization would save on investments in urban infrastructure, every centre aims to construct a complete set of urban infrastructure such as streets, department store, movie theatre, water treatment plant, etc. which may not all be put to full use. Valuable and scarce funds have thus been thinly scattered over large areas in the countryside.

But the duplication involves an even more irrational problem, which is that the small towns are basically of the same order in the urban hierarchy, as each constitutes the centre of its own local community, and its hinterland is defined by the administrative boundaries of the local community. Due to the need for each rural community to have its own industrial base, the forces of competition that would lead to the establishment of a rational hierarchy of urban places, and therefore a more integrative urban and economic network, have been shut out.

5 Limitation of Rural Urbanization Programme

Small-town development is very much a matter of combining the exploitation of local comparative advantage and historical experience with the overcoming of human, physical, and locational liabilities. Southern Jiangsu's pattern of "leaving the soil but not the village, entering the factory but not the town" is firmly founded on the human geography of the region. The high population density has long meant a small portion per capita of cultivated land, and an age-old history of development of handicrafts and other non-farm activities, mutual support to the small towns, and close linkages with nearby cities. The rural population is distributed in evenly scattered villages in the countryside. For example, over the 1,763 km^2 of Wujin County, there are 8,303 villages averaging a population of 149 for each village. For every 100 km^2, there are 471 villages, and the distance between the villages is less than 500 m (Jin 1986). This type of population distribution allows small-town employees to take a leisurely bicycle ride on the numerous rural tracts between their home villages and their places of work in the towns.

This type of rural-urban relations is not being repeated, for example, in the Northeast. This author's study of small towns in Central Liaoning (Tan 1990a) shows that, because of the recency of settlement and the dominance of the large cities, there is a particularly deep gulf between the countryside and the city. One group of towns, while being rejuvenated, are mainly relying on trade in their periodic market. Rural industries are primarily based on the household, and undertaken in the peasants' spare time. "Leaving the soil" has barely begun. A second group of towns, while industrializing, have little direct involvement with the rural economy. They are in the course of expansion due to decentralization of industries from the large cities. Such expansion results in the conversion of adjacent farmland for urban use and in transforming the affected peasants into urban workers. Because the village is now turned into an urban district, it can be said that "leaving the soil *and* the village" has taken place.

Other areas of the coast which are experiencing rural industrialization and small-town development, and which apparently share the same historical and geographical conditions with Southern Jiangsu, have gone beyond the principle of "leaving the soil but not the village, entering the factory but not the town". For example, in the Wenzhou region (Tan 1991), as industries develop in the small towns along the coast, and the hundreds and thousands of traders travel to all parts of the country to promote and sell Wenzhou products, many peasants from the less accessible parts of the municipality have taken advantage of the opportunities created and have flowed into the coastal region. Some of them have taken over agricultural production left by those who have themselves taken to the towns, others have entered the towns directly as employees of the numerous industries that have mushroomed. At the current rate of absorption of rural population, it is estimated that within five years almost half of the rural population in the area would be located in the small towns.

Testifying to the accelerating process of "leaving the soil *and* the village" in the Wenzhou region is the growth of Longgang. Referred to as a "peasant city", Longgang was originally a fishing village of 200 houses and a population of one thousand. Its construction as a designated town was approved of in April 1984, but by October 1986 it had become a bustling urban centre of multi-storey buildings, with 570,000 m^2 of finished floor space, a network of 23 km of paved roads, a harbour, integrated water and power supply systems, and educational and health facilities. More than 1,300 enterprises had been located here. A total investment of about 160 million Yuan had been made, six-sevenths of which had come from peasants, who had congregated from all corners of the Wenzhou area, unrestricted by any administrative boundary as long as they possessed the 20 to 30 thousand Yuan capital needed to set themselves up in the town.

Zhujiang River Delta towns are experiencing a similar process. Here non-local labourers have entered farming as share-croppers. They have taken over from the local households the management of the responsibility plots, allowing the local peasants to leave farming for secondary and tertiary jobs in the towns (Lu 1985). Non-local labour has also become an important component of the small-town industrial labour force (Xi, Xueqiang et al 1988).

Even in the case of Southern Jiangsu, there are signs that "leaving the soil but not the village" is being superseded. Here the upward spiralling of the development process, and the need to retain some labour force on the farms to meet the state procurement quota in foodgrains and other agricultural products have jointly restricted the labour supply available to the township and village enterprises. To resolve the problem of labour shortage, small-town enterprises have had to resort to the importation of labour from Northern Jiangsu and adjacent provinces. In many townships and villages, the size of the local labour force has been exceeded by outsiders. Housing and other amenities adjacent to the industrial enterprises in the town have had to be provided for these non-local workers (Chen 1987). It is possible that the expanding resident population and the newly emerging way of life in the small towns may provide enough attraction to the redeployed labourers to move out of their rural households and become part of the town population.

Thus, the very success of Southern Jiangsu requires that it modifies a concept whose universal applicability throughout China it is supposed to demonstrate. In view of the many breaches of the principle of "leaving the soil but not the village, entering the factory but not the town", many scholars are urging that "leaving the soil *and* the village" should be accepted officially as another principle defining China's rural-urban relations.

It is suggested that in areas where "leaving the soil but not the village" has been in operation, "leaving the soil *and* the village" should be seen as the next logical phase of rural-urban relations (Qi 1989). In those parts of the country which have difficulty instituting the former, such as the less developed and depressed areas where local rural diversification has little opportunity of success, and/or where economic stagnation is caused by an overwhelming ratio of rural labour force to cultivated land, "leaving the soil *and* the village" should constitute an independent alternative, so that these areas can export their surplus labour either to the nearby small towns or beyond (Xu, Fangkuan 1987). This type of relocation does not have to cause difficulties to the receiving urban centres because, as shown in Southern Jiangsu, non-local labour can also help in the development of the recipient areas. Advanced regions may also, through "leaving the soil *and* the village", send out workers to help stimulate development elsewhere, as in the case of the large numbers of traders from the eastern coastal belt promoting commerce in the interior areas of Qinghai and Xinjiang (Zhao 1987).

There are yet others who argue that the relocation of peasants into designated towns and rural market towns does not qualify them as having "left the soil *and* the village" (Meng 1990). "Leaving the village" is thought to mean making a clear break with the rural community, which can only be achieved by relocation to urban centres at the county seat level and higher, physically and socio-culturally far away from the home village of the migrating peasant.

Asserting that the closed system of peasant mobility has been responsible for cutting off the rural areas from the civilizing influence of the towns and cities and thus for the stagnation of China's rural areas, some are arguing that the system of rural-urban segregation must be completely abolished and replaced by an open system of free movement of labour. The city should be opened to everyone who has the means to live, invest and develop. To achieve this, the state should cease to assume exclusive responsibility over the construction and provision of urban infrastructure and amenities, and drop the policy of guaranteeing every urban resident officially subsidized food and essential materials, health care, welfare protection, and employment (Zhou 1990).

In an attempt to present a case of the inevitability of the need to lift the city gates, one advocate (Cai 1985) suggests that in any situation where rural economic transformation takes place, as it is true of much of the Chinese countryside since the late 1970s, there will be a transfer of rural labour out of agriculture. For a while perhaps the job opportunities in processing, commerce and transportation in the countryside may absorb the initial wave of transferees, allowing them to remain as rural residents. But eventually, as soon as economic take-off occurs, even these sectors may not be large enough for the transferees. Given the huge size of the surplus rural labour force in China, this situation may come earlier rather than later. When such an eventuality arises, it becomes necessary to organize a second transfer, involving not just a change of jobs as the first, but also a change of location of residence from the rural to the urban, beginning in the small towns as the first stop. This second transfer cannot be avoided, or the upward spiralling effect of the rural economic transformation would all be wasted. As a matter of state policy small towns, and eventually cities, must be opened to receive these surplus labourers for both employment and settlement.

6 Rural-Urban Integration

Since the inauguration of the People's Republic of China, the official line has always been that the state is concerned with the resolution of the contradictions between the countryside and the city. Yet during its first three decades, China saw a widening of the rural-urban gap. Despite notable improvements since the late 1970s, rural-urban relations still need considerable development before the commodity economy, which is the objective of the current series of reforms, can operate smoothly. Indeed, the need for continuous improvement of rural-urban relations cannot be overemphasized. It is estimated that by 2000, the surplus rural labour force in China could reach 250 million (*Nongmin Ribao* 1988). As current symptoms of this problem, the large size of the "floating population",[1] and especially the occasional spontaneous "blind flow" of millions of rural folks into the major cities seeking employments,[2] provide a powerful argument that rural-urban relations not only have to be improved, but must be improved without delay.

If the series of systemic weaknesses in both the rural economy and the enterprises resulting from the persistence of rural-urban dualism are allowed to continue, rather than serving as a facilitator of national economic integration as has been hoped, the new rural non-farm acitivities could settle down as the second sector within the rural economy, opposed to agriculture. In such an eventuality, in addition to the existing rural-urban cleavage, there would be a new order of duality within the rural sector. Like the first order of duality, this second order would lead to further depression of the agricultural sector (Rural Industrialization 1988).

A closer relationship between the rural enterprises and the state-owned urban industries is necessary. For large parts of China, an ideal relationship between rural enterprises and the state-owned industries would be a division of labour under which the former handles the initial stages of processing of agricultural and industrial raw materials, leaving the advanced stages to the latter. By depending more on rural primary production and not having to compete with urban industries, rural enterprises may be able to better exploit their comparative advantage, and bring about a more rational use of the rural environment. For the advanced regions where rural industrialization is already underway, extension of state planning and coordination of the production of rural enterprises is urgently needed. As the rural industries eventually enter into a division of labour with state-owned urban industries, and the rural economy is integrated more closely with the urban economy in this process, rationalization of industrial production, in terms of both structure and distribution, may take place.

This should facilitate the rationalization of small towns, and should be treated as mutually supportive. Under the general strategy of small-town development, there is now a consensus that rationalization has to be carried out through a concentration of effort on a smaller number of towns. In practice, each region would have to be encouraged to make its own decision about the type of towns worthy of this effort. Such decision would have to take into account the local socio-economic situation and urban structure. For example, along the more advanced coastal region, where the rural economy is either in the course of taking-off or has already done so, and where small towns are duplicating and competing among themselves, it is widely believed that rationalization can be achieved by first developing the county seat, so that a strong intermediate centre can be created between the regional cities and the numerous small towns. Thus, Jiangsu has awarded city status to some of its county seats such as Yangshe and Yixing. In other provinces like Yunnan, where the county seats constitute the lowest order of urban places due to a very low level of urbanization, market towns which until now have been rural places, have been given the urban designation of *zhen* in order that they may serve as focus of a commodity economy involving the countryside around them. Because in China a rise in administrative status often results in a corresponding increase in economic centrality, this type of political action should set in motion a process of rationalization of urban centres in the countryside. If this was coupled with the declaring of certain designated towns as rural industrial centres, and some market towns as lower-level industrial districts, thus encouraging the trend of industrial agglomeration of different types and orders, a well-balanced and integrated system of small urban centres would very soon emerge in the countryside. The development of these centres and districts for peasant economic activity as well as residence should satisfy, for the time being at least, the peasants' need to break out of their rural confines.

This type of action does not have to involve massive state investment. Longgang, the "peasant city" in the Wenzhou region was completely built by peasants who were permitted to move into the town to establish rural enterprises. Having the rural people construct their own towns and cities, instead of leaving it to the state to make all the necessary arrangements for urban construction and livelihood, may ensure that both the urban and rural "ills" found in China today are effectively remedied. The breakdown of the rural-urban barrier through the construction of other "peasant cities" like Longgang at the county and sub-county levels is one way of promoting a stepwise rural-urban movement of people, and an effective means of preventing a large wave of rural migrants from pouring into the cities. It would also give the urban-oriented regions based on the former prefectural city or the township seat substantial meaning.

But this should be followed by a gradual opening of the higher regional and national order of cities. It should be done especially in those regions whose urban system at the lower end is too weak to provide the necessary jobs, even if it were through various kinds of ad hoc arrangement in effect now.

A final breakdown of economic dualism and rural-urban segregation does not have to mean lifting the city gates fully and immediately. What is necessary now is a determined effort to continue with the process of integration initiated with the recent reforms. But it should be pointed out that in the Chinese situation where rural-urban and regional transportation bottlenecks are expected to persist for many years to come, basic self-sufficiency at all levels will continue, and the commercial rate of agriculture will remain low. Within the foreseeable future, rural-urban relations cannot be expected to develop to a level comparable to that of fully functioning commodity economies in developed countries.

Notes

1) People who are in the city without official permission to establish permanent residence there. In major cities like Beijing and Shanghai, this group can exceed one million.
2) During the Lunar New Year of 1989, more than one million peasants from all over China congregated into Guangzhou seeking odd jobs, while many others entered other major cities.

References

Cai, Long (1985): "On 'leaving the soil and the village'", *Nongye Jingji Wenti* (Problems of Agricultural Economy), 7: 4-8

Chen, Yi (1987): "Rural labour redeployment: new tendencies and choice of objectives", *Jingji Yanjiu* (Economic Research), 10: 77-80 & 50

Deng, Yiming (1989): "On the growth of agriculture and the changes in employment structure under economic dualism", *Zhongguo Nongcun Wenti* (Chinese Rural Economy), 7: 15-25

Ding, Jiaxin (1990): "An enquiry into the rationalization of Chinese rural-urban economic relations", *Jingji Yanjiu* (Economic Research), 3: 64-67

Fan, Honggen and Zhu, Guangfu (1989): "Some thoughts on two glaring problems of the rural enterprises", *Zhongguo Nongcun Jingji* (Chinese Rural Economy), 7: 11-14 and 54

Gu, Yikang; Huang, Zuhui and Xu, Jia (1989): "An historical evaluation of the rural enterprise - small town development road", *Nongye Jingji Wenti* (Problems of Agricultural Economy), 3: 11-16

Jin, Daqin (1986): "Rural urbanization needs many models: a sceptical look at 'leaving the soil but not the village, entering the factory but not the town'", *Jianzhu Xuebao* (Architecture Journal), 12: 43-45

Li, Keqiang (1991): "On China's trilateral economic structure", *Zhongguo Shehui Kexue* (Chinese Social Science), 3: 65-82

Li, Sihui (1987): "Models of surplus rural labour force redeployment and their theoretical differences", *Nongye Jingji Wenti* (Problems of Agricultural Economy), 1: 49-53

Li, Xiangzhang (1989): "On double dualistic structure and agricultural development", *Zhongguo Noncun Jingji* (Chinese Rural Economy), 2: 3-16

Liu, Chunbin (1988): "Step out of dualism, the only way to change fundamentally China's irrational rural-urban relations", *Nongye Jingji Wenti* (Problems in Agricultural Economy), 4: 22-26

Lu, Wen (1985): "Certain questions relating to the rural economic development of China's coastal developed areas", *Nongye Jingji Wenti* (Problems of Agricultural Economy), 1: 12-16 & 50

Ma, Xia (1990): "Types of Chinese population migration and their changes", *Zhongguo Shehui Kexue* (Chinese Social Science), 5: 141-154

Meng, Xiaochun (1990): "The route to the unification of the double tracks in China's urbanization", *Chengshi Wenti* (Urban Problems), 1: 10-13

Nongmin Ribao (Peasants Daily) (1988), May 28

Qi, Haotong (1989): "On the historical reality and future options of China's dualistic economy", *Zhongguo Nongcun Jingji* (Chinese Rural Economy), 7: 26-32

Rural Industrialization and Urbanization Study Group, Economic Policy Research Centre, Ministry of Agriculture (1988): "Certain suggestions concerning the accelerated realization of China's rural industrialization, urbanization and agricultural modernization", *Nongcun Jingji Wenti* (Problems of Agricultural Economy), 10: 15-17 and 46

Tan, Kok Chiang (1986a): "Revitalized small towns in China", *Geographical Review*, 76: 138-148

Tan, Kok Chiang (1986b): "Small towns in Chinese urbanization", *Geographical Review*, 76: 265-275

Tan, Kok Chiang (1989): "China's new spatial approach to economic development"; *Chinese Geography and Environment*, 4: 3-21

Tan, Kok Chiang (1990a): Small towns in China's metropolitan regions. A paper presented at the annual conference of the Canadian Association of Geographers, University of Edmonton, Edmonton, Alberta, June

Tan, Kok Chiang (1990b): Rural enterprises and small town development in China, problems and prospects. A paper presented to the IGU Regional Conference, Beijing, August

Tan, Kok Chiang (1991): "Small towns and regional development in Wenzhou", in: Greg Veeck (ed.): *Uneven Landscapes: Geographical Studies of Post Reform China*, Baton Rouge: Geoscience Publications, Louisiana State University, 207-234

Xu, Boyuan (1991): "A preliminary analysis of the integration of rural enterprises into the system which has the urban industries as its core", *Chengshi Wenti* (Urban Problems), 3: 23-25 & 37

Xu, Fangkuan (1987): "Promotion of rural population mobility is the key to the deepening of rural reform", *Fazhan Zhanlue Bao* (Development Strategy), May 9

Xu, Xueqiang et al (1988): *Zhujiang sanjiaozhou chengshi huanjing yu chengshi fazhan* (Urban environment and development in the Zhujiang River Delta), Guangzhou: Zhongshan Daxue Chubanshe

Zhang, Gengsheng (1988): "Some thoughts on the long-term development of rural enterprises in China", *Zhongguo Nongcun Jingji* (Chinese Rural Economy), 1: 1-11

Zhao Dequn (1987): "East-west relations and surplus rural labour force redeployment", *Zhongguo Qingnian Jingji Luntan* (Chinese Young Economists Forum), 4: 48-56

Zhou, Yixing (1990): Evaluation and rethinking about the national urban growth policy of China. A paper presented at the IGU Regional Conference on Asia and the Pacific, University of Beijing, Beijing, August

Trends of Urbanization in the Pearl River Delta

by Peter C.J. Druijven

I would especially like to thank Professor Xu and Professor Lin and Mrs. Zhong and Hou of the Guangzhou Institute of Geography, CAS, for their support and advice and Mr. Zhou, vice-director of the TVE Statistical Bureau, Guangdong, for his information and introduction to officials in the Pearl River Delta region.

1 Introduction

In this paper the Pearl River or Zhujiang Delta, situated at the southern part of Guangdong Province, is conceived as consisting of the Pearl River Delta Open Economic Development Zone, the urban area of Guangzhou and the Special Economic Zones (SEZ) of Shenzhen and Zhuhai. Its total population of about 15 million (more than 20% of the province's total) inhabits an area of more than 25.000 km² (about 12% of Guangdong). Its favourable physical conditions - semitropical monsoon climate, extensive irrigation and transport network, fertility of the soil - together with the region's proximity to Hong Kong and Macau make the area one of the most prosperous regions of China. The gross industrial and agricultural output amounts to 70% of Guangdong's total (in 1990: 31,000 million US$) which equals the export share (*FEER*, 5-16-1991).

The urban system of the Pearl River Delta thus conceived has been described by some authors as large, complex, and dynamic (Pannell & Veeck 1989, 37). Since 1978 the region's urban population grew by 7.7% per year (1978-1986) and the urbanization level lies well above the province's average of 37%. However, the rate of increase is rather unevenly distributed among the various urban places. The Special Economic Zones of Shenzhen and Zhuhai grew fast with an average rate of 31%. The capital Guangzhou showed a very modest rate of growth, only 3.2%. But the small cities and towns experienced an average growth rate of 5.4%, which means that the share of small towns and small and medium-sized cities increased from 32.8% in 1978 to 59.7% in 1986. At the same time Guangzhou's share declined from 67.1% (1978) to 50.3% in 1986 (Xu & Li 1990, 53). Thus, the degree of primacy of the region's urban system has obviously diminished since the liberalization policies of 1978. The restructuring of the rural economy together with the gradual opening of the region to the outside world have resulted in much faster urban growth rates especially for the smaller urban places. This process of reversed polarization amidst a substantial penetration of foreign capital is remarkable and such a trend is a rather unexpected phenomenon in terms of conventional development theories.

Figure 1: The Pearl River or Zhujiang Delta Region

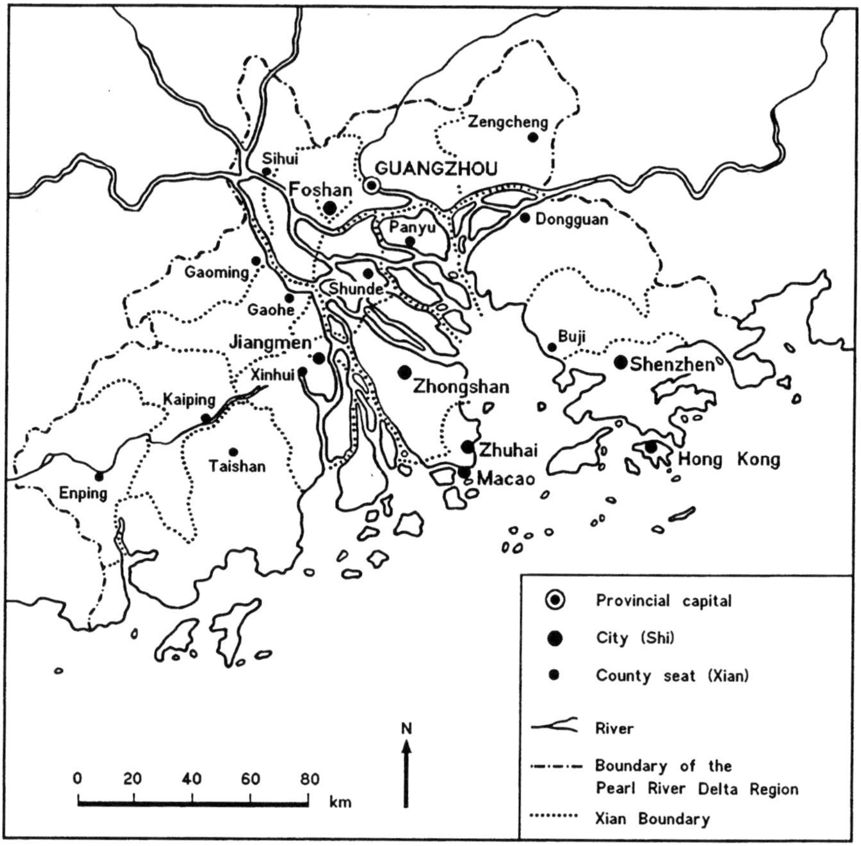

Source: Xu & Li, 1990.

According to Lo (1989a, 29) the decentralized territorial or agropolitan approach in the Zhujiang Delta is obvious. He claims that the conditions for agropolitan development would be present like for instance self-sufficiency and self-reliance in decisionmaking at county level, diversification of employment, small-scale labor-intensive market-oriented rural industrialization, and the maximum utilization of the local resources. For this author the most interesting urban development is the generation of a hierarchy of market towns of varying sizes which relates upwards with the central city of Guangzhou. Xu and Li (1990), however, completely disagree with this view. According to them the reorganization of the regional administrative structure on a nodal region basis may facilitate the development of a market-oriented economy, of which commercially organized rural industrialization forms a part. Part of the profits generated by rural industrial enterprises owned by local governments could be used for investments in infrastructure construction and urban amenities in small rural towns. The economic external dependence of a major part of these industrial enterprises however is obvious, both in terms of raw materials, labor and capital as well as commercialization as will be shown in this paper. Xu and Li perceive this development as a far cry from anything approaching a self-reliant agropolitan community: "instead one sees substantial progress amid increasing penetration by world capital." (Xu & Li 1990, 68).

Fincher (1990, 54-56) discerns a tendency among Chinese policy makers towards a rural bias in spatial planning by stressing the fast development of small and medium cities because of "over-urbanization". "Along with the downward fluctuations in annual grain production figures, and double-digit inflation, the rise in China's urbanization rate has greatly alarmed many important political figures" (Fincher 1990, 54). This view of "rural bias" or "anti-urbanism" in spatial planning has been criticized by Kirkby (1985) who points to the focussing until recently by Chinese planners on urban industrial development and on urban employment problems, often to the exclusion of non-agricultural development and employment in small and medium-sized cities in rural areas. The fast growth of medium-sized cities and rural towns as a means to retain rural people in the countryside should be considered as a consequence of safe-guarding the urban industrialization by avoiding a rural mass migration to the big cities. Instead of a rural bias a bias to big cities was and still is in vigour within Chinese spatial planning.

As one can see, the combination of the increasing role of foreign capital in the regional economy and the simultaneously rising importance of secondary cities cause a lot of confusion and contradictory explanations by regional planners.

In this paper attention will be paid to two processes fundamental to the recent growth and functioning of small and intermediate cities in the Zhujiang Delta, i.e. the characteristics of demographic growth and the nature and spatial impact of industrialization. Three factors are described which offer these latter urban places greater flexibility and space of manoeuvre to adapt to and profit from changing circumstances: the reforms of the rural economy, the open door policy and the accompanying political and administrati ve reforms. Notwithstanding the economic progress and rising welfare, the fast urban growth within the Pearl River Delta occurs not without problems. Attention will be paid to some of these problems like the stagnation of the capital and regional node Guangzhou, the external dependency of the industrialization of intermediate cities and some spatial problems like pollution, congestion and the lack of coordination in spatial planning. At last some brief notes will be made on the foreseeable urban development.

2 Demographic Processes and Their Impact on Urbanization

The rising share of small and intermediate cities in the urban population of the Zhujiang Delta is partly caused by changes in the urban administrative structure. In November 1984 the 1963 criteria for town designation were released in order to revitalize the small towns. The 1984 criteria for designation were as follows:

1. seats of county government;

2. seats of township government, where the total township population was below 20,000, of which 2,000 non-agricultural persons reside in the township seat, or where the total township population was more than 20,000 and the number of non-agricultural residents in the township seat was more than 10 per cent of the total township population;

3. seats of township government located in areas of national minorities in sparsely populated frontier and/or mountainous areas, in a scenic area or a harbour even if their non-agricultural population was below 2,000.

This relaxation augmented the number of towns in the Zhujiang Delta enormously: According to the 1982 Census only 18 towns were counted but in 1985 the total number of new towns amounted to 115. Figure 2 based on the Public Security Department statistics (1985) and developed by Lo (1989a, b) shows the size and distribution pattern of these towns.

Another administrative change which resulted in a sudden expansion of the town population was the introduction of the governing measure of "town administering village" (*zhen guan cun*). The administrative boundary of a designated town was enlarged beyond the built-up area of the town itself to include its surrounding villages (Lee 1989, 784). By this expansion of urban administrative areas a huge agricultural population is counted as urban.

The differences in natural growth rate was another factor which resulted in a faster population growth of small and intermediate cities. In Guangzhou the natural growth rate in the early 80s averaged eight to ten per thousand per year, whereas those of smaller cities were about twelve to fifteen per thousand per year (Xu & Li 1990, 55). Besides the age composition and level of education, less stringent execution of the population policy in the rural areas seems the main reason for these differences.

Next to the differential natural growth the differences in the rate of population immigration are by far the most important factor resulting in the changing demographic and economic position of small and intermediate cities in the Zhu-

Figure 2: Spatial Distribution of Designated Towns in Zhujiang Delta by Population Size, 1984

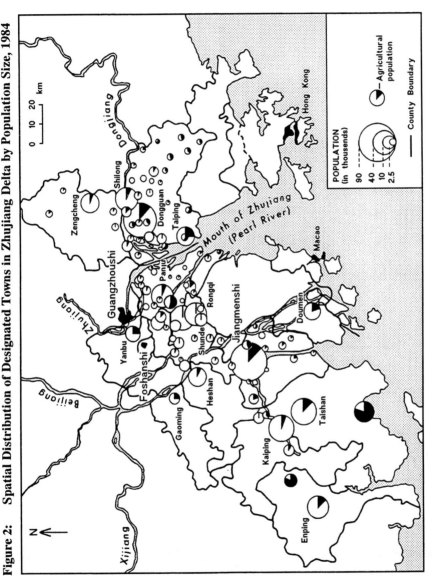

Source: Lo 1989b.

jiang Delta. The extent and different types of migration or in general the spatial mobility of labor is strongly related to the national urban policy of: "... containing growth of large cities, selective development of medium-sized cities and actively promoting growth of small cities". Confronted with the existence and rapid expansion of a rural labor surplus after the rural reforms of 1978 and with spectacular production increases in agriculture as well as an overwhelming growth of rural non-agricultural enterprises the Chinese government introduced more liberal policies towards population movements.

We can distinguish three types of population movement: the category which is known as peasants who are allowed to reside in towns providing their own food needs (*zili kouliang hu*); a second group of laborers on a temporary contract; a third group of the so-called "floating population" among which "blindful migrants" (*liumin* or *mangliu* or *liudong renkou*), i.e. migrants nobody asked for but came along on their own decision.

The first group of *zili kouliang hu* originally consisted of peasants who could take care of their own food needs and housing. They were allowed to reside in certain cities and towns, but officially, in terms of the household registration system, they still belonged to the rural population. The increase in agricultural production and the opening of free markets since the end of the 70s made finding food relatively less difficult. However, the availability of housing and job opportunities was and still is the critical factor influencing this migration flow. Because of the past emphasis on the maintenance and expansion of the urban productive capacity, which has often occurred at the expense of urban amenities, urban housing was in short supply. Moreover, the major part of urban housing is state-owned and not available for rent by the *zili kouliang hu*. Finding a job is much easier, especially because of the rapid rise of industrial enterprises in rural towns and small cities.

The Pearl River Delta cities and counties which are in urgent need of labor like Panyu, Zhongshan, Nanhai and Siyi are even encouraging this type of migration and provide potential migrants with information about housing and job opportunities. The latter place offered residence to the majority of the *zili kouliang hu* until 1984: about 70 per cent of the total (Xu & Li 1990, 55). On the other hand cities like Guangzhou, Zhuhai, Shenzhen and Dongguan have not yet given permission to such migration but use the second form of migration, the contract labor system.

A second group of temporary migrants is organized by a contract labor system which involves a fixed-term contract between employer and employee for specific activities (agriculture, construction, or industrial activities). Sklair (1991, 201) estimates that the number of contract laborers in whole China amounts to more than ten million. Some temporary workers go to the city often in teams to earn enough money to be able to spend the winter period more comfortably at home. This seasonal contract system of "temporary urbanization" evolves more and more in the direction of a three-to-five year contract system which sometimes is renewable. These prolongated contracts occur especially in export processing industries and main construction works. If running well, this system not only relieves some rural areas of the population pressure, but it also satisfies urban demand for cheap and easily dismissable labor force. Sometimes it eventually brings new resources (skills, management, capital, market and product information and personal contacts) into the depressed rural areas.

However, this system of contract labor is not without problems. From the viewpoint of the receiving urban place the system enhances the manageability of urban construction and development. But sometimes it is rather difficult to expel these migrants as they get accustomed to the urban way of life. This is the more so because the loosening of social and economic controls has enhanced their possibilities to survive in the informal urban society and economy. Seen from the contract laborer himself, he or she is in the city in a better position than earlier in the place of origin, notwithstanding the relatively lower-grade jobs and harsh working conditions offered in the urban regions and the poor housing conditions like overcrowded dormitories and squalid shacks.

The third group of temporal residents is a mixed one composed on the one hand of tourists or people on business or official mission but on the other hand of increasing numbers of so-called "blindful migrants" looking for jobs or education or simply to find out what city life is all about.

The first group often consists of salesmen and seekers for market information for rural enterprises. Because the majority of rural enterprises have to take care of their raw materials and equipment by themselves and are dependent on the market, their performance is strongly dependent on the success of their purchasing agents, salesmen and information seekers. These travel agents often amount to about ten per cent of the total labor force of a rural enterprise (Chang 1987, 27). This impressive number of travel agents and the like is partly due to the inadequate condition of China's tele-communication system. But even after the amelioration of tele-communication in the near future in the Pearl River Delta, face-to-face contact in doing business will continue to be of great importance.

The latter group of the so-called "blindful migrants" is increasing rapidly in the Zhujiang Delta. About 1.5 to 2 million people from the rural and urban areas elsewhere in Guangdong or in other provinces, like Guangxi and Sichuan, flooded into Guangzhou after Chinese New Year in 1989 and 1990 (Yeh e.a. 1989, 4; JPRS-CAR 8-17-90). They were trying to find jobs in the capital itself or were using Guangzhou as a springboard to look for jobs elsewhere in the Pearl River Delta.

In periods of a shortage of labor the arrival of an abundant cheap, young and often well-educated labor force from elsewhere can be employed for the benefit of urban development. However, nowadays the amount of jobseekers is overwhelming and with a temporary stagnation of economic growth in Guangzhou this "floating population" forms an ever-increasing burden for the urban economy and society (JPRS-CAR 8-17-90). Squatter problems and illegal practices (theft, smuggling, robbery, prostitution) to survive are augmenting in Guangzhou, although until now not as severe as elsewhere in big Third World cities. The recently started process of organizing and registering these outside laborers met with resistance not only from the workers themselves but also from managers of export processing enterprises. According to the latter the long waiting period for a working permit from the provincial government would cause a loss of foreign orders (JPRS-CAR, 8-17-90).

In sum, the demographic processes described above (a redefinition of township boundaries, the natural growth rate and the relaxation of population movements) besides the fast growth of the SEZs due to a huge inmigration have resulted in a faster growth of small and intermediate towns. In comparison with Guangzhou the small and medium-sized urban places could benefit from the attraction of cheap, relatively skilled, young people to solve the problem of a shortage of local labor. This shortage of labor was due to the diversification of the local economy and the rapid expansion of the township and village enterprises, especially those directed, to export processing.

3 Selective Impact of Industrialization

3.1 Introduction

During the 1980s Guangdong Province registered a average economic growth rate of 9% a year. In roughly the same period the Pearl River Delta has undergone a fundamental change of society: from a society of substantially subsistence--farming peasants before 1978 to a society in which commercialized foreign demand-led industry is predominant. In 1978, 90 percent of the province's total output was derived from agriculture and 10 percent from industry. In 1990, the relative positions of both sectors were nearly reversed and industry amounted to about 70 percent of the gross provincial output.

The Pearl River Delta with roughly one quarter of the province's total population of 63 million in 1990 accounted for 70 percent of the province's total export and gross output (Table 1). Another indicator for the economic prosperity in this region is the average wage level. In 1990, the average urban wage was Rmb. 3,500 a year (province's average 2,900) while the average rural wage was 1,600 (province's average 950) (*FEER*, 5-16-91, 66). The annual economic growth rate after 1978 however showed substantial differences within the Delta. The SEZs of Shenzhen and Zhuhai during the period 1978-1984 registered an average industrial growth rate of 95 percent a year (Xu & Li 1990, 58). After a slight recession in 1985-1986, due to the designation of the Zhujiang Delta Open Economic Zone which diverted many potential investors from the SEZs, and after the massacre in Beijing in mid-1989, the growth rate of both zones recovered and recorded a growth rate above 60 percent (Sklair 1991, 204).

Guangzhou, the traditional urban node of the Delta Region registered the lowest increase during 1978-1984, namely 10.3 percent a year. In 1988, a top year for Guangzhou's industrial growth due to large investments in 1985, the growth rate was 26%. However, this rate dropped enormously with 40 percent in 1989 (JPRS-CAR 7-26-90). At the same time industrial production costs rose by 20 percent and this trend will probably be continued in the near future.

Table 1: Demographic and economic characteristics of cities of the Pearl River Delta, 1990

City	Pop. (mil)	Pop. dens.	GVIAO *	GVIAO p.c.#	Export % GVIAO	Foreign invest*
Guangzhou	3.6	480	7,750	2153	17	300
Shenzhen	1.0	500	3,610	3610	83	520
Zhuhai	0.5	385	950	1900	52	110
Dongguan	1.3	520	1,350	1038	12	100
Foshan	2.7	711	4,160	1541	31	140
Zhongshan	1.1	647	1,350	1227	32	280
Jiangmen	3.4	362	2,680	788	19	70
Huizhou	2.2	196	570	259	54	160
Guangdong	63.0	297	31,000	492	34	2,000

* = US$ million; # = US$; GVIAO = Gross Value of Industrial and Agricultural Output.
Source: Guangdong Provincial Statistics.

The small and medium-sized towns and cities during 1978-1984 recorded industrial growth rates averaging more than 20 percent a year (Xu & Li 1990, 58). Within the industrial structure of the secondary and tertiary cities the role of the township and village enterprises (TVEs) is predominant. This industrial subsector registered an average annual growth rate of 33% during 1978-1987 (Guangzhou Institute of Geography, 1991).

These diffential growth rates have resulted in a change in relative positions of the constituent elements of the regional industrial structure. The share of Guangzhou has dropped from 63% in 1980 to less than 50% since 1985; the share of small towns' industry rose in the same period from 20% to roughly 25%, whereas that of the secondary cities including Shenzhen and Zhuhai grew from 16% to above 25% (Xu & Li 1990, 58).

In this part attention will be paid to these regional differences in industrial growth rate among urban places of distinct population size and economic structure. In the following description emphasis will be laid on the selective impact of three policies (open door policy, rural reform and administrative restructuring) on regional industrialization for three distinct zones: the SEZs, the capital of Guangzhou and the secondary cities in the Zhujiang Delta Open Economic Zone. As will be shown, particularly the smaller urban places in the latter region have significantly profited from these economic and political changes by their flexibility and dynamism to react on and to adapt to changing circumstances. The description will be focussed on local industrialization and on township and village enterprises (TVEs) in particular. These enterprises recorded an impressive growth rate, partly because of strong backward and forward linkages with a dynamic rural economy but especially because of attractive arrangements with outlying places like on the one hand Hong Kong, Shenzhen and Guangzhou for investment, management and commerce, and on the other hand with marginal areas with abundant cheap labor. Although the export-oriented strategy for development has laid the foundation for local industrialization, this industrial progress should be conceived of as an intermingling of local initiative and external ties.

3.2 The Special Economic Zones of Shenzhen and Zhuhai

The central aim of the SEZs of which Shenzhen is by far the largest in terms of industrial output (in 1990: 18.9 billion yuan *FEER*, 8-8-91) as well as in surface, has always been to promote exports in order to earn foreign currency and upgrade Chinese manufacturing industry to be able to compete at the world market (Sklair 1991, 202). This export-led type of industrialization had to be realized by the attraction of foreign investment and high-grade technology and management. In order to attract foreign capital the Chinese government invests much in infrastructure and talented technical and administrative cadres from elsewhere in China have been allocated. Moreover, like elsewhere in the Third World foreign enterprises were offered attractive financial arrangements. Cheap labor is being recruited from the countryside, partly from areas with a rural labor process - a pressing problem since the introduction of the household responsibility system in the rural economy - on a temporary contract basis.

However, the reactions of transnationals with high-grade technology and management so far have been rather unsatisfactory for China. The hesitance to settle in Shenzhen and Zhuhai was due to two factors. Particularly in the beginning the time- and nerve-consuming bureaucratic organization and the insecurity of the repatriation of capital, the amount of extra charges for overhead costs, the labor arrangements, a lack of patent protection, etc., discouraged the big foreign companies of the U.S.A., Japan and Europe. Although the procedure nowadays has been improved significantly, another factor, i.e. the closure of the large Chinese market by the government in order to protect the domestic industry, did not convince foreign companies to leave the other export zones in Asia and to relocate in South China.

Although the degree of technology remained less than hoped for, the foreign investment attracted and the rate of economic growth have been impressive. Shenzhen's foreign trade recently overtook Shanghai and total output and exports from the zone both increased more than tenfold between 1984 and 1989. The actual foreign investment amounts roughly to three billion U.S. dollars, spread over more than 6,000 enterprises of which 2,500 are foreign and 4,000 Chinese ones (Sklair 1991, 204).

Notwithstanding the enclave character of Shenzhen the economic relations with other parts of China and with the Pearl River Delta in particular are very important. For the surrounding rural counties the urban population forms a huge market for high-grade agricultural produce. Part of the temporary laborers has been recruited from nearby counties like Baoshan. Sometimes the contract labor is performed by laborers who are in excess of local demand; sometimes the shortage of local labor caused by the departure to Shenzhen is in turn compensated by cheap labor from elsewhere. Remittances from contract laborers could enhance local welfare and/or local capital accumulation (Li 1989, 35, Lo 1989a).

Many enterprises in other parts of China have established footholds in Shenzhen, attracted by lower tax rates and the permission to retain a greater share of their profits and 90 percent of the earned foreign exchange. Shenzhen also proved to be an attractive location for state as well as collective and private enterprises for the final preparation of goods for export and for gaining information about technology and export markets (Vogel 1989, 141).

The characteristics of an export-enclave are obvious, not only by the difficulty and sometimes even prohibition for foreign enterprises to sell products made in Shenzhen on the Chinese market but also by the strict rules of admission of Chinese laborers and the control on smuggling by the construction of an iron fence in 1982. The existence of this fence in the north is in strong contrast with the invitation by Shenzhen to the people from Hong Kong at the southern border. Therefore, Shenzhen can be considered more and more as a natural expansion of Hong Kong - even before the return of the latter to China in 1997. The major part of investments originates from Hong Kong: Many companies are attracted by lower land prices and labor costs. Moreover, an ever-increasing number of Hong Kong citizens prefer to live in Shenzhen and leave their overcrowded and more expensive hometown.

The presence of foreign companies and residents, the modern urban amenities and the influence from near-by Hong Kong exert a powerful attraction upon people from elsewhere in China. Shenzhen and Zhuhai, to a lesser degree, therefore are a symbol of the modern urban way of life in a productive as well as in a consumptive sense.

To conclude, on the other hand, Shenzhen as an export-enclave economy has not completely been able to attract the highly-advanced technology which China dreamed of. On the other hand Shenzhen exerts a dynamic influence on other parts of China, particularly on the surrounding counties and cities of the Pearl River Delta. In this latter sense Shenzhen can be considered as a growth pole which stimulates the local, regional and national economy.

3.3 The Old Capital of Guangzhou

In comparison with a few years ago, the increasing prosperity of Guangzhou's households is remarkable. In 1986, for instance, only 7% of them disposed of an income of 7,200 RMB or more a year, whereas in 1990 the percentage rose to 66%. In 1990, 90% of the households owned a colour tv; last year-end more than 75% owned a refrigerator (*FEER*, 5-16-91, 66). However, this rise in living standard obscures the structural economic problems of Guangzhou now and in the near future.

Vogel (1989) gives a lively description of some of these structural problems in which he depicts Guangzhou as an old tired man struggling for revival but missing some vital elements to achieve its rejuvenation. He gives an overview of the following infirmities in 1978, at the start of the liberalization:

- congestion and old fabrics: its large population was diffi cult to move and its heavy industrial plants with their 1950 equipment expensive to replace;
- old age of industrial laborers: the plants had aged workers less amenable to innovation and retired workers who required housing and welfare;
- old housing stock: replacing the city's run-down housing would require a large capital investment, new infrastructure and difficult decisions about financing and priorities;
- complicated bureaucracy: Guangzhou was slowed down by complex issues and four layers of bureaucracy above its enterprises;

- local versus provincial spheres of influence: Guangzhou had a lot of responsibility as the capital of its own metropolitan region, and as the provincial capital; this led sometimes to a stagnation and delay in decision-making;
- less attractive tax arrangements: revenue payments from a city or county to higher levels were generally set for five years using one year's production as a base line. This meant that counties or small cities that began with hardly any industry and grew rapidly had virtually a tax holiday for five years. As a large city beginning (in 1978) with a large base that was being slowly replaced, Guangzhou had no such advantage (Vogel 1989, 196).

It would be a mistake to conclude from this description that Guangzhou did not make any progress since 1978. On the contrary: particularly the amelioration of its commercial and service functions and urban amenities in general are quite impressive. However, the economic structure is featured by a high degree of external dependency. In the past decade Guangzhou gradually restored its traditional role as a transit port and became once again South China's largest commerce and trade centre. About 40 percent of Guangzhou's products are sold to other regions of China and roughly 20 percent are directly exported. Most of the raw and semi-finished materials needed for production come from elsewhere in China or from abroad. About a third of its purchasing power is from outside (JPRS-CAR 7-26-90). Therefore, changes in the domestic market but at the same time in the international market have a great influence on Guangzhou's economy. The protective policies adopted in various other parts of China to protect their regional economies has diminished the sale of goods from Guangzhou. Moreover, the international reactions after the June 4 incident in Beijing also had a negative impact.

Next to this external dependency, the industrial structure is hindered by old equipment and by a large state sector with little dynamics and a lot of social obligations like guaranteed employment, cheap housing and the provision of other services. Whereas the industrial production costs in Guangzhou have increased at an annual rate of 20 percent, the product mix continued to be little competitive and has remained predominantly traditional and of low and medium quality.

In sheer contrast with the old industrial structure of Guangzhou City stands the performance of the Guangzhou Economic and Technological Development Zone. This zone, situated in Huangpu 35 km from the city centre along the Pearl River, was initiated in 1984. The realization occurs stepwise, based on the lessons learned from Shenzhen and is aimed at attracting only high-technology industry and services. The project started rather successfully and until 1988, 4 years after its start, 607 million RMB yuan were invested. As in Shenzhen and in the Inner Delta's cities and counties Hong Kong investors took the lion's share with 66 percent. However, to persuade skilled technicians and managers from Guangzhou to relocate to Huangpu seems rather difficult. By means of bonuses Guangzhou tries to attract highly qualified workers to settle in this new and very well-equipped industrial zone, which until now is difficult to reach due to overcrowded roads.

Although the urban character of Guangzhou has been strengthened and the amenities have been greatly improved, Guangzhou functions no longer as the only or the major urban spot to which people are attracted to. Shenzhen and especially the information from Hong Kong by newspaper, television, commerce and personal contacts exert more influence in social and cultural terms. Yet as a provincial capital and as a commercial hub for domestic trade Guangzhou remains the most important centre in the Pearl River Delta.

3.4 Inner Delta Cities and Counties

The Inner Delta is densely populated and richly endowed with natural resources. Fertile land and water resources, the advantages of a large and cheap labor force as well as proximity to Hong Kong and Macau have long existed in the Pearl River Delta. However, it was not until the rural reforms and the "Open Door" policy since 1978 that economic development accelerated (Yeh e.a. 1989, 2). In comparison with the special economic zones of Shenzhen and Zhuhai the Inner Delta has some disadvantages. Shenzhen and Zhuhai are developed with significant assistance from skilled technical and administrative cadres, they have generous financial support from national ministries and famous architects participate especially in Shenzhen to make it an attractive modern city. Guangzhou, as the provincial capital and the commercial and service node of Southern China, is, setting aside the negative points mentioned earlier in some respects, particularly for enterprises oriented toward the domestic market, more attractive than the Inner Delta secondary cities. In contrast, the Inner Delta counties are the "country cousins" encouraged to rely on their own strength (Vogel 1989, 161).

However, this relying on their own strength proves to be a certain advantage as well. The counties are primarily working outside state plans and in general higher-level officials respond more quickly because county requests for funds are lower. Although this local cadre is not always profound and thorough in their decision making they are ready to respond more quickly and flexibly than their big city cousins. Moreover, the Zhujiang Inner Delta is found to be more attractive than the two SEZs which are facing problems of increasing living expenses as well as soaring labor and land costs. The relatively lower production costs in the Delta (wage rates are 20 percent of those in Hong Kong) has attracted some of the middle-sized and smaller factories and enterprises in Hong Kong and Macau to move either all or part of their production lines to the Delta or to subcontract their production there. A rough estimation tells us that in 1989 about 2.5 million workers in the Delta were serving industries in Hong Kong which has a population of roughly six million (Yeh e.a.1989, 2).

Table 2: Performance of rural industry for rural enterprises in general and township and village enterprises, per enterprise or per laborer in 1988 (in 10,000 yuan 1980)

City	Number lab. ent.		Output val. ent.		lab.		Net profit ent.	
	tot	tve	tot	tve	tot	tve	tot	tve
Guangzhou	24.3	43.5	28.2	47.4	1.2	1.1	2.1	3.6
Shenzhen	82.9	85.9	26.2	25.7	0.3	0.3	5.6	5.8
Zhuhai	31.1	58.3	51.0	97.9	0.8	1.7	2.3	4.3
Dongguan	43.4	62.4	35.2	48.2	0.8	0.8	3.1	4.3
Foshan	27.8	49.1	55.8	108.5	0.8	2.2	2.5	4.5
Zhongshan	29.3	53.6	62.3	98.1	2.1	1.8	2.7	3.7
Jiangmen	12.0	29.0	16.0	48.5	1.3	1.7	0.5	0.8
Huizhou	7.3	24.8	4.6	15.7	0.6	0.6	0.3	1.0
Guangdong	10.2	35.7	9.5	38.9	0.9	1.1	0.6	2.1

ent. = per enterprise; lab. = per laborer; tot = total rural industry; tve = township and village enterprises.
Source: Guangdong Department of Township and Village Enterprises.

Among these industrial enterprises the township and village enterprises (TVEs) play an essential role (Table 2). In comparison with the province's average number of TVEs those situated in the Pearl River Delta are well above this average. The same, and even more pronouncedly, holds true with regard to the output value and the profit, although the share of Huizhou is in some respects slightly below average. In 1988, with a population share of 15 percent of the province's total, the number of industrial TVEs located in the Inner Delta amounted to 46 percent, whereas the share of the number of laborers registered 63 percent of the province's whole. In terms of total income the industrial TVEs recorded 85 percent of Guangdong's total income generated by those enterprises (Guangdong TVE Bureau 1991). With regard to their productivity: in 1988, the TVEs accounted for 10.2% of the total number with a share in output value of 67.1 percent (Guangzhou Institute of Geography 1991).

In contrast with the majority of other rural areas in China, the Inner Delta has a permanent shortage of local labor which has to be compensated by laborers from elsewhere. In the TVEs as a whole, 30 to 50 percent of the labor force in 1988 was recruited from elsewhere.

A very important implication of the economic reforms and greater local responsibility is that the fruits of the economic development are for a major part kept at the local level rather than fuelled away to far-off financial and government centres. If a factory makes profit, a reasonable proportion of that money could be spent locally and can be invested not only in productive infrastructure but also on public amenities, social security funds and housing. Two changes in the administrative system had a great impact on the functioning and performance of local enterprises: the relaxing of criteria for designated towns and the adoption of the "town administering village" principle.

By the designation of a market town into a designated town this place may receive a sum of the county's industrial and infrastructure investment funds and attract urban and industrial cadre as well. This could lead to increased industrial employment opportunities and to the construction and improvement of infrastructural facilities, like transport and communication and electricity and social amenities such as banks, schools and hospitals. However, the designation originally resulted in some disadvantages as well, especially for the TVEs. The tax rates for TVEs were and are more favourable in undesignated towns. Moreover, by designation the town becomes administratively separated from its main source of revenue: the TVEs.

The second administrative change, the introduction of the "town administering village" lessened these disadvantages. Also, by way of enlargement of the administrative territory the town's nodal influence can be used to help invigorate the rural economy. With regard to rural industrial enterprises, groups of enterprises can be formed which can share and exchange technology and management and can collaborate by putting-out links. Moreover, the tax base of the central towns is enhanced so that they can collect part of the rural resources to invest in town construction (Lee 1989, 780).

Although many township and village enterprises developed from local initiatives, a lot of these enterprises are organized by a confluence of local and Hong Kong initiatives. By the late 1980s all the counties in the Inner Delta had export processing factories that made goods with materials delivered by Hong Kong and the finished products transported back to Hong Kong to be sold on the world market. Small and middle-sized Hong Kong companies in particular are able to participate very well in the world market by planning, designing, marketing and sales handled in Hong Kong and labor-intensive work done cheaply in China. The contracts are often arranged with former compatriots or fellow-citizens who fled from their home-town to Hong Kong. Commonly the contracts cover one year. In general the Hong Kong side supplies the materials, the model of what is to be done, and the equipment that has to be imported into China. The Chinese side supplies the building, electricity and other local utilities and the labor force. Lump sums are paid by Hong Kong for a certain quantity of goods contracted with final payment when the products are completed. In some contracts the machinery brought in from Hong Kong will revert to Chinese ownership after about ten years.

Sometimes, as in Dongguan, the supply of employment in the export processing industry is so abundant that the local labor is exhausted and labor begins flowing in from elsewhere. However, the best jobs go first to locals, and the least desirable jobs, in construction, in agriculture and in export processing as well, overwhelmingly go to outsiders.

The blooming export processing industry, mainly in textiles, electronics and plastic items, has brought about corresponding changes in the other economic sectors. In particular, the construction industry and the transport sector flourish as a result. Also, agricultural production has experienced structural changes, with a significant increase in commercial farming. The increase in rural incomes generated an uprising in savings. Most of the savings are deposited in the Agricultural Bank of China or the Rural Credit Cooperative and the money could be recycled for investment, particularly for township, village and private industries. However, the individual accounts also reflect the increase in family-income and the ability to invest in housing and to purchase more consumption goods.

The Agricultural Bank of China began to invest more in rural community industry than in agriculture. Due to the fact that the Agricultural Bank has branches in every county its officials quickly became familiar with local enterprises. Moreover, although the Bank's total lending is linked to deposits, it can move funds from one county to another to make promising loans.

The Agricultural Bank is often the key source of initial investments in rural enterprises. However once an enterprise is successful it can generate its own funds for expansion. At last the local community can also draw on the profits from one enterprise to invest in other local ones or to invest in infrastructure. Accompanying the economic growth are improvements in urban infrastructure provisions, particularly in the small rural towns. Rapid growth in industry and trade has encouraged peasants in the nearby farms to leave their land to work in towns (Vogel 1989, 172).

However, economic growth and prosperity have not spread equally throughout the Inner Delta. The spatial inequality is clearly brought out by Figure 3 showing the spatial distribution of gross value of industrial and agricultural output per capita for 1982. The two city areas of Foshan and Jiangmen had the greatest GVIAO per capita of RMB 4,260 and RMB 4,082, respectively. Shunde, Nanhai, Zhongshan, Panyu, Doumen and Dongguan were counties that showed a GVIAO per capita exceeding RMB 1,000. Clearly they represented the wealthy core area of the Delta. On the other hand the lowest value occurred in Zengcheng (RMB 513), followed by Gaoming (RMB 550) (Lo 1989a, 24).

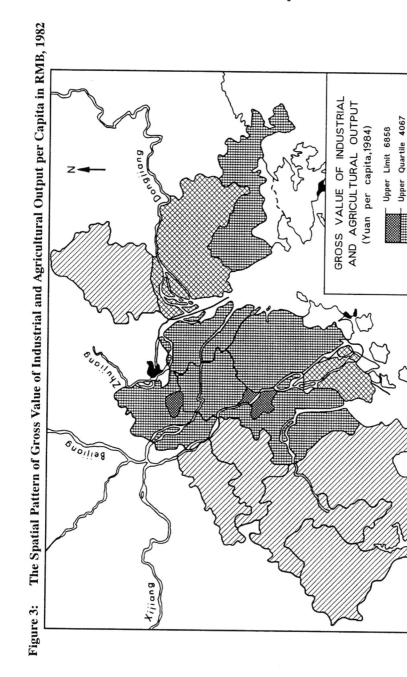

Figure 3: The Spatial Pattern of Gross Value of Industrial and Agricultural Output per Capita in RMB, 1982

Source: Lo, 1989b.

Another classification has been composed by Vogel (1989, 192-95), using the criteria of accessibility to and the accompanying dependence on Hong Kong together with the role of local government in industrial development. The first tier consists of counties whose economies are most integrated with that of Hong Kong. Their ready accessibility by truck and boat and the presence of recent migrants from these counties makes it easy to develop export-processing arrangements with Hong Kong. However the speed and depth with which they take advantage of this favorable situation depends to a great deal on the attitude and ability of the county leaders. Counties with a unified leadership as in Dongguan have made more progress than those that are equally close but without a strong commitment as, e.g. in Panyu.

The second tier contains places like Foshan, Nanhai, Shunde, and Zhongshan which are less close to Hong Kong. For them it is less easy to attract simple processing plants. In comparison with the first layer they have larger towns, a history of more light industry and more experienced workers. They orientate themselves more to Guangzhou and make use of its expertise and its network of internal Chinese markets. These counties produce not only for the world market via Hong Kong, but they also produce, and far more than the first layer, for the rest of Guangdong and other provinces. The second tier has also developed more entrepreneurship, because it faces more complex issues of capital, technology and marketing. They followed different routes to develop industry. Nanhai started quickly with many small village industries. Shunde with the help of Hong Kong capital installed several industries on a larger scale than those in Nanhai. Zhongshan relied more on larger, county-run state factories because a major part of its population was centered in the county capital. However, in the late 1980s Shunde and Zhongshan began to converge in their approaches. Shunde county, impressed that the Zhongshan government received more income from its state industries and could undertake county-wide infrastructural projects, decided to develop more state enterprises. On the other hand Zhongshan was impressed by the vitality and local initiative of Shunde's town industries and changed its route toward more town-led industries. At last the third layer consists of counties farthest away from Hong Kong and they were generally also farther from Guangzhou. The counties are poorer and the cadres are often less willing to take risks. When the transportation by the mid-1980s improved and the cost of labor was rising in the first- and second-tier counties they took their chance. This occurred especially in Jiangmen, the second largest urban center in the Inner Delta (see also Figure 1 and Table 2).

4 Spatial Problems

After the static period of a predominantly self-sufficient society during which the construction and maintenance of basic infrastructure and urban facilities had been discouraged and neglected, the reform period since 1978 has led to an outburst of construction of housing, roads, bridges, waterways, ports, factories and (tele)communication systems. The economic development occurs so rapidly that planning often cannot adequately anticipate or react to the needs of inhabitants and/or enterprises.

Broadly we can make a distinction between the spatial planning problems of big cities and those of the secondary cities and small towns. Big cities like Guangzhou are confronted with the neglect in the recent past of housing and urban amenities. From 1954 onwards the emphasis in urban planning in Guangzhou as well as elsewhere was to change those urban places from a "consumption city" status to an industrial city. Therefore, since 1958 Guangzhou has become the industrial base for South China. It was expected and hoped that once heavy industry succeeded there would be benefits for the citizens' livelihood but this approach failed. The housing stock is inadequate, both in quantitative (number of houses, number of rooms) as in qualitative (maintenance, amenities) terms. Almost no new housing was built between 1949 and 1979 except for some new cadre and some apartments for workers at newly built factories. For the construction, maintenance and allocation of dwelling units the work unit (predominantly state-enterprises) monopoly still exists. Residents themselves have little capital, few construction materials and almost no incentive to repair housing which is not their property. In the meantime the urban population more than doubled and this resulted in an acute shortage of space (Vogel 1989, 197).

This system of allocation which guarantees a cheap dwelling unit for the present employee and even after his/her retirement is harmful and inadequate to adapt to changing circumstances. This is the more so if state-enterprises are in a bad shape and could not or would not set aside money for construction and repair of housing.

The same holds true for infrastructural facilities like roads, bridges, electricity, sewage systems and telephone service. Although the progress made in the enlargement and maintenance of these infrastructural facilities is quite impressive, the congestion and overcrowding still continues. The overburdening of the transport system is, next to the near neglect by the government, largely due to the fact that commercial travellers, peasant-workers and market information seekers are obliged to move with whatever vehicle available or to stay for short periods in hotels or guesthouses, because of the obstacles they face in establishing more regular means of supplying their operations (Fincher 1990, 53).

The huge flood of "blindful migrants" puts the existing facilities under even more pressure. In times of booming construction activities, like in 1985-1987, these migrants were a benefit for Guangzhou. However, since 1989, the urban economy has not been able to absorb those migrants anymore. Squatting and rising poverty among them are already manifest and will cause a growing problem for the municipal government.

Guangzhou, like other big cities in the coastal zone, quite often is not capable of planning and managing the suburban areas around the city, the so-called urban fringe. Incompatible land-use, residential areas mixed up with farmland, roads and open-air deposits of urban factories can be seen very often. Due to this chaotic planning or the absence of efficient planning valuable resources are wasted and the functioning of services and factories is hindered. Moreover, the costs ensuing afterwards to regain the area and to create a more efficient and compatible land use will be enormous.

As described above, urban growth in the Inner Delta mainly occurs in small and medium-sized cities. These places and their surrounding rural areas are very attractive to small and medium investors from Hong Kong and Macau. Not only because of lower labor and land costs but also because the environmental control measures are less stringent in these smaller urban places.

The competition among the smaller cities with regard to foreign investments is enormous. Means to surpass nearby places are financial preferential treatments (tax exemption, low fees for public amenities) and high investments in the construction and maintenance of roads, ports and telecom facilities. These infrastructural investments, the so-called "five linkages and one levelling" (provision of road links, sea links, water supply, electricity and telecom plus land levelling) are resulting in rising overhead costs. This uprise in overhead costs plus the shortage of local labor and the accompanying rising labor costs however undermine the low cost factor for settlement. Moreover, development plans are mostly formulated for the land use within the boundaries of the respective local government with little consideration to the overall development of the broader region.

Rapid urbanisation of these small and medium urban places also leads to rapid encroachment of urban land onto fertile agricultural land. If however the local government will not succeed in attracting foreign investments, much of this land will be abandoned and it will be very difficult and expensive to restore the agricultural land.

The individualistic way of spatial policy and planning also gives rise to a substantial duplication of facilities and land use or, in other words, to a waste of financial and land resources. The dispersal of factories and urban facilities carry high economic costs like higher transport costs and industrial pollution.

The less stringent environmental control measures have caused a relocation of polluting industries such as tannery and dyeing from Hong Kong and Macau and even from Guangzhou into the small towns and the countryside of the Pearl River Delta.

So there clearly exists a trade-off between the flexibility in dealing with foreign investment and careful, efficient spatial planning in local as well as in regional perspective and in short- as well as long-term development. From the viewpoint of the regional economy a closer coordination based on local comparative advantages between Guangzhou, the SEZs and the Inner Delta towns and counties is of primary importance.

5 Concluding Remarks

The spatial organization of the Pearl River Delta in the 1980s and the beginning of the 1990s has been characterized by a process of reversed polarization in which the degree of primacy of the region's city system has declined substantially. In conventional regional planning this phenomenon of reversal is associated with self-sustained economic and spatial development. In this respect the development within the Delta seems an anomaly: a more balanced urban hierarchy occurs together with a strong influx of foreign capital. According to the conventional models of regional development, however, it is exactly this penetration of capital which results in more polarizised spatial development.

This anomaly can be explained by the interference of several factors. Firstly, the rigid political and administrative system in China has hindered the penetration of foreign capital in big urban places and has avoided the take-over or predominance by foreign capital of the domestic production and markets. This selective use of foreign capital and know-how, described as the ELIFFIT strategy ("export-led industrialization fuelled by foreign investment and technology" and by the mobilization of massive cheap local labor or labor to be recruited from elsewhere) could be considered as a selective territorial closure harvesting the benefits while diminishing the evils or dangers of foreign influence.

Secondly, the liberalization policy after 1978 (Open Door Policy and the Rural Reforms in agricultural as well as non-agricultural activities) and the administrative reforms (more room for local decision-making, the relaxation of designation of towns and town administering villages) have given local governments more space of manoeuvre for local economic development by attracting foreign investments and by retaining the fruits of this local economic progress.

In the third place, the realization of this economic development depends very much on local resources, the relative location vis-à-vis foreign investors and markets and personal contacts with potential investors. In all these respects the Pearl River Delta discerns itself positively from other regions by its rich natural and human resources, the proximity to Hong Kong and Macau and the personal relationships with former refugees. As described in this article the small urban places and middle-sized cities have profited the most because of their flexibility in attracting and bargaining with foreign investors, particularly the medium-scale investors from Hong Kong.

However, the regional economy of the Delta is very strongly externally dependent and therefore rather vulnerable, not only in terms of foreign dependence like investment, know-how and commercialization, but also in terms of dependence on other regions elsewhere in China with regard to cheap labor and domestic markets. Moreover, the attitude and resulting policy of the central government of China towards the economic development in Guangdong Province and the Pearl River Delta is of primary significance and changes in policies are sometimes difficult to foresee. Recently a change in emphasis could be discerned to strengthen the industrial development of Shanghai and moderate the industrial growth of Guangdong.

Next to this external dependence another weakness of the regional economic development of the Pearl River Delta is the duplication or waste of investments in infrastructure. This is closely associated with the greater local responsibility and room for manoeuvre and could at best be considered as a transitional problem. As a next step forward in the development of the Delta a spatial division of tasks among the urban places of different size and the surrounding rural areas seems of utmost importance. After 1997, the role of Hong Kong could be one which lies predominantly in finance and services; that of the SEZs of Shenzhen and Zhuhai as well as the Guangzhou Economic and Technological Development Zone could be a specialization in high-grade industry and services; the Inner Delta towns and counties could specialize in less high-tech industries and intensive agriculture, while Guangzhou could enhance its position as regional commercial centre as well as its function as a hub in the growing domestic market.

At last, the reversal of polarization which obviously takes place nowadays within the Pearl River Delta, has to be evaluated very carefully and with some caution. As described above, the greater equality in spatial development within the region has resulted in a greater disparity between the Delta and other regions in Guangdong and the surrounding provinces. Moreover, even within the Delta the differences in economic development and the potentialities for the future are significant. Next to this spatial perspective, seen in the perspective of time, the economic development in the Delta has taken off only recently and it is not unthinkable that the recent reversed polarization together with a growing importance of the increasing domestic market in the long run could be turned into a more polarizised development pattern.

References

Chang Sen-dou: Implications of Nonagricultural Development in Rural China, unpublished Paper, Conference on Chinese Cities in Asian Context, Hong Kong 1987
FEER/Far Eastern Economic Review, nos. 16th May and 8th August 1991
Fincher, J.: "Rural Bias and the Renaissance of Coastal China", in: Linge G. & D. Forbes: *China's Spatial Economy*, Hong Kong: Oxford University Press, 1990
Guangzhou Institute of Geography, oral communication from Prof. Chen Ningxun
Guangdong Township and Village Enterprises Bureau Statistics and oral communication from Mr. Zhou, Vice-Director
JPRS-CAR 26th July and 17th August 1990
Kirkby, R.: *Urbanisation in China: Town and Country in a Developing Economy 1949-2000 AD*, London: Croom Helm 1985
Lee, Y.: "Small Towns and China's Urbanization Level", in: *The China Quarterly*, Vol.120, December 1989
Lo, C.P.: "Population Change and Urban Development in the Pearl River Delta: Spatial Policy Implications", in: *Asian Geographer*, Volume 8, nos. 1 & 2, 1989 (a)
Lo, C.P.: "Recent Spatial Restructuring in Zhujiang Delta, South China: A Study of Socialist Regional Development Strategy", in: *Annals of the Association of Americam Geographers* 79 (2), 1989 (b)
Pannell, C & G. Veeck: "Zhujiang Delta and Sunan: A Comparative Analysis of Regional Urban Systems and Their Development, in: *Asian Geographer*, Volume 8, nos. 1 & 2, 1989
Sklair, L.: "Problems of Socialist Development: the Significance of Shenzhen Special Economic Zone for China's Open Door Development Strategy", in: *International Journal of Urban and Regional Research*, Vol.15, no. 2, 1991
Vogel, E.: *One step ahead in China. Guangdong under Reform*, Cambridge, Mass.: Harvard University Press, 1989
Xu X.Q. & S. Li: "China's Open Door Policy and Urbanization in the Pearl River Delta Region", in: *International Journal of Urban and Regional Research*, Vol.14, no. 1, 1990
Yeh A. e.a.: "Spatial Development in the Pearl River Delta: Development Issues and Research Agenda", in: *Asian Geographer*, Volume 8, nos. 1 & 2, 1989

Social Transformation in Rural China
An Alternative Pattern of Urbanization

by Bingyu Shen

1 The Problem

Presently most of the developing countries are faced with a dilemma. Development in these countries naturally involves urbanization, and excessive growth of large cities unavoidably results in many social diseases which threaten the socio-economic health of the population.

There may be two different approaches to this problem: First, determining the factors which cause the excessive growth of large cities and attempting to remedy each separately. Unfortunately, hard work and cost-effective programs failed to negate the problem, because no organization or agency had been successful. Is there an alternative approach? Could administrative measures serve to prevent the excessive growth of large cities? This method was also attempted with national development, and resulted in strong resentment from the rural population. Secondly, the conclusion was that a comprehensive approach aimed primarily at the development of small towns in the nearby countryside, was a better strategy for both promotion of rural development and prevention of over-urbanization with its social polarization between the urban and the rural areas. The strategy desired is to create urbanization in small cities and towns, rather than relocate the surplus agrarian labor force into the big cities.

Over the past 35 years, small towns in the rural areas of China have passed through a process of rise-fall-revival. During the early years of the People's Republic, small towns in the rural areas to a considerable degree developed along with the recovery and development of China's national economy. According to the statistics of 1954, there were 5,400 small towns spread across the country. Afterwards, leftist policies were implemented and grain became the major crop of agriculture which resulted in a single-product economy. Private commerce and rural markets were disrupted, and the peasants had no chance to sell their products in the markets. As a result the small towns no longer served as distribution centers for agricultural and sideline products. The traditional multiple channels of commodity circulation were meanwhile blocked and altered into unitary channels which were controlled by state-run commercial enterprises. Small towns were unable to provide job opportunities for their residents because of the reduction of the commodity economy and the restriction of private enterprises. The decline of small towns therefore became inevitable. The towns recuperated after the Third Plenary Session of the 11th Central Committee of the Chinese Communist Party in 1978. New decisions on economic reforms were then made. The contract system of agricultural production was introduced across the country; this caused an immense increase in agricultural production.

The failure of the policy of industrialization clearly resulted in a vicious circle in the rural areas: a downgraded agriculture and industry, and a decline of small towns. 2,819 small towns remained in China by the end of 1982, because of the rural economic stagnation over the past twenty years. This was approximately half of the number in 1954. The prosperity of agriculture over the past six years called the development of small towns back on the agenda. Small towns increased to about 12,000 by the end of 1989. Eighty percent of China's one billion people, as is known, inhabit the countryside. If sixty percent of the rural population in the process of urbanization (more than twice the U.S. population) will according to some predictions flow into large cities, then the grave consequences would remain difficult to predict. The urbanization of the country therefore seems to depend upon the countryside and rural residents' trend towards modernization. This paper attempts to study the process of small town transformation in terms of socio-economic changes.

2 Background

Experiments have been made since 1979 in order to reform the economic mechanism, beginning in the rural areas. The economic reform allowed the coexistence and development of multiple forms of economy and management which included the collective, jointly owned, and individual economies of various forms. Its purpose was to invigorate the rural economy. The responsibility system for agricultural production soon proved its vitality. It was adopted universally in order to replace the existing communes with their distribution system of "eating from one big pot" (i.e., egalitarian distribution). The contract system as a new form of responsibility, linked to output on a household basis, had been applied to more than 90 percent of China's farming households by 1983. The significant growth in agricultural productivity was due to the rise of enthusiasm and initiative of the producer. The positive results were caused by the guarantee of greater independence and autonomy in work. The *total* growth in agricultural labor productivity from 1952 to 1978, for example, was 2.7 percent, meanwhile the average *annual* growth from 1979 to 1981, after the adoption of the contract system, was also 2.7 percent.[1] Almost 1/3 to 1/2 of the peasants as a result were able to quit farming and become part- or full-time commodity producers in various economic sectors.

The rapid development of rural town industries in the delta region of the Yangzi River exceeded the average in terms of size and capital. These industries after their establishment in 1958 had had difficulties and had been faced with interference, therefore their actual development began only after 1978. The policy was that any processing of agricultural and sideline products which could be accomplished in the countryside, was to be gradually turned over to industries in rural towns. The urban factories should also transfer to these small industries those parts of their production which were suitable for processing in the countryside. The rural factories had to pay minimal taxes or were exempted for the first three years. Afterwards, the rural town enterprises rapidly developed. The enterprises generated a remarkable contribution of 48.8 percent of the 143,800 million RMB net increase in rural China's total output value in 1983.[2] These rural town enterprises became the buttresses of China's rural economy. They influenced the expansion of commodity production, altered the economic structure, and created a new form for the peri-urban small towns and villages. Parallel to this they also provided the material basis for alterations in traditional attitudes of the rural society.

3 Methodology

I selected one *xiang*[3] and one village in Suzhou prefecture in the Yangzi Delta. Both locations are above the medium level in terms of economic development and have well-developed rural town industries. In most local households occurred a shift from agriculture to industry. The number of farm laborers has gradually decreased while industrialization has increased.

Local government offices provided statistics and data which present a longitudinal perspective on these changes. I additionally conducted a consecutive random sampling survey in March 1985 and 1986, by the use of questionnaires to which 50 peasant workers responded. These were the first to discontinue farming and their answers were of great significance. Nevertheless, these peasant-workers were not accustomed to surveys of this kind, so many were a little suspicious. Every item on the questionnaires therefore had to be explained. The rural resident workers were also informed of the purpose of my survey. Anonymity was guaranteed so that there would be authentic answers. It was requested that they check their answers, and after having collected the questionnaires the answers were double-checked with the participants. A new copy was supplied for them if the questionnaire was not properly filled in. These measures were used in order to reduce the bias to a minimum. Most of the villagers were cooperative and the results were satisfactory. In March 1986, identical questionnaires were used again in a random sampling of 36 peasants in Ouqiao Village for comparative purposes. The geographical situation and the economic conditions of Ouqiao Village are similar to those of Bixi Xiang.

4 General Situation of Bixi Xiang

Bixi Xiang, in which Bixi Market Town is located, is in Suzhou Prefecture in the southern province of Jiangsu. Communication and transportation are convenient. Highways built after 1979 connect it with other *xiang*. The geographical advantages of Bixi are comparable to those of the cities of Suzhou and Wuxi.

Bixi was originally a small *xiang*. In 1958 it joined with three other *xiang* to form Bixi People's Commune. In April 1983 the commune was abolished and the *xiang* was restored as an administrative unit. It consisted of twenty-two villages (production brigades) and one market town, also named Bixi, which served as its administrative seat. The *xiang* was very limited in land resources. The 1982 census showed that there was only 0.8 mu (less than one-fifteenth of a hectare) of land per capita for a population of 27,765. Nevertheless, for a long period of time the entire labor force had been constrained to the land by ultra-left policies. Annual per capita income was consequently below 100 RMB before 1970; it was a poverty-stricken commune. After 1979, reforms in agricultural production were instituted which encouraged the peasants to diversify their operations: truck farming, animal husbandry, weaving, knitting, services, transportation, processing, etc. Rural town industries also rapidly developed. Each village engaged in a form of industrial venture, so a network of industries was formed. Knitting was the most prominent industry among the 61 trades which included machine-building, building materials, electric appliances, plastic goods, etc.

Bixi Market Town had a population of more than 6,000 in 1983. 3,030 were peasant-workers who lived in surrounding villages; they daily went by bicycle to work in the factories. These industries attracted the peasants to the market town and also promoted construction. They performed an important function in transforming the *xiang* into a town. Bixi Market Town, formerly poverty-stricken, underdeveloped and consisting of a single street, less than 200 meters long, had emerged as a moderately prosperous town and became a prototype of an urban town. Bixi Xiang was abolished in March 1986 as a result of this development. The People's Government of Bixi Town was established and Bixi Market Town appointed as its seat. This formally marked the change of Bixi's status from a rural unit to an urban one in terms of government administration.

5 Changes in Bixi Xiang

5.1 Economic Changes

Table 1 demonstrates the significant changes in the economic structure after the late 1970s. Against a background of increased total output value, the proportion of agriculture steadily decreased, while that of industry continued to rapidly increase. Bixi's agricultural output value amounted to 6.3 percent of the *xiang*'s total output in 1985. The total industrial output value increased to 91.2 percent, which was thirteen times higher than that of agriculture. The concepts and modes of production that had been a tradition for thousands of years in the countryside - predominance of agriculture - were broken through. Bixi was transformed into an industrialized *xiang*.

Table 1: Changes in Economic Structure, Bixi Xiang

Year	Total Output Value (in Y.10.000)	Agriculture (%)	Industry (%)	Sideline (%)
1966	638	10.9		
1970	615		20.7	
1975	572			
1979	3.044	25.8	71.5	2.7
1980	4.446	14.4	76.4	9.2
1982	5.977	14.8	79.2	6.0
1984	10.212	10.9	82.7	6.4
1985	14.000	6.3	91.2	2.5

Source: Bixi Xiang Government.

This state of affairs also reflects the structure of the labor force (Table 2).

Table 2: Changes in Labor Force Structure (%)

Year	Agriculture	Industry	Sideline
1960	92.8	1.1	6.1
1970	88.4	5.3	6.3
1979	57.0	35.9	7.1
1982	43.2	47.8	9.0
1984	32.5	58.3	9.2
1985	25.8	64.8	9.4

Source: Bixi Xiang Government.

Table 2 shows that the agricultural laborers who dominated the scene, comprising 92.8 percent of the total labor force in 1960, sharply decreased. Industrial workers, only 5.3 percent of the total labor force in Bixi by the end of 1970, accounted for ca. 65 percent at the end of 1985. At this time 18.503 laborers were present and 11.991 were engaged in industrial production. These changes in the labor force served as catalyst in the economic development, which promoted the peasants' desires and opportunities to leave the farming sector for non-farming activities. Furthermore, Bixi which had had a surplus of labor, had a shortage of manpower and hired residents from the outside.

Table 3: Changes in Income Structure (%)

Year	Annual Income per capita (RMB)	Agriculture (%)	Industry (%)	Sideline (%)
1954	88.0	100.0	0	0
1958	90.0	100.0	0	0
1978	172.5	46.1	43.5	10.4
1980	274.5	47.9	43.7	8.4
1982	383.0	50.5	47.0	2.5
1984	768.0	35.0	46.0	19.0
1985	820.0	25.0	61.0	14.0

Source: Bixi Xiang Government.

One result of this economic growth was that the peasants' income increased in 1985, though it was a year of severe natural disasters. Per capita income amounted to 820 RMB, an increase of 6 percent compared to that of the previous year (see Table 3). In comparison with 1978, per capita income had increased by 19.5 percent.

Table 3 also demonstrates that the income of agriculture accounted for only 25 percent of the total income, while the income of industry production consistently increased after 1979. It replaced the agricultural income as the main source of income and hence employment. These structural changes mark a new trend in China.

Private deposits by Bixi peasants by the end of 1985 totalled 8,200,000 RMB in the local bank, an average of 305 RMB per capita. Individual investments in local rural town collective enterprises amounted to 3,670,000 RMB which averaged 137 RMB per capita and were used by the enterprises for the expansion of reproduction. In this process, the surplus labor force, as well as idle funds in the surrounding villages, were attracted to and collected from the market town for more expansion of production. Bixi thus functioned as a reservoir for creating a positive force which contributes an important share to the prosperity of the market town and surrounding countryside.

The industrial profits of Bixi Xiang totalled 44,260,000 RMB for the period 1978 - 1985. 24.2 percent of this was allocated for construction in the market town and 14.5 percent for the expansion of the market town's industry. The data show that the rural town enterprises function as the buttress for market town development. The market town uses these funds in order to build factories, stores, schools, housing plots, etc. A total of 150,103 square meters of new construction is 2.45 times of that which the market town had in 1978.

Industrial development caused changes in both the nature and scope of the market town's circulation: Imports from other regions were no longer limited to articles of daily usage or means of production for agriculture but consisted in the main of industrial materials and construction materials. The exports of the urban area included industrial commodities as well as farm products. Its exchanges transcended the original economic and administrative boundaries and in some cases entered the international market. The circulation also expanded in another direction absorbing urban talents, technology, and information. Skilled and experienced retired workers were invited to serve as consultants and aids in order to solve technical problems which might exist in production.

The constant increase of economic prosperity of the market town of Bixi aids in the development of the surrounding rural areas; this includes the mechanization of farm work, which provides manpower resources for the market town. As a result, the market town grew in both population and area. Its population tripled in 1985, as compared to that of 1978, and its area more than quadrupled (Table 4). Thus the market town evolved into the economic and cultural center of the *xiang*.

Table 4: Expansion of the Market Town of Bixi in Area and Population

Year	Area (in sq.kilometer)	Population (in person)
1978	0.13	2,500
1980	0.22	3,500
1982	0.33	6,000
1984	0.50	7,500
1985	0.53	8,420

Source: Bixi Xiang Government.

The facts and figures above demonstrate that Bixi Xiang has experienced a great change within eight years (from 1978-1986).

An important question is whether or not cultural changes in conjunction with economic development can be found. In March 1985, I investigated 50 Bixi peasant-workers. The youngest was 19, and the oldest 64.52% were between 19 and 29,40% were between 30 and 49, and 8% between 50 and 65. In educational terms, the most educated were those between 19 and 29, having had secondary or higher education. Three illiterates were found in the two older age groups.

In March 1986, the identical questionnaires were used in an investigation of 36 peasants in Ouqiao Village for comparative purposes. Most of the peasants were drastically different from the peasant-workers in both age and education. Of the

36 peasants 92% were older than 40 years, 8% were between 30 and 40. None engaged in farming was below 30. In educational terms 61% of them were illiterate, 33% had four years of schooling, and 5% were junior middle school graduates.

The data demonstrate that the first people to abandon farming for industrial careers were usually educated young people, who are different from the traditional peasants in terms of life-style and values. These differences are most evident in the following aspects.

5.2 Value Changes

5.2.1 Shifts Away from Traditional Ethics

The data obtained through the survey demonstrates that 80% of the married Bixi peasant-workers live in their own nuclear families, away from their immediate relatives. Present-day household production, with its enlarged scale and broadened scope of operation, seems to have made a gradual transition from a self-sufficient natural economy into a commodity economy of which more production is shifted to productive operations. Family members begin to consciously observe the arrangements made by those who are economically aware, those who understand production and good management. As a result, the traditional model of the family structure with an elder as the head of the household is replaced by a new model with an able person as the head of a family. The institution of the responsibility system linked to the output has abolished the practice of the collective "eating from one big pot", however, it has not resolved the problem of domestic distribution among brothers and sisters and in-laws. Therefore, increasing impatience leads many to leave the extended family and live separately. The rejection of the large family forced parents to live alone, or with different sons on a rotating basis, or with one son only.

The emergence of nuclear families has eliminated the traditional power of the extended family, in which the senior person, the family elder controls the family finances, marriages, and childbirths. These controls were used in order to preserve the authority of the family head, to build a network of social ties to consolidate the family, and to solve the problem of family planning. These matters were all closely linked, however the shift of economic rights within the family helped young couples gain control over their nuclear families and to strengthen their position in the extended family. The patriarchal system and Confucian ethics having prevailed in the countryside for thousands of years are being shattered.

5.2.2 Changes in the Institution of Marriage

Of the 50 peasant-workers 35 were married and 10 of the remaining 15 are all under the age of 25 and engaged to be married. An analysis of the patterns of marriage or engagement shows that arranged marriages amounted to 12% of the total, love-marriages accounted for 70%. Half of those who had married out of love were between the age of 19 and 29. In comparison, 92% of the 36 peasants of Ouqiao had their marriages arranged. The others orphaned at an early age were allowed to choose for themselves.

The marriages of young people in traditional families were always arranged by the parents, who built a solid network of social relationships. As patriarchal authority is losing its economic power, parental interference in marriages has diminished.

Furthermore, the industrial development in the countryside has lifted the limitations of the small-producer economy based on the traditional family in rural China. It provides more opportunities for contact between young people of the opposite sex thus stimulating the demand for autonomy in marriage. As a result, even arranged marriages have changed the traditional pattern: They are not finalized until both prospective partners converge and agree to the marriage.

5.2.3   Changes in Attitudes toward Childbirth

Eighteen respondents of Bixi Town are satisfied with single-child families, they are mostly in the age-group between 19 and 29. Twenty residents said that the infants' sex was of no importance, and these residents were also between the age of 19 and 29. Of the 36 peasants who responded all were married, had children, and were over the age of 33. 30 desired two children; only three were satisfied with one child. There was a great difference between the two groups of respondents. However, between the majority of both peasant-workers and peasants there was no preference of sons or daughters. This was related to the one-child family planning. Acceptance of such matters represents a major change in the traditional concept of male superiority in which a male descendent continues the family line.

The changes in attitude toward childbirth may be related to a certain degree of modernization in the countryside. Some elderly still insist upon a male descendent to continue the family line, however, a mother-in-law's pressure upon a daughter-in-law for the birth of a male has abated somewhat due to the changes in family structures. Furthermore, the rapid development of village-run industries enabled some villages to establish a welfare fund for members of the community; part of it was designated for medical care and old-age pensions. Many old people have basic provisions today, so they no longer feel the need to depend upon their descendents as much as before. The local knitting industry is relatively well developed and has many women workers. Wage-earner status has contributed to the advancement of women's participation in deciding family affairs together with their husbands. Families have realized that fewer children are advantageous. These two trends have promoted family planning, and allowed the realization of China's single-child program in both places by 1984.

Table 5: Attitudes toward Childbirth

	Satisfied with One		Want to Have Two		Prefer Boy(s)		No Preference between Boys & Girls	
Age	P.-w. Bixi	P. Ouqiao	P.-w. Bixi	P. Ouqiao	P.-w. Bixi	P. Ouqiao	P.-w. Bixi	P. Ouqiao
16-29	12	0	3	0	1	0	13	0
30-39	3	0	9	3	1	0	3	0
40-49	2	5	5	13	1	0	3	10
50+	1	1	2	14	0	2	1	9
Total	18	6	19	30	3	2	20	19
%	30	10	32	53	5	4	33	33

Table 6: Sense of Time and Attitude toward Work

	Peasant-workers Bixi		Peasants Ouqiao	
	No.	%	No.	%
Sense of Time				
Not Enough	35	70	14	39
More Than Enough	9	18	18	50
Indifferent	6	12	4	11
No Answer	0	0	0	0
Total	50	100	36	100
Attitude toward Work				
Should be as Industrious as Possible	37	74	13	36
Should Take it Easy	6	12	5	14
Should Just do same as Everyone Else	5	10	17	47
No Answer	2	4	1	3
Total	50	100	36	100

5.2.4 Changes in the Sense of Time

70% percent of the peasant-workers expressed their dissatisfaction due to the lack of spare time, 74% believed that they should have more time in order to accomplish things (Table 6). 50% of the peasants expressed that they had enough time and another 47% attempted not to force their pace of work in order to avoid conspicuousness. These differences seem to stem from the different modes of production. The peasants no longer engaged in traditional small-peasant economy are not yet engaged in large-scale fully mechanized production.

Traditionally peasants simply divided the day according to necessities. Important for them were the seasonal changes. Peasants living in an emerging commodity economy in the countryside, especially those engaged in diversified operations, realize the importance of time and information gained through their operations. The slogan "Time is money, time is life" also appeals to them. This marks a new consciousness of the peasants.

5.2.5 Changes in Cultural Life

What changes have occurred in the cultural life of the peasant-workers? How do they use spare time, and what are their expectations? Table 7 demonstrates that the peasant-workers utilize their spare time primarily for housework, reading, and television. The peasants also use their spare time primarily for housework, however, their second and third priorities were sideline production and tea-house visits. Note that none of them reads.

An agricultural society in the countryside tends to be culturally underdeveloped. Illiteracy is widespread, and peasants are characterized by ignorance. However, the emergence of a large number of peasant-workers and the development of commodity economy all forced the peasants to improve the general cultural level in order to obtain better results in production and operations. Today it is common for peasants to invite college lecturers to their villages. This all stems from the peasants' desire to learn more for the modernization of the countryside.

What are the aspirations of the peasant-workers?

The three prominent aspirations for the Ouqiao peasants are: higher financial income, construction of new houses, and finding a more ideal job. It thus seems that the peasant-workers put more stress on the immaterial side of life in their aspirations, while those of the peasants were more materialistic. Note that only one person in Bixi desired a job in the city. How might this be explained? An important consideration is that the peasants are better off than town-dwellers in terms of income and housing.

For the peasants the pull-effect of the city is generally the expectation of a higher material and spiritual civilization. This desire increases, if the gap between the urban and rural standard of living expands. The modernization of the countryside narrows the urban-rural gap and reduces the pull-effect of the city. The peasants enjoy a better material and spiritual life and do not aspire after city careers, as the rural economy develops.

Table 7 (a):   Spare-Time Activities

Peasant-Workers (Bixi) Priorities	1st	2nd	3rd	Total	%
Housework	28	9	2	39	30
Farming	2	1	0	3	2
Sideline Production	8	7	4	19	15
Reading	9	12	6	27	21
Watching Television	0	11	17	28	22
Visiting Friends	0	1	5	6	4
Tea-house Visits	2	0	0	2	1.5
Sports	1	0	3	4	3
Other Activities	0	0	2	2	1.5
Total				130	100

Table 7 (b):   Spare-Time Activities

Peasants (Ouqiao) Priorities	1st	2nd	3rd	Total	%
Housework	19	13	0	32	26
Farming	36	0	0	36	29
Sideline Production	17	10	0	27	22
Reading	0	0	0	0	0
Watching Television	0	4	5	9	7
Visiting Friends	0	3	6	9	7
Tea-house Visits	0	5	6	11	9
Sports	0	0	0	0	0
Other Activities	0	0	0	0	0
Total				124	100

The wish for filial and obedient children reflects traditional values. However, this was no choice of anyone in Bixi, only of one person in Ouqiao. The modern peasant seems to pursue his own success. The collective now is prosperous enough in order to provide for its senior citizens. People no longer heavily rely upon their children for financial support.

Table 8: Aspirations

	Peasant-workers Bixi		Peasants Ouqiao	
	No.	%	No.	%
Study	12	24	0	0
Successful Career	9	18	0	0
Get Rich	7	14	16	44
Pleasant Life	1	2	0	0
Domestic Happiness	12	24	0	0
Urban Job	1	2	0	0
Happy Old Age	0	0	2	6
Filial Children	0	0	1	3
New House	4	8	9	25
Good Marriage	2	4	0	0
Other	2	4	8*	22
Total	50	100	36	100

*) All 8 peasants expressed the hope for more ideal jobs.

5.2.6 Changes in Material Life-Style

Bicycles and watches are quite common in the countryside. Each family (in both places) possesses on the average more than two of these durable goods. The number of durable goods per household is generally identical. Approximately each peasant household in Ouqiao had a son or daughter working in a plant. The number of durable goods possessed in peasant-worker households was similar to that of the peasants. An investigation would demonstrate that in households of younger couples living with their parents, the durable goods were usually the property of the younger generation. The young prefer a modern life-style opposed to the older peasants' preference of simple appliances and decorations. The appearance of electric appliances in the villages is recent.

Chinese peasants like other groups had to have sufficient provisions of food and clothing before improving their livelihood in other respects. However, peasants now say, "We can learn about world affairs just sitting at home," referring to television which has expanded their horizons. Economic reforms have transformed the urban-rural relationship. Urban areas now send the countryside not only manufactured goods as in the past but also technical information. The rural areas send the cities manufactured goods as well as farm and sideline products. This new situation inevitably has had noticeable effects upon the mobility and way of thinking of the peasants. Presently closely linked to the urban culture and in an improved financial position, the peasants attempt to keep up with the urban way of life.

Table 9: Durable Household Goods

Item	Peasant-workers (Bixi) No. per family	Peasants (Ouqiao) No. per family
Watch	2.7	2.7
Bicycle	2.2	2.0
Radio	1.1	0.7
Clock	1.0	1.1
Electric Fan	0.5	0.6
Sewing Machine	0.4	0.6
Television	0.3	0.4
Recorder	0.2	0.3
Camera	0.1	0
Washing Machine	0.2	0.3
Modern Furniture*	0.6	0.8
Sofa and Chairs*	0.3	0.7

*) These items are counted in sets, the rest in pieces.

6 Discussion

The case-study may prove the process of urbanization to be a process of social transformation in economic and cultural terms. The development of Bixi Xiang demonstrates the advantages of an alternative strategy for a diversified urbanization program.

6.1 It Contributes to More Rapid Economic Growth

The majority of the population in most developing countries lives in the countryside. Modernization of the country ultimately serves the modernization of those regions in which the majority of the people reside. However, all development economists know that the modernization of the rural areas demands both immense capital investment and continuous transfer of technology which are insurmountable barriers. China's development strategy in recent years has enabled hundreds of millions of peasants to accumulate the needed capital in order to invest in small industries. It also led to non-agricultural employment of the surplus labor force in rural areas through the development of small towns. For example, in Jiangsu Province, there is a large population, but a lack of land. Rural industry in Jiangsu Province developed rapidly during the past few years and was responsible for 1,100 million RMB (15%) of the province's revenue of 7,280 million RMB in 1983.[4] The development of small-town industry is a process which concentrates on both the rural households' capital and the surplus labor force in the countryside.

6.2 Social Stability is Retained During the Process of Urbanization

Workers are usually separated from their relatives, families, and friends when the surplus labor force is transferred from rural areas to large cities. These workers adopt new life-styles in the city. The uprooting of peasants from the rural community may result in social maladjustment and problems. Now, with the growth of small towns, urbanization occurs within the homes of the peasants. The peasants work in near-by towns and many live in their own houses. All social bonds and networks remain intact. This ensures a stable and healthy social environment for smooth social transformation.

6.3 Small Towns Serve as an Intermediary between City and Countryside

Small towns function as conveyor belts for modern science, technology, and education, spreading these to the remote underdeveloped areas. The development of small-town industry is a process of disseminating science, technology, and knowledge of management from the large cities to rural areas, a process breaking up the closed circuit of an autarky or semi-autarky and building up China's countryside in the commodity economy. It exerts a wide-range impact upon the countryside. The rapidly growing small towns, with newly acquired capital and skilled laborers, have power plants, paved roads, department stores, schools, clinics, reading rooms, cinemas, etc. Soon they will become centers of modern technology, culture, and new life-styles. The traditional customs, psychology, behavioral patterns, and value concepts of the peasants begin to change.

6.4 A Reservoir of Manpower is Provided

Sideline production, industry, and commerce compose a diversified economy and enable small towns to offer ample job opportunities for the surplus labor force in the countryside. Additionally, small towns utilize local capital and form a rational layout of productive forces. Therefore, in the urbanization process they function as a reservoir for the surplus rural labor force possibly preventing job-hunting peasants to overpopulate urban areas.

6.5 Women's Social Status is Elevated

The eldest member in traditional peasant families is usually the head of the family. He or she has the highest authority in all important decisions concerning family affairs such as finances, marriages, etc. Sons and daughters are subordinate to him or her. Daughters-in-law, coming from other families, have a low status and usually must abide by the wishes and opinions of the mother-in-law. Despite the participation of women in production teams for approximately 30 years after collectivization, in the year-end distribution - chiefly grain and cash - women still remained under the control of the family head. With the development of small-town industries, particularly after 1979, factories have employed women and payed cash. Like the young men these women now have their own incomes, so it is more difficult for the patriarch/matriarch to continue his/her control over younger family members. This is particularly significant for daughters-in-law. Now these family members are able to buy the articles they require. It is no longer necessary for them to care for the opinion of their mother-in-law. Relationships between these two generations of women in the family are changing. The elder generation is gradually losing its patriarchal status as the nuclear family replaces the extended family and the patriarchal system is reduced.

The changes within the family in combination with job opportunities in the factories of rural market towns have also had a strong impact on the institution of arranged marriages. Young men and women are now active in larger social circles and meet with more people. Consequently more autonomy is demanded in marriages.

6.6 Family Planning Occurs More Spontaneously

A large family was traditionally regarded as a standard of prosperity: "A big family brings great happiness." People married young and had as many children as possible. Family planning was unknown or ignored. In the past few years the single-child family has been more successful, because the economic conditions have improved in many towns. People in the towns say: "The poorer one is, the more children one wants. Now that life has become better, one does not want so many children." This once again shows the impact of the economy and culture on fertility. This new perspective of child-birth will eventually replace the traditional ideas.

The advantages of China's pattern of diversified urbanization are numerous (some of which have been mentioned above). China's past efforts of development of small-scale industries demonstrate that the present growth depends upon certain preconditions:

1) A government policy increasing the income of the peasants so that there is a sufficient amount of surplus cash for them to create small industries or other trades.

2) The necessary infrastructure for the development of small industries, such as electricity, roads, etc.

3) A government policy which supports the exemption or reduction of taxes for small industries in the initial stage and which provides a certain amount of raw materials, energy supply, etc.

4) Information concerning markets, guidance for the development of small industries, and provision with technical personnel which aids the underdeveloped areas for a certain period of time.

Development is nevertheless unevenly dispersed across the vast territory of China. Some regions are more developed, others are relatively underdeveloped. Bixi Xiang investigated in this report is representative of communities in the coastal zone. However, the trends of development may be taken as an indicator of what will occur in China's vast countryside.

Notes

1) Economy Yearbook of China, 1984, Beijing, Economic Management Publishers, 1985, p.V-6 (Chin.).
2) Zhang Yi, "Rural Town Enterprises and Construction of Market Towns in the Countryside," 1985 (Chin.).
3) *Xiang* is an administrative unit in the countryside. It is under the administration of the county (*xian*) and higher than a village (*cun*). It was abolished during the period of 1958 - 1983, when it was replaced by the people's commune. It is usually translated as "township".
4) Han Peixin, "The Five Years When Output Doubled in Rural Jiangsu", *Reports From Practice*, Jiangsu People's Publishing House, 1985, p.3 (Chin.).

Recent Development of the Urban Private Economy in China

by Thomas Heberer

Introduction

The following article deals with the recent trends of the private economic sector in China. As the history of this sector, the bureaucratic obstacles to its development, and negative factors towards the society were already analyzed elsewhere,[1] I will limit this article to the functions and perspectives of this sector.

If we analyse the individual and private economy in China in the light of the theory discussion in the West, we find many similarities with the "parallel" or "shadow economy" in socialist countries as well as with the "informal sector" in developing countries. The "shadow economy" includes all goods and services which are produced *outside the officially registered sector*, and are economically not countable. "Parallel" or "second economy" means all goods and services which are produced *outside the socialist*, i.e. outside the state-owned and collective sector and which are also not countable. The latter is a supplement, not an antipode to the official economy.[2]

Besides the dominating socialist sector in China there exists an officially accepted private economic sector. This private sector is organized in a different way from the socialist sector and is controlled by the state. It cannot be equated with the inofficial sector which is not controlled by the state. Thus we may subdivide the non-socialist sector in a parallel economic one (which is accepted and can be controlled) and a shadow economic one (which is not accepted and cannot be controlled).

In the case of China, the shadow economy contains the so-called underground economy (non-registered private economy, illegal economic activities, non-registered sideline occupation, moonlighting) and self-supply of households (farming on private plots, household handicraft production). The shadow economy evades control by the state, is officially not registered, and does not pay taxes and fees. The parallel economy, on the other hand, includes the legal private sector, registered sideline occupation and the leasing of state-owned enterprises.

In contrast to the shadow economy in capitalist countries, it is not the evading of taxes and unemployment that give the primary impulse for the rise of underground activities but the scarcity of consumer goods and services.[3]

Supply deficiencies, employment problems, low efficiency of the state-owned sector and high costs caused by deficitary operation, especially in the microeconomy, are the reasons for the reestablishment and expansion of the parallel and shadow economies. Parallel and shadow economies are functionally connected with the inefficient operation of the socialist sector. Rising production costs and declining efficiency and flexibility in the state-owned enterprises were the result of the takeover of the retail trade and the small industries by the state. The Chinese leadership therefore concluded to release the microeconomy from state-ownership to a certain extent.

Development policy has only in the last years realized the potential of small industries for economic development. In Western theories about urbanization and development in developing countries, the concept of the "informal sector" plays an important role.[4] This theory starts from the fact that migration from the country to the towns and the lack of jobs in the cities produced a latent jobless mass of urban inhabitants who live under conditions of absolute poverty. The urban economy tends towards a dual structure: it is divided into a "formal" sector, i.e. one which is regulated through contracts, laws etc., and an "informal sector", which gives people without jobs and without any income the chance of surviving.[5] "Informal sector" means the self-organization of the urban poor and is based mainly on unpaid family-work. Such enterprises are mainly managed on a family basis, use indigenous resources and are small in respect to their scale of operation. They produce for small, local markets and have no direct entry to formalized supply (capital, resources) or to translocal sale markets. This definition resembles to a high degree that of the individual economic sector in China.[6]

Although there are considerable differences between the Chinese private sector and the informal sector in other developing countries, not only with regard to the correlation mechanisms of the economic sectors (state, collective, private) but also as far as the relationship between the individual sector and the state is concerned (in China the state exercises a stronger supervision and direction of the private enterprises than in developing countries with a market economy), there are quite a lot of similarities, for instance the function of creating jobs and the closing of supply gaps through self-organization of urban dwellers.

We do not intend to discuss those theories here. It is, however, noteworthy that the explanation for the existence of the parallel and shadow economies in socialist countries, or for the existence of the informal sector in developing economies seems to be identical with that of the private sector in China after 1979, i.e.:

- supply gaps,
- employment problems,
- low efficiency and high costs of the state-owned sector (especially in socialist countries),
- income for social groups with low or no income (retired or jobless people, housewives).

It is interesting that the World Bank sees one of its main functions now in the stronger promotion of the private sector in developing countries, because this sector seems to be a motor for growth and therefore stimulates economic development.[7] Thus it may be possible that the World Bank will assist in developing this sector in China.

When speaking about the function of the individual or private economy in China, we find three main problems in Chinese cities which make this sector nearly indispensable:

- the growing employment problem, i.e. an oversupply of labour as a result of economic development deficits and a faster growth of the population relative to the economy;

- problems of supplying the urban population with agricultural and consumer goods as well as with services;

- the scarcity of funds.

Latest Developments

In the following we try to explain the recent developments in the private sector and its contribution to reducing these problems. Finally, we will make some comments on possible perspectives and functions of this sector for the Chinese economy.

Up to 1988, the private economy, which was abolished or nationalized after 1957, was the most dynamic and fastest developing sector of the Chinese economy. What we call "private economy" according to Chinese definitions consists of the so-called "individual economy" (*geti jingji*, with less than eight employed people) and the "private economy" (*siren jingji*, with more than seven employed people). In the following we refer to both as "private economy". By the end of 1988, some 14.135 million "individual" and 225,000 "private" businesses had officially been registered, with a workforce of 22.224 million in the "individual" and of 3.6 million people in the "private" economy.[8] If we add the non-registered (i.e. illegal) businesses with their non-registered labourers, assisting family members, people with a second job or 'moonlighters'[9], and the huge number of companies which are by name state- or collective-owned, but in fact privately owned, there may well be between 70 and 80 million people engaged in the private sector. Furthermore, if we accept Chinese reports that a considerable part of the rural collective industry is in fact privately owned, the actual figures on private businesses are significantly higher.[10] According to Chinese sources, 90% of the 18.7 million "village and town enterprises" (*xiangzhen qiye*) in 1989, with a working force of 97 million people, were owned by private persons (peasants) or a group of peasant households.[11] If this really were to have been the case, the private sector would be the absolutely dominating sector in the countryside.

The austerity policy of the Chinese government and the political development in 1989 in fact brought about a considerable decline of the people engaged in the private economy: At the end of 1989 the number of individual households had decreased by about 2.06 million (-14.2%) and the number of employed persons by about 3.64 million (-15.8%). The decrease in the rural part (households: -17.1%, employed persons: - 20.0%) was much higher than that of the urban one (households: -3.7%, employed persons: -3.1%).[12]

Yet the economic situation (growing urban unemployment, supply problems, growing budget deficit, increasing number of state enterprises in the red) made it necessary to encourage the private sector once more. So in 1990 and 1991 the "individual sector" grew again, at the end of 1991 up to 14.145 million households with 22.46 million employed persons, of which 4.19 million were urban households. The registered "private sector" at the end of 1991 consisted of only 180,000 households with 1.84 million people.[13] Bo Yibo, one of the veteran leaders, declared in spring 1991 the number of individual businesses were far too little.[14]

In 1990 the growth rate of the gross value output was led by the private sector with 21.6%, followed by the collective sector (9.1%). The growth rate of the state-owned sector was the lowest one (2.9%).[15] In the first five months of 1991, economic growth was again led by the private sector. Compared with a year ago, e.g., the industrial growth of the private sector was up 43%, that of the collective sector 19%, and that of the state enterprises only by a mere 9%.[16]

The reestablishment of the private sector after 1978 brought about a rapid increase in this sector. The annual growth rates exceeded by far those of state- or collective-owned enterprises. Although the rural individual sector by far exceeded the urban one (in 1985 there were 76.1% rural households engaged in the individual sector, as opposed to 23.9% urban households; accordingly 78.3% of all employed persons in rural enterprises were in the individual sector, as against 21.7% in urban ones), in the years after 1986 the urban sector increased vis-à-vis the rural one, especially in 1989 (up to 29.6% of the households and 28.9% of the employed people; 1988: 26.4% of the households and 25.1% of the employed people).

The development of the individual economy in small towns is more rapid than in big cities. In small towns the catchment area may stimulate this process, and the better possibilities of shop and stall placement, more uncomplicated and less rigid administrative structures and regulations also allow a larger number of rural inhabitants to do business in urban areas.

The larger private enterprises are mainly situated in the countryside (1989: more than 80%).[17]

Individual economy and employment problems

With regard to employment, terminology and definition already raise difficulties. In China one differentiates between "employed" (*jiuye*), "job-waiting" (*daiye*) and "unemployed" (*shiye*). "Employed" are able-bodied persons, who for payment carry out a regular occupation, either in a state-owned or collective enterprise or institution, or in a registered business of their own. "Job-waiting" is the term for able-bodied male persons between 16 and 50 years as well as female persons between 16 and 45 years who want to be employed.[18] Here again, there is a difference between "job-waiting youth" (*daiye qingnian*), who are between 16 and 25 years, and "other job-waiting people" (*daiye renyuan*). People with rural permanent residence (*hukou*) living in urban areas are not registered as "unemployed". Therefore the official data for unemployment are incorrect.

As to the category *daiye* only persons with registered urban permanent residence belong to it.[19] Unemployed with rural permanent residence are not recognized or registered as "unemployed". This group is not entitled to receive a job through the government.

Middle school graduates constitute the majority of urban unemployed. The share of females by far exceeds the share of males.[20]

One main problem (which is not included in the statistics) is underemployment, i.e., the overstaffing of jobs in state-owned enterprises. According to Chinese economists, up to 40% of those employed in state-owned industries are "surplus labour force".[21] While statistics show that the government created 13.8 million jobs in urban areas in 1989 and 1990,[22] factory managers complain that huge numbers of workers are actually sitting idle at their jobs and pulling down productivity.

Furthermore, there will soon be increased pressure from rural areas, because about 210 million labourers will leave their farmland and look for jobs outside agriculture between 1990 and 2000.[23] Including urban job-seekers, there may be about 280 million people seeking a job in that period.[24] Yet according to Chinese sources, only 30 million new jobs will be created by the year 2000.[25]

At the end of 1990, the official urban unemployment rate was 3.0%, up from 1.8% in 1985.[26] Experts meanwhile admit that the actual rate may be about 12%, with an open urban unemployment rate of about 2%, a hidden one of 10.7% and a hidden one in the countryside of 15.4%.[27] Yet even this figure may be much too low, as special groups, such as those with permanent rural residence, are excluded from the official statistics, and the hidden unemployment reaches up to 40% of the whole labour force.

The increase of unemployment after 1985 on the one hand results from the constantly high number of young people leaving school, whereas at the same time the absorption capacities of the state enterprises are more or less exhausted. On the other hand, it is the result of the reduction of jobs in the state sector as well as economic difficulties in enterprises of every form of ownership. Accordingly the group of job-seekers in the city of Guangzhou in 1989 was composed of 80.000 who had just left school and 50.000 unemployed, who had been dismissed or whose contracts had not been prolonged.[28]

In this respect the private sector plays an indispensable role.

Between 1980 and 1990, 61.5% of the newly employed found a job in the state-owned sector, 28.8% in the collective, 8.8% in the private sector and 0.9% in other forms of ownership. 38.5% were employed in the non-state sector.[29]

An analysis shows that the role of the private sector in providing jobs differs according to regions. In cities with developed large-scale industry, the demand for jobs in the private sector is not as great as in less developed areas and in small towns. In big and medium-sized cities the employment pressure has decreased. It is at present most pressing in county- and *zhen*-towns.[30] The share of those "job-waiting" people in urban areas who were still jobless at the end of the year in large and middle cities dropped from 50% (1980) to 44% (1986) of all job-seekers in the related year. In county- and *zhen*-towns, however, it increased from 42% to 56%.[31]

In the context of employment reform, which among other things implies personnel reduction in state-owned enterprises, the number of jobless people will increase. Collective and private enterprises are, in this respect, the main channel for absorbing labour.

In the nineties it may be difficult for the Chinese state to provide such a large number of people with jobs, especially since because of the baby-boom between 1970 and 1975 once again a large number of students leaving school need jobs. Between 1990 and 1995 alone this will affect about 100 million people. While in rural areas the core of non-agrarian employment is in the private and small collective enterprises, in urban areas state and collective enterprises will further have to provide the majority of new jobs. Here the private economy serves only a complementary, but not unimportant function: While in 1984 15.1% of the newly employed people found a job in the private sector, the figure was only 6.0% in 1989 and 5.1% in 1990.[32]

Economic development and modernization require a rise in labour productivity. This, again, requires the reduction of the labour force in overstaffed enterprises. For this reason, the contract labour system, the bankruptcy law, and limited possibilities for dismissals were created. These reforms, the increasing possibilities of job-seeking on one's own, and employment in the private sector are bringing about a labour market. Unemployment up to a certain degree is intended. At present some economists speak about a possible tolerance of four to six percent of unemployment.[33] A rigid employment policy and the providing of jobs for the majority in state-owned enterprises will not solve the problems, but will only increase the economic difficulties of the enterprises, which are already overstaffed. Thus, employment problems alone push for a further expansion of the private sector.

Private economy and urban supply

One main reason for the reestablishment of the private sector was the inability of the state-owned and collective sector to satisfy the demand of urban consumers. A centralized planned economy with a single-track ownership structure is not able to plan and satisfy the demand of the whole society through state-owned enterprises, especially under conditions of economic underdevelopment. With the present financial preconditions the state is not able to help the tertiary sector in its attempts to satisfy the demand quantitatively and qualitatively.

At present the private economy plays only a minor role in the Chinese economic structure. At the end of 1990, 3.7% (1988: 4.2%) of all urban employed were engaged in the registered private economy.[34] If the non-registered are included, there may be about 10-15% of all employed people who are engaged in the private sector. When counted by the number of enterprises, the majority is already owned by private persons, with an increasing tendency. There are more rural private enterprises than urban ones, and the share of private enterprises in light industry exceeds that in heavy industry.[35]

Private enterprises in the industrial and construction sectors are, however, mostly small or tiny ones. Accordingly, the share of private enterprises in the industrial gross output value and the industrial employment is, especially in urban areas, small. In 1991 only 1.4% of all industrial workers were employed in the private sector, and only 0.5% in the construction sector.[36]

In the tertiary sector, the share of the private economy in the "total value of retail sales" (*shehui shangpin lingshou zong'e*), i.e. the total volume of retail sales in the fields of trade, catering, retail sales of industry and handicrafts, and service trades, in 1989 amounted already to 18.6% (1978: 0.1%); if retail trades from peasants to urban dwellers are included, the amount is 28.2%. The break-down according to branch is: trade 20.1%, catering 51.2%, industrial retail sales 10.7%. The state-owned trade had only a share of 39.1% (down from 90.5% in 1978).[37] Of course, there are considerable regional disparities. In South and Southwest China, the share of the total value of retail sales surpasses the national average, in North, Northwest and the most developed parts of East China, as well as in the urban metropoles, it is below that average.[38] In the urban areas it is normally also below this average. This is due to the more developed state-owned and collective tertiary sector in the urban areas. The private tertiary enterprises are mostly small or tiny ones.

Economic operations in the tertiary sector are better organized in small and private enterprises than in big and state-owned ones. In addition, small and private enterprises need only small investments and less qualification of management and labour force. The supply with materials and goods is less problematic, and the administrative barriers for the acquisition of a licence and the risks of business are smaller. Moreover, the profits are quite high.

The private economy has shown remarkable growth in the supply of the urban population with agrarian products. In the cities we have investigated, about 50-60% of the fruit and vegetables were already privately marketed. In the county towns, the private share in this respect is higher than in large towns. Countrywide in 1985 already 73.5% of the whole vegetable sales were sold on free markets. The larger a town, the more is sold through state channels. In 1985 50.4% of the poultry, 37% of the fruit, 22.1% of the eggs and 21.2% of the aquatic products, but only 12.9% of the vegetables and 2.8% of the meat were sold through private channels in Shanghai, much less than in the country's average.[39] In the first six months of 1991 the urban free markets sold - compared with the urban state-owned shops (given 100%):

vegetables	193,2%
aquatic products	220,0%
poultry	169,0%
beef/mutton	153,3%
eggs	135,0%
pork	62,8%[40]

In large cities the state-owned and collective trade net is much better developed than in small towns. The larger the net of the state-owned and collective trade, the smaller the number of private traders and vice versa.

Providing Funds

The urban population has for a long time been familiar with the phenomenon that state-owned enterprises without any competition are not interested in production that satisfies the demand of the consumers. The state enterprises, which often produce inefficiently, had to be subsidized by the government. Funds which could have been used to create jobs were thus tied up. The policy of single-track state ownership copied from the Soviet Union, has - as everywhere - failed. So it was not astonishing that Chinese economists as early as 1978 began to discuss the diversification of the ownership structure. Property was no longer considered a "social-political original sin which brings evil to the world".[41]

Private business, it was conceded, meets the needs of the people which the state sector is not able to satisfy. They create jobs and offer the possibility of professional training, at no cost to the government.[42] They are an incentive to the state-owned enterprises to improve their operation and management and to consider the needs of the customers. In addition, as taxpaying enterprises, they provide the government with considerable funds (1980-89: 49 billion Yuan; e.g. 1991 17,9 billion yuan).[43] A reform of the ownership system and the extension of the private sector is necessary for a lasting improvement in economic efficiency and for the easing of the public finances. Moreover, the private economy may take over the function of a supplier of the state-owned and collective enterprises. It may produce and sell traditional products and export articles which have disappeared from the market but which are nonetheless urgently needed.

The function of the private economy for urban development

With the expansion of private economic activities, the exchange between the sectors under the various forms of ownership as well as the importance of the market itself have been increasing.

The private economy is neither an isolated sector nor an economic circuit in itself. It not only competes with the state-owned or collectively-owned sectors, but there are many connections between these three sectors of economic ownership, and they are interwoven, particularly in the areas of supply and marketing.

Let us demonstrate this by some examples: Business connections are usually established through middlemen (relatives, friends, acquaintances). Many private businessmen were formerly employed in the same state-owned or collectively-owned enterprises they are now conducting business with. Private workshops provide some types of processing and sub-contract work for state-owned and collectively-owned enterprises. These industries are interested in private maintenance, repair and other service trades because the private sector is quicker, cheaper, and more flexible.

On the other hand, individual businesses are to a large extent dependent on state-owned wholesale departments for obtaining raw materials etc., as well as fuel and energy, unless their needs are catered for either by the free market itself, or by legal or illegal middlemen. Very often private industries have to put up with competitive disadvantages: They have to pay higher prices than state-owned or collectively-owned enterprises, and often they receive poorer quality in return. Moreover, the state-owned wholesale network is very inflexible. For certain categories of products there are already private wholesalers.

Above all, commodities in short supply and high-quality products frequently flow into illegal channels. A Chinese investigation showed that in Shanghai every individual businessman had on average more than five "suppliers" from the state-owned or collectively-owned sector.[44]

Such forms of supply have emerged because in many fields the state has a monopoly. Thus, the private sector and the market are restricted in many respects. As a result, various forms of internal economic relationships came into existence. Production, distribution, transport, and wholesale and retail trade have already been partly organized within the private sector. For instance, one such network is now operating in the garment industry: The garment is produced in the coastal areas, transported to the hinterland, and sold on the local markets. Private entrepreneurs achieve a speed of circulation and distribution which is n-times higher than that of the sluggish state-owned distribution system.

As a result of the existence of the private economy, the supply of the urban and rural population with foodstuffs and commodities of daily use has undoubtedly improved. Private traders can often supply goods which are hard to obtain elsewhere or are only available in lower quality from state-run shops. The high mobility of the migrant traders contributes to the rapid distribution of, for instance, modern clothing or newly-available commodities, even into the remote rural areas of the West, a region which has so far been undersupplied or has been supplied only with outdated products. In 1988, about 80% of the privately produced clothing from the coastal areas was sold in other parts of China.

The increasing share of the private market in supplying the urban inhabitants with foodstuffs, especially fruit and vegetables, is particularly remarkable. In 1987, about three-quarters of the vegetable supply in the cities were marketed privately. The share of the free-market supply in the total urban marketing of foodstuffs amounts from 20 to 46% of the total supply, depending on the size of a city.[45] Though free-market prices are considerably higher than those in state-run shops, the free-market products are of better quality, and the waiting time for customers is much shorter.

In some of the retail and service branches, the private economy is no longer a complementary sector to the state-owned and collectively-owned economy, but has become the leading factor in supply, turnover, and ownership. This holds true, in particular, for certain localities, e.g. Wenzhou. The 1987 figures for the

'Wenzhou model' were as follows: In industry the private share in output value amounted to 34.3% as compared to 48.5% for the collectively-owned, and 17.2% for the state-owned sector, and for rural private industry the figure was even higher: 61.6%. The respective figures for private transport were 74.4%, for retail sales 73.6%, and for catering 68.8% of the total output value.[46] Since a considerable part of the private industry in Wenzhou is in fact registered as collectively-owned, the actual figures might be much higher.

The Wenzhou development is no longer an isolated case. The remote county of Zhuozi in Inner Mongolia had by 1989 become the most eminent case. This county had almost done away with all of its state-owned enterprises, and had abolished all but six of its formerly 127 separate government offices. All prices were deregulated, including those of grain and key raw materials, and all urban housing was privatized. Thus, Zhuozi County may have been the only genuine free market in China.[47]

The development of the private economic sector does, however, bring about several social implications which provoke changes in the urban social structure: e.g. weakening of the *danwei* organization structure, diminishing of party control; new social values (e.g. wealth, money-making) and a new life-style, which promotes a trend towards individualism and privatization; the development, in the long run, of a new middle class (most of the *getihu* today are people with a low grade of education, but in the future money-making will require more professional and technical skills; this will increase the demand for education) which demands service trades on a middle level (e.g. not only luxurious hotels, restaurants and other services); social mobility and migration into the urban centres, and so on. Bruun points to the fact that "the real potential for change in Chinese society lies in the challenge of the private sector and its affiliated value system to formal society. The existence of a successful private sector indicates that there are other paths to privilege than conformity, that an easy life can be attained without sacrificing personal freedom".[48]

The diversification of the ownership system brought about - mainly in the villages - a dualism of economic and political power. This trend was confirmed by veteran Communist Wang Zhen in an internal speech in 1991.[49] Especially in the countryside, the private entrepreneurs endeavour to get more political power, while cadres try to get more economical power via entrance into the private economy. Finally, private entrepreneurs are trying to frustrate policies that challenge their interests through "pervasive informal networks".[50] This process (especially in Southern China) developes more and more via the traditional structure of the patriarchal clan power.[51] Property becomes increasingly a sign of political power and an indication of the social status of a person.

That this process is also developing in urban areas is demonstrated by reports about cities in Southern China, where the majority of newly appointed cadres consists of individual entrepreneurs.[52]

Prospects

The private economy in China exists because the inability of the socialist sector to satisfy the needs of society. Moreover, the state-owned and collective enterprises operate very inefficiently. Private economic activities are characterized by much higher motivation and efficiency than state-owned enterprises. It is therefore not surprising that the motivation push evoked by the economic reform is largely the result of a stronger privatization of economic activities.

Yet I doubt the prognosis of Chinese economists that the higher grade of flexibility and efficiency in private business may stimulate the socialist sector, nor is it likely that the element of competition will improve the efficiency and the management of the state-owned sector. Firstly, there is no real competition between the socialist and the private sector due to restrictions of the latter one and favourable treatment of the first one. Secondly, low incomes, low material incentives, and bureaucratic control and intervention, to name only a few, prevent the socialist sector from improving its efficiency, thus hindering real competition between the various forms of ownership. The lessons learned from state enterprises in market as well as in planned economies show that inefficiency arises when the control through a stock market no longer exists, because necessary restructuring processes are left undone. So in the long run, a planned economy that reacts to market forces seems to be highly problematic.[53]

An orderly economic development will, in the last consequence, only be possible if the reformers succeed in embedding the private economy as a complementary factor into the whole economy in such a manner that it becomes an integral part of the economic system. In this way the private enterprises could form a net of small and medium enterprises which supplement the large enterprises in the fields of supply, marketing, services, and processing. As private small and medium enterprises are more able than the centralized socialist sector to react to the fluctuations of the market, they could contribute to a more efficient and more flexible adjustment of the economy to the market. In this way they would make it easier for the large enterprises to respond more flexibly to the changing demands of the market.

Scientific research, high technology, and highly skilled staff may be better concentrated in large state-owned enterprises, while labour-intensive and dispersed activities are a strong point of small and medium private enterprises. What the small enterprises ("individual enterprises") are not able to carry out, middle ones ("private enterprises") may take over. Thus a dual economic model could develop, with modern state-owned, large-size enterprises on the one hand, which determine the development process of industrialization and the technological development, and with millions of private enterprises with economic complementary function on the other hand. A precondition for such a development is a genuine free market or - as Milton Friedman put it - "free markets, where 'free' means open to competition, from both abroad and domestic sources. In particular, individuals or groups should be free to establish any enterprise producing or selling any good that is legal to buy and sell without requiring permission from any official."[54]

The market and the private economy are pressing for expansion. This process can only be reversed by direct state intervention. Protagonists of private economic enterprise want the state to refrain from such intervention. If, however, intervention of some sort is necessary, the application of economic regulating levers should be preferred to any administrative measure. This would make necessary a detailed concept with a proper perspective, in order to specify how the private economy could be made use of effectively. If private economy were given a free hand, this would - in the long run - have not only economic but also political consequences. According to Eucken's economic theory of the "Interdependence of Orders", economic changes lead to changes in the political system.[55] A monopolized political system and a deregulated economy lead to permanent contradiction.

The decentralization of the economy may well bring about the decentralization of the existing political order, i.e., the power monopoly of the party will be challenged. From time to time, the Chinese leadership intervenes in the economic process in order to preserve economic stability, a balanced development, and "social harmony", all of which indeed require some kind of systematic planning and intervention, or, as Myrdal put it, a strong state.[56] A "strong state", in this sense, does not mean that the state controls and determines everything, but that it strategically sets the cornerstones for further development and regulates the macro-economy. As could be expected, the Chinese Communist Party tried to intervene exactly in those fields where economic power threatened to change into political power.

Yet inevitably, a mixed system of plan and market economy and competition between different forms of ownership contain so many incompatibilities that they will cause conflicts again and again.

The admission of private economic activities to such an extent is astonishing for a socialist country. Before 1989 we asked ourselves if China in the long run would return to Sun Yat-Sen's thesis, according to which only those parts of the economy are to be transformed into state property that could not, or should not, be handled by private enterprises.[57] Sun referred to sectors that could be monopolized by private enterprises or that involve national interests, like defence or needs of the general public, as well as to enterprises too large for private activities. All the rest was to be left in private hands.

By number, the majority of enterprises is already in private hands, with an increasing tendency (1990 in the industrial sector officially: 77.6%; this rate may in fact be much higher). In 1990, the private economy's share of the industrial gross output value amounted to 5.40% (1987: 3.64%), and that of the total value of the total retail volume 18.9% (1987: 17.4%), although there is a wide range of regional differences, e.g. in 1990 from 4.6% for Shanghai and 5.7% for Beijing to 33.5% for Hainan, 27.8% for Guangxi and 25.0% for Guizhou (figures including retail trades from peasants to urban dwellers: Shanghai 10.4%, Peking 11.0%, Hainan 48.9%, Guangxi 37.9% and Guizhou 37.5%).[58]

Although it may at present be pure speculation, I want to make some brief remarks about prospects which once might become a reality. Chinese economists had already proposed that in the future the state-run economy should only represent 30% of the national economy, leaving 70% to the private and collectively organized sectors. In remote and poor areas, as well as those inhabited by ethnic minorities, the private economy could well become the sole sector.[59] Such proposals do not find a majority now, but if they could be[60] implemented later, they would advocate a model coming close to the economic system of Taiwan, as Taiwan also has some kind of centralized economic planning, even though the state-owned sector comprises only 20% at present; it once was much higher, 50% (in the fifties).[61] Both economies could then, under certain circumstances, meet on the basis of Sun Yat-Sen's conception, according to which only the key industries remain state-owned, whereas the rest would be privately or collectively-owned. If the economies of Mainland China and Taiwan were to develop in this way, the two political systems could in the long run converge.

Notes

1) Heberer/Taubmann 1988; Jamann/Menkhoff 1988; Heberer 1989; Kraus 1989; Heberer 1990.
2) See e.g. Wiles 1981; Hedtkamp 1983; Weck/Pommerehne/Frey 1984; Gretschmann/Heinze/Mittelsiefen 1984; Schäfer 1984; Grossmann 1984; Gaertner/Wenig 1985; Cassel/Cichy 1985; Haffner 1985; Allessandrini/Dallago 1987; Schrage 1987; Jessen/Siebel 1988; Cassel/Jaworski/Kath et al. 1989.
3) Compare Cichy/Paffenholz 1986: p.91; the causes of supply shortages are analysed by Kornai 1979: pp.801 ff., Kornai 1980 and Maresse/Mitchell 1984: pp.74 ff.
4) See e.g. Mazumdar 1976; Sethuraman 1976; Bromley 1978; Moser 1978; Herrle 1983; Elwert/Evers/Wilkens 1983; Portes 1983; Mathur/Moser 1984; Acharya 1984; Ferman et al. 1987; Gaghan/Ferman 1987; Gerry 1987; Miller 1987; Pahl 1987.
5) See e.g. Remy/Weeks 1973: pp.295 ff.; Weeks 1975: pp.1 ff.; Mazunda 1979: pp.655 ff.; Elwert/Evers/Wilkens 1979: pp.281 ff.; Herrle 1983, pp.49 ff.; Portes 1983: pp.295 ff.
6) Cf. Bromley 1978: pp.1033 ff.; Mehta 1985: p.328.
7) Vuylsteke 1988; Nankani 1988; Candoy-Sekse 1988; Pfeffermann 1988; *Frankfurter Allgemeine Zeitung*, 2.7.91.
8) According to statistics of the State Administration of Industry and Commerce.
9) In 1988 about 16.3% of the workers in Shanghai, 20% of those in Guangzhou and 70% of the workers in Tianjin had a "second job", compare *Gongren Ribao*, 7.8.88, *Dangzheng Luntan*, 6/1989, pp.18 ff.; Wei 1991: p.16. Chinese economists in 1988 reckoned that between 10 and 20% of all employed people had a second job, *Jingji Cankao*, 8.5.88, *Gongren Ribao*, 7.8.88. But as most employed people do not openly admit that they are moonlighters, the actual figure may be much higher.
10) Jia/Wang/Tang 1987: pp.41 f.; *Jingji Cankao*, 3.11.88; *Zhongguo Gongshang Bao* 25.2.91; *Renmin Ribao*, 9.3.91.
11) Shehuizhuyi chuji jieduan yanjiu ketizu 1991: p.21.
12) According to statistics of the State Administration of Industry and Commerce.
13) According to information of the State Administration of Industry and Commerce given to the author in February 1992.
14) *Zhongguo Gongshang Bao*, 18.4.91.
15) Cf. Funcken 1991: p.380.
16) Cheng 1991: p.30.
17) Liang 1990: p.14; Wang, Kechong 1990: pp.2 ff. Chinese authorities define private enterprises as ones with more than seven labourers. In 1990 there existed 98.000 officially registered private enterprises with a workforce of about 1.703 million people, cf. *Jingji Cankao Bao*, 10.3.91. This would have been 17.000 enterprises less than in 1987 and probably 127.000 less than in 1988.

18) Liu, Zhuanqi 1986: p.81; Liu, Xingran 1987: pp.639 f.
19) See *Zhonghua Renmin Gongheguo ladong fagui xuanbian* 1986: pp.31 f.
20) *Zhongguo 1982 nian renkou pucha ziliao* 1985: p.468.
21) Yang 1991,1.
22) *Zhongguo Gongshang Bao*, 12.8.91.
23) Cf. i.a. *Beijing Daxue Xuebao*, 4/1989: pp.26 ff.; *China Daily*, 30.7.91.
24) *China Daily*, 30.7.91.
25) Bundesstelle für Außenhandelsinformationen (1991): p.6.
26) Yang, Yiyong 1991,2: p.8.
27) Zhang, Changgong 1991: p.41.
28) *Jingji Cankao*, 18.4.89.
29) Cf. *Zhongguo tongji nianjian 1991*: p.116.
30) Lin/He 1986: p.37.
31) *Ibid.*
32) *Zhongguo tongji nianjian 1991*: p.116.
33) *Jingji Guanli*, 5/1989: p.14.
34) *Zhongguo tongji nianjian 1991*: pp.91, 95, 108.
35) Cf. *Zhongguo tongji nianjian 1991*: p.391.
36) *Ibid.*: pp.105 ff.
37) *Zhongguo guonei shichang tongji nianjian 1990*: pp.118 f.; *Zhongguo maoyi wujia tongji ziliao 1952-83*: p.65.
38) *Zhongguo tongji nianjian 1988*: p.690.
39) Cf. Heberer 1989: p.382 f.
40) *Zhongguo Gongshang Bao*, 7.10.91.
41) Röglin 1991.
42) See, e.g., Xue 1979: pp.28 ff.; Xue 1980: pp.39 ff.; Xu, Dixin 1981: pp.118 ff.; Ma/Sun 1981, vol.1: pp.44 ff.
43) According to statistics of the State Administration of Industry and Commerce in Beijing on April 8, 1990, and *Renmin Ribao*, 16.1.92.
44) Chen, Baoming 1985: p.4.
45) *China Daily*, 15.4.87.
46) See Xu/Ye 1987: p.37; *Renmin Ribao*, 8.1.88.
47) *Far Eastern Economic Review*, 27.4.89.
48) Bruun 1990: p.42.
49) Cf. *South China Morning Post*, 14.3.91 and *China heute*, 5/1991: p.118.
50) Manion 1991: p.253.
51) Chen/Li 1991: pp.35 f.
52) *Gongren Ribao*, 12.1.92.
53) Brus 1972; Kloten 1985: pp.37 ff.; Prybyla 1987; Wong 1987: pp.385 ff.
54) Friedman 1990: p.124.
55) Eucken 1965; for Prybyla a price reform will lead to pluralism and, possibly, even to democracy, Prybyla 1987: p.199.
56) Myrdal 1980.
57) Sun 1963: pp.130-135.
58) *Zhongguo tongji nianjian 1991*: pp.391, 591 f., 595.
59) So an article in *Renmin Ribao*, 17.10.88.

60) *Nongye Jingji Wenti*, 10/1988: p.58.
61) Cf. e.g. Menzel 1983: pp.98 ff.

References

Acharya, S. (1984): "The Informal Sector in Developing Countries - A Macro Viewpoint", in: *Journal of Contemporary Asia*, vol.13 (1984): pp.432 ff.
Alessandrini, S./Dallago, B. (1987), eds.: *The Unofficial Economy. Consequences and Perspectives in Different Economic Systems*, Aldershot 1987
Beijing Daxue Xuebao (Journal of Peking University), Peking
Bromley, R. (1978): "Introduction - The Urban Informal Sector: Why is it worth discussing?", in: *World Development*, 9-10/1978: pp.1033 ff.
Brus, W. (1972): *The Market in a Socialist Economy*, London/Boston 1972
Bruun, O. (1990): "Urban Individual Households and Cultural Change in China: When 'Losers' Become 'Winners'", *Copenhagen Papers in East and Southeast Asian Studies*, 5/1990: pp.29-47
Bundesstelle für Außenhandelsinformationen (1991), ed.: *VR China. China. Wirtschaftsentwicklung 1990*, Köln 1991
Candoy-Seeke, R. (1988): Techniques of Privatization of State-Owned Enterprises, vol.II. World Bank Technical Paper Number 90, Washington 1988
Cassel, D./Cichy, E.U. (1985): The Shadow Economy and Economic Policy in East and West: A Comparative System Approach, Diskussionsbeiträge des Fachbereichs Wirtschaftswissenschaft der Universität-Gesamthochschule Duisburg, Nr.75, Duisburg 1985
Cassel, D./Jaworski, W./Kath, D./Kierczynski, T./Lutkowski, K./Paffenholz, H.-J. (1989), eds.: *Inflation und Schattenwirtschaft im Sozialismus*, Hamburg 1989
Chen, Baoming (1985): "Getihu dui guannian de tiaozhan" ("Ideological Challenge of the Individual Economy"), in: *Shehui* (Society) 3/1985: pp.4-7
Chen, Yongping/Li, Weisha (1991): "Zongzu shili: Dangqian nongcun shequ shenghuo zhong yige tizai de pohuai liliang" ("Patriarchal Clan Power: The Present Latent Destructive Capacity in Rural Community Life"), in: *Shehuixue Yanjiu* (Sociological Studies), 5/1991: pp.31-36
Cheng, E. (1991): "Credit needs fuel inflation", in: *Far Eastern Economic Review*, 8.8.91: pp.28-32
China Daily, Peking
Cichy, E.U./Paffenholz, H.J. (1986): "Schattenwirtschaften in sozialistischen Planwirtschaften", in: *Verbraucherpolitische Hefte*, 3/1986: pp.91 ff.
Dangzheng Luntan (Party Policy Forum), Peking
Elwert, G./Evers, H.D./Wilkens, W. (1983): "Die Suche nach Sicherheit: Kombinierte Produktionsformen im sogenannten informellen Sektor", in: *Zeitschrift für Soziologie*, 4/1983: pp.281 ff.
Eucken, W. (1965): *Grundsätze der Wirtschaftspolitik*, Reinbek 1965

Ferman, L.A. et al. (1987): "Issues and Prospects for the Study of Informal Economies: Concepts, Research Strategies, and Policy", in: *Annals of the American Academy of Political and Social Science*, 493/1987: pp.154 ff.
Friedman, M. (1990): *Friedman in China*, Hongkong 1990
Funcken, K. (1991): "China - zurück auf dem wirtschaftspolitischen Reformpfad", in: *Vierteljahresberichte*, 126/1991, pp.377-384
Gaertner, W./Wenig, A., eds.: *The Economics of the Shadow Economy*, Berlin et al. 1985
Gaughan, J.P./Ferman, L.A. (1987): "Toward an Understanding of the Informal Economy", in: *The Annals of the American Academy of Political and Social Science*, 493/1987: pp.15 ff.
Gerry, Ch. (1987): "Developing Economies and the Informal Sector in Historical Perspective", in: *The Annals of the American Academy of Political and Social Science*, 493/1987: pp.100 ff.
Gold, T. B. (1991): "Urban Private Business and China's Reforms", in: Baum, R., ed.: *Reform and Reaction in Post-Mao China*, New York/London 1991: pp.-84-103
Gongren Ribao (Worker's Daily), Peking
Gretschmann, K./Heinze, R.G./Mettelsiefen, B. (1984), eds.: *Schattenwirtschaft. Wirtschafts- und sozialwissenschaftliche Aspekte, internationale Erfahrungen*, Göttingen 1984
Grossmann, G. (1984): *Die "zweite Wirtschaft" und die sowjetische Wirtschaftsplanung*, Berichte des Bundesinstituts für ostwissenschaftliche und internationale Studien, 6, Köln 1984
Haffner, F. (1985): "Ist die Schattenwirtschaft ein Reformansatz? Das Verhältnis der Wirtschaftsreformen in Osteuropa zur Schattenwirtschaft", in: *Vierteljahreshefte zur Wirtschaftsforschung*: pp.177-187
Heberer, T. (1989): *Die Rolle des Individualsektors für Arbeitsmarkt und Stadtwirtschaft in der VR China*, Bremer Beiträge zur Geographie und Raumplanung, Bremen 1989
Heberer, T. (1990): "Belebung durch privatwirtschaftliche Tätigkeiten", in: Heberer, T./Weigelin, R. (1990), eds.: *Xiandaihua. Versuch einer Modernisierung. Entwicklungsprobleme der VR China*, Bad Honnef 1990: pp.95-122
Heberer, T. (1991): *Korruption in China. Analyse eines politischen, ökonomischen und sozialen Problems*, Opladen 1991
Heberer, T./Taubmann, W. (1988): "Die städtische Privatwirtschaft in der VR China - 'Second Economy' zwischen Markt und Plan", in: Leng, G./Taubmann, W. (1988), eds.: *Geographische Entwicklungsforschung im interdisziplinären Dialog*, Bremen 1988: pp.233-262
Hedtkamp, G. (1983), ed.: *Beiträge zum Problem der Schattenwirtschaft*, Berlin 1983
Herrle, P. (1983): "Der informelle Sektor: Die Ökonomie des Überlebens in den Metropolen der Dritten Welt", in: *Materialien zum Internationalen Kulturaustausch* Bd.18, ed.: Institut für Auslandsbeziehungen, Stuttgart 1983

Jamann, W./Menkhoff, T. (1988): "*Make big Profits with a small capital*". *Die Rolle der Privatwirtschaft und des "Informellen Sektors" für die urbane Entwicklung der VR China*, München 1988

Jessen, J./Siebel, W., et al. (1988): *Arbeit nach der Arbeit. Schattenwirtschaft, Wertewandel und Industriearbeit*, Opladen 1988

Jia, Ting/Wang, Dekuan/Tang, Baoling (1987): "Dui Liaoning siren qiye de diaocha yu sikao" ("Private Enterprises in Liaoning Province: Investigation and Reflections"), in: *Shehuixue Yanjiu* (Sociological Studies), 6/1987: pp.28-32

Jingji Cankao (Economic Information), Peking

Jingji Cankao Bao (Economic Information Daily), Peking

Jingji Guanli (Economic Management), Peking

Kloten, N. (1986): "Der Plan-Markt-Mechanismus Chinas", in: Schüller, A. (1985), ed., *China im Konflikt zwischen verschiedenen Ordnungsprinzipien*, Berlin 1985

Kornai, J. (1979): "Resource-Constrained versus Demand-Constrained Systems", in: *Econometrica* 4/1979: pp.801 ff.

Kornai, J. (1980): *Economics of Shortage*, 2 vols., New York 1980

Kraus, W. (1989): *Private Unternehmerschaft in der Volksrepublik China*, Hamburg 1989

Liang, Chuanyun (1990), ed.: *Zhongguo siying qiye jingying guanli zhinan* (Guidebook for Management and Running of Private Enterprises in China), Peking 1990

Lin, Jixiao/He, Weisheng (1986): "Dangqian laodong jiuye de renwu he duice" ("Tasks and Policy of Present Employment"), in: *Jingji Wenti Tansuo* (Inquiry into Economic Problems), 12/1986: pp.37-38

Liu, Xingran (1987), ed.: *Laodong renshi wenti jieda* (Questions and Answers About Labour and Personnel), Changchun 1987

Liu, Zhuanqi (1986), ed.: *Laodong jingjixue cidian* (Dictionary of Labour Economy), Zhengzhou 1986

Ma, Hong/Sun, Shangqing (1981), eds.: *Zhongguo jingji jiegou wenti yanjiu* (Studies of Problems of China's Economic Structure), 2 vols., Peking 1981

Manion, M. (1991): "Policy Implementation in the People's Republic of China: Authoritative Decisions versus Individual Interests", in: *The Journal of Asian Studies*, 2/1991: pp.253-279

Marresse, M./Mitchell, J.L. (1984): "Kornai's Resource-Constrained Economy: A Survey and an Appraisal", in: *Journal of Comparative Economics*, 8/1984: pp.74 ff.

Mathur, O.P./Moser, C.O.N. (1984), eds.: *The Informal Sector. Regional Development Dialogue*, vol.5, No.2 (1984)

Mazumdar, D. (1976): "The Urban Informal Sector", in: *World Development* 8/1976: pp.655 ff.

Mehta, M. (1985): "Urban Informal Sector. Concepts, Indian Evidence and Policy Implication", in: *Economic and Political Weekly*, 8/1985: pp.326 ff.

Menzel, U. (1983): *Länderstudie Taiwan*, Bremen 1983

Miller, S.M. (1987): "The Pursuit of Informal Economies", in: *The Annals of the American Academy of Political and Social Science*, 493/1987: pp.26 ff.

Moser, C.O.N. (1978): "Informal Sector or Petty Commodity Production: Dualism or Dependence in Urban Development?", in: *World Development*, 9-10/1978: pp.1041 ff.
Myrdal, G. (1980): *Asiatisches Drama*, Frankfurt/M. 1980
Nankani, H. (1988): Techniques of Privatization of State-Owned Enterprises, vol.III, World Bank Technical Paper Number 89, Washington 1988
Nee, V./Young, F.W. (1991): "Peasant Entrepreneurs in China's 'Second Economy': An Institutional Analysis", in: *Economic Development and Cultural Change*, 2/1991: pp.293-310
Nongye Jingji Wenti (Problems of Agriculture), Peking
Pahl, R.E. (1987): "Does Jobless Mean Workless? Unemployment and Informal Work", in: *The Annals of the American Academy of Political and Social Science*, 493/1987: pp.36 ff.
Pfeffermann, G.P. (1988): *Private Business in Developing Countries. Improved Prospects*, ed. by World Bank, Washington 1988
Portes, A. (1983): "The Informal Sector. Definition, Controversy, and Relations to National Development", in: *Cultures et Development*, 2/1983: pp.297 ff.
Prybyla, J.S. (1987): *Market and Plan Under Socialism. The Bird in the Cage*, Stanford 1987
Remy, D./Weeks, J. (1973): "Employment, Occupation and Inequality in a Nonindustrial City", in: Wohlmuth, K. (1973), ed.: *Employment Creation in Developing Societies*, New York 1973: pp.293 ff.
Renmin Ribao (People's Daily), Peking
Röglin, H.-C. (1991): "Eigentum in einer gerechten Welt", in: *Frankfurter Allgemeine Zeitung*, 8.6.91
Schäfer, W. (1984), ed.: *Schattenökonomie, Theoretische Grundlagen und wirtschaftspolitische Konsequenzen*, Göttingen 1984
Schrage, H. (1987): *Theoretische Grundlagen der Schattenwirtschaft*, Frankfurt/Bern/New York/Paris 1987
Sethuraman, S.V. (1976): "The Urban Informal Sector: Concept, Measurement and Policy", in: *International Labour Review*, 1/1976: pp.69 ff.
Shehui Kexue (Social Sciences), Shanghai
Shehuizhuyi chuji jieduan yanjiu ketizu (Discussion group for studying the primary stage of socialism) (1991), "Zhongguo shehuizhuyi chuji jieduan de suoyouzhi tese" ("Characteristics of the ownership system in the primary stage of Chinese socialism"), in: *Longjiang Shehui Kexue* (Longjiang Social Sciences), 3/1991: pp.21-27
Sun, Yatsen (1963): "Chinas Internationale Entwicklung", in: Kindermann, G.K. (1963), ed.: *Konfuzianismus, Sunyatsenismus und chinesischer Kommunismus*, Freiburg 1963: pp.130 ff.
Vuylsteke, Ch. (1988): Techniques of Privatization of State-Owned Enterprises, vol.I, World Bank Technical Paper, Number 90, Washington 1988
Wang, Kechong (1990), ed.: *Zhongguo xian jieduan siying jingji tansuo* (Discussion About China's Private Economy in the Present Period), Shanghai 1990
Weck, H./Pommerehne, W.W./Frey, B.S. (1984): *Schattenwirtschaft*, München 1984

Weeks, J. (1975): "Policies for Expanding Employment in the Informal Urban Sector of Developing Economies, in: *International Labour Review*, 1/1975: pp.1 ff.
Wei, Guojian (1991): "'Di er zhiye re' zai Zhongguo" ("The 'Second-Job-Feaver' in China"), in: Zhou, Jing, ed.: *90 niandai: Zhongguo shehui xianxiang* (Social Phenomenons in China in the Nineties), Peking 1991: pp.16-18
Wiles, P. (1981): *Die Parallelwirtschaft: Eine Einschätzung des systemwidrigen Verhaltens im Bereich der Wirtschaft unter besonderer Berücksichtigung der UdSSR*, Sonderveröffentlichung des Bundesinstituts für ostwissenschaftliche und internationale Studien, Köln 1981
Wong, C.P.W. (1987): "Between Plan and Market: The Role of the Local Sector in Post-Mao China", in: *Journal of Comparative Economics*, 3/1987: pp.385 ff.
Xu, Dixin (1981): *Zhongguo guomin jingji fazhan zhong de wenti* (Development Problems of China's Economy), Peking 1981
Xu, Tianji/Ye, Zhendong (1987): "Nongcun laodongli zhuanyi moshi shitan" ("A Probe into the Shift Pattern of Labour Force in China's Rural Areas"), in: *Renkou Yu Jingji* (Population and Economics), 2/1987: pp.37-42
Xue, Muqiao (1979): *Zhongguo shehuizhuyi jingji wenti yanjiu* (Studies About Problems of China's Socialist Economy), Peking 1979
Xue, Muqiao (1980): *Dangqian wo guo jingji ruogan wenti* (Some Problems of the Present Economy of our Country), Peking 1980
Yang, Yiyong (1991,1): "Jinhou shinian laodong jiuye gongzuo de xingshi yu renwu" ("Forms und Tasks of Employment Work in the Next ten Years"), in: *Gongren Ribao* (Worker's Daily), 16.8.91
Yang, Yiyong (1991,2): "Jin ji nian chengzhen daiyelü shangsheng de yuanyin ji duice" ("Causes and policy of the urban unemployment rate in recent years"), in: *Jingji Yuce Yu Xinxi* (Economic Prognosis and Information), 7/1991: pp.8-9, 24
Young, S. (1991): "Wealth but not Security: Attitudes Towards Private Business in China in the 1980s", in: *The Australian Journal of Chinese Affairs*, No.25, January 1991: pp.115-137
Zhang, Changgong (1991): "Dangqian wo guo de shiye xianxiang ji qi xingcheng yuanyin chutan" ("The Phenomenon of Unemployment in Our Country and Its Forms and Origins"), in: *Sichuan Daxue Xuebao* (Journal of Sichuan University), 1/1991, pp.41-46
Zhongguo Gongshang Bao (China's Industry and Commerce), Peking
Zhongguo guonei shichang tongji nianjian (1990) (Statistical Yearbook of the Chinese Domestic Market), Peking 1990
Zhongguo laodong gongzi tongji nianjian (1990) (Statistical Yearbook of Labour and Wages in China), Peking 1990
Zhongguo maoyi wujia tongji ziliao (1984) (Statistical Material About Commerce and Prices in China), 1952-83, Peking 1984
Zhongguo tongji nianjian (Statistical Yearbooks) (1987-91), Peking 1987-91
Zhongguo 1982 nian renkou pucha ziliao (1985) (1982 Population Census of China), Peking 1985
Zhonghua Renmin Gongheguo laodong fagui xuanbian (1986) (Selected Labour Laws and Regulations of the PR of China), Peking 1986

Suburbanization of Megalopolis and Spatial Change of Urban-Rural Fringe.
A Case Study on Shanghai

by Zhongmin Yan

1 Introduction

China in comparison to other countries of the Third World in the last decade, has not had a rapid urbanization. For example, up to the time of 1985 the average annual growth of the urban population in China was 2.78%,[1] while the annual growth of the urban population in South America after World War II was 4.5%, in India 3.3%, and in Algeria 5.9%.[2] According to China's 3rd and 4th Population Census, the urban population accounted for 20.6% and 26.23% of the country's total population.[3] These data cannot reflect the exact level of China's urbanization, due to variations in the statistical definitions. One can, however, conclude the following inferences from such differences in the results of the censuses:

1. In spite of its relative low level of urbanization, China has a large population and its total urban population amounts to 296 million residents.[4]

2. Due to the implementation of reform, the policy of opening to the outside world, and the development of industries, the number of cities and towns, as well as the urban areas have been greatly expanded. During the period from 1980 to 1990, the number of China's cities or municipalities formally established by the government, had increased from 223 to 467. The total number of urban areas increased by the same amount. Their total built-up area extended to 12,855.7 km².[5] The number of towns formally established, expanded from 2,874 in 1980 to 11,873 in 1989, an increase of 313%.[6] This demonstrates that there has been a considerable development in China's urbanization in the past ten years. In this period the size of population in the metropolises and megalopolises have also gradually expanded.

Shanghai's total population increased from 11.9 million in 1982 to 13.3 million in 1990. Its urban population had increased from 6,975,100 to 8,395,700, i.e. the ratio of Shanghai's urban population in relation to the total population increased from 58.81% to 62.93%.[7] The suburbanization, due to the expansion of the urbanized area and the wide urbanization in the rural area, has caused a change in the spatial structure between urban and rural areas. (The most noticeable changes occurred in the urban fringe, which experienced an alteration from the rural area to the urban-rural transitional belt.) In the case of Shanghai, the central city comprised 82.4 sq.km in 1949. Due to the development of industry, housing, and transportation, this urbanized area has continuously expanded, incorporating neighbouring towns or villages merged into the central city. Until 1990 the 10 districts belonging to the central city had a total area of 280 sq.km (its urban population had increased to 7,555,493 in 1990). At the same time a number of rural residents (engaged in agriculture) received a non-agricultural household registration due to the change of the land-use structure. This shows that the formation of the urban fringe, a transitional belt between the urban and rural areas, is a product of urbanization. Although this urban structure in China has many similarities with the pattern of urbanization in other countries, it has maintained its unique features. Shanghai will be discussed as an example in the following:

2 Shanghai's Urban Fringe: Structural Changes and Actual Land-Use

There are diverse opinions among experts concerning the boundaries of the suburban area. In China as a rule a zone of about 5 km in width around the city proper may be regarded as its fringe, when considering the following aspects:

- the relative low levels of suburbanization in the metropolitan areas of China;

- underdevelopment of urban transportation facilities; a relative low average of travel distances, bicycles as the main means of private transportation;

- other features, such as the ratio of non-agricultural population, population density, building density, land-use, infrastructure, linkages with the central city, existing well-formed administrative districts, etc.

Shanghai's urban fringe includes 26 townships/towns, which belong to three counties: Shanghai County, Jiading County, and Chuansha County (see Map 1). The Baoshan District is also a part of the urban fringe. These administrative units were incorporated into the central city because of their transitional characteristics.

The urban fringe can be characterized by the following features:

(1) Generally, the area for non-agricultural land-use accounts for more than 40% of the total fringe area; of that over 10% are utilized for industry and warehouses; and over 4% for transportation.

(2) More than 40% of the agricultural land-use are utilized for vegetable gardening.

Map 1: Shanghai - Administrative map of the urban fringe

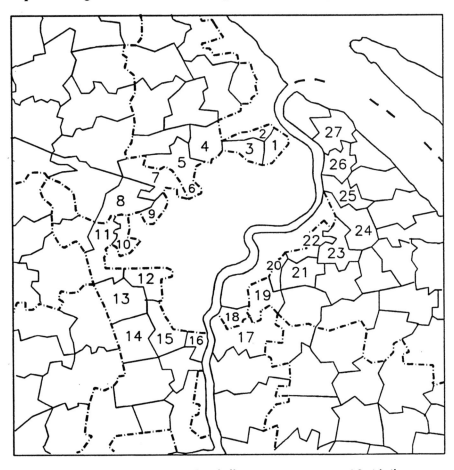

1 Wujiaochang	10 Xinjing	19 Liuli
2 Songnan	11 Huaqing	20 Yanqiao
3 Jiangwan	12 Hongqiao	21 Huamu
4 Miaohang	13 Qibao	22 Yangjing
5 Dachang	14 Xingzhuang	23 Jinqiao
6 Pengpu	15 Meilong	24 Zhangqiao
7 Taopu	16 Longhua	25 Donggou
8 Jiangqiao	17 Sanlin	26 Gaonan
9 Changzheng	18 Yangsi	27 Gaoqiao

(3) The actual non-agricultural population (including a part of the mobile population) may come up to as much as 40-50% of the total population, while the non-agricultural population, according to the census, accounts for only 15-20%. The non-agricultural income is now the main source of income. The townships/towns of the distant suburbs apparently differ in their land-use features, when compared to the area of the urban fringe (see Table 1).

Table 1: A Comparison of Land-Use between the Urban Fringe (Near Suburbs) and Far Suburbs 1984

Item	26 towns/townships in the urban fringe	Remaining towns/ townships of Shanghai, Jiading, Baoshan and Chuansha Counties
Cultivated land	56.0	64.9
Gardens, forests and waters	10.5	11.5
Canals, ditches etc.	3.3	5.3
Industry and warehouses	10.5	2.2
Transportation	4.5	2.5
Housing	12.6	12.2
Special land-use	2.7	1.4
Vegetable gardening in % of total cultivated area	46.0	7.3
Total area %	100.0	100.0
skm	(410)	(1,802)

Since 1984, the suburban village/town industry has rapidly developed and a large amount of cultivated land has been used for industrial sites and warehouses. Analytical studies dealing with these changes and the present situation of land-usage in Shanghai County (7 towns/townships), Jiading County (3 towns/townships), Chuansha County (10 towns/townships), and Baosha District (5 towns/ townships) examined this matter more closely (see Map 1):

The total area of these 25 towns/townships, mentioned above, is 32,706 hectares (327 km^2). Originally, there was a predominant agricultural economy in these areas. The economic reform and open policy following the 1980s, have demonstrated a rapid development in the mainstay economy in the village and town industry. The development of agriculture, industry, and trade in the urban fringe intensifies the urban-rural interchange. The total social output rose from 643 million RMB in 1980, to 4,258 million RMB in 1988. In the same period, the number of factories rose from 730 to 2,324, among which 118 factories were run by the municipality and the rest by the villages and towns. The proportion of labour force engaged in industrial production in relation to the total labour force rose from 30.6% in 1981, to 52.4% in 1988. At the same time, however, the cultivated area decreased from 20,360 hectares to 20,150 hectares (1988). The average annual decrease of 26.3 hectares, includes 70.8%, accounting for industrial utilization (in particular for village industry), storage and poultry farming purposes; 17.9% for housing; 6.8% and 3.8% for fish ponds and road construction, respectively.

Taking the density of population and buildings, as well as the distribution of factories, warehouses, and cultivated land as criteria, the urban fringe may be divided into 6 quarters according to their different functions and spatial structure (see Map 2):

(1) The Northern Industrial Quarter. It consists of Dachang and Taopu industrial districts, which are adjacent to Wusong and Pengpu industrial districts. 13% or more of the area are absorbed by factories and warehouses; and 15.2% by housing. The land under cultivation is relatively limited; therefore the percentage of the agricultural labour force in relation to the total population is low.

(2) The Western Quarter of Warehouses and Vegetable Gardening. Vegetable Gardening accounts for 90% of the land under cultivation. Half of this area is utilized for storage land-use (8.5%) being greater than the industrial land-use (5.7%).

(3) The Southwestern Cropland Quarter. The cultivation of paddy rice is predominant. Factories and store places account for 4.6% of land-use.

(4) The Northeastern Riparian Industrial Quarter. Industrial and storage land-use covers more than 10% of the total area, mainly located east of the Huangpu River and west of the Yanggao Road, including the Gaoqiao Industrial District. The land-use east of the Yanggao Road is dominated by farmland; housing accounts for 15.1%.

(5) The Eastern Vegetable Gardening and Housing Mixed Quarter. It is adjacent to the Pudong urban area. Markets, public buildings, and housing compose 18.5% of the land-use. The high percentage is related to the movement of inhabitants from the city proper to the outskirts of Shanghai.

(6) The Pudong Farmland Quarter. It has a high percentage of reclamation land and paddy rice fields.

Map 2: Shanghai - A functional classification of the urban fringe

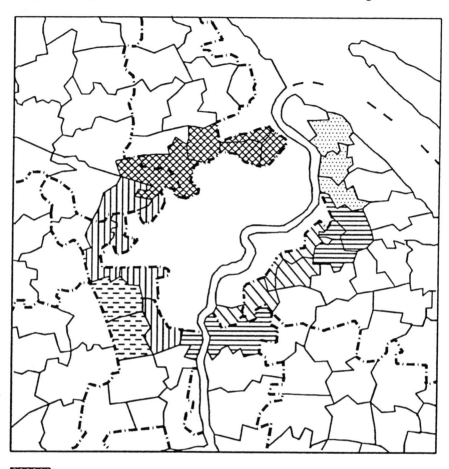

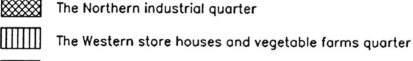 The Northern industrial quarter

 The Western store houses and vegetable farms quarter

The Southwestern cropland quarter

 The Northeastern riparian industrial quarter

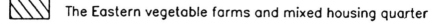 The Eastern vegetable farms and mixed housing quarter

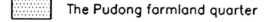 The Pudong farmland quarter

The overall landscape of the urban fringe presents a mixed arrangement of farmland and gardens, factories and warehouses, newly-built residential quarters, schools and research institutions. The formation of the urban fringe is mainly the result of two factors: the expansion of the central city and the force of attraction around it. The different quarters in the urban fringe have received distinct influences resulting from the changes in the rural economy. The difference in (1) locational conditions, (2) original economical basis, and (3) characteristics of the functions with which they are linked to the central city will lead to the different patterns within the urban fringe. For example, the northern part of the city proper has a better developed industry and transportation. This facilitates the industrial development of the neighbouring quarters of the urban fringe. Changzheng township, which is adjacent to Putuo District in the west of the city, has gained in locational superiority and has vigorously developed. The tertiary sector of the economy had a turnover of 23.9 million RMB or more in 1988. Due to the development and implementation of the open-door policy in the Pudong Area the original urban fringe will be rapidly altered.

3 Functions of the Urban Fringe

The urban fringe of Shanghai and other cities in China has the following functions:

(1) As a belt for developing external transportation.
(2) As a region for expansion of the industrial district of the city proper after appropriate reformation.
(3) As a primary area to be developed for storage service.
(4) As a newly-built residential quarter.
(5) As a base for supply and produce of vegetables and non-staple food.
(6) As a region for rapidly developing commerce, catering trade, repairing, and other services.

These different urban fringe functions can alleviate the difficulties of the central city's traffic, housing, environment, provision of vegetables, non-staple food-preserves and can improve the urban environment. The countryside in contrast receives support from the city in funds, technology, and equipment, thus facilitating the development of the rural economy and accelerating the progress of integration of urban with rural areas. Therefore, the urban fringe functions as "bridge" or "hub" which connects the urban economy with the rural economy. The urban fringe is thereby subjected to the impact of a two-way development from both the city and the countryside. There is a dynamic change occurring in the socio-economic development of the urban fringe. Competition increases a series of conflicts and problems. Currently, the urban fringe is confronted with the following crucial problems:

(1) The area of cultivated land has decreased, so that the selfsufficient level of staple food production has drastically been reduced. Also, its function as a supply base for vegetable and non-staple foodstuff failed.

(2) The agricultural labour force decreased, while a rise in the agricultural productivity remains an important necessity.

(3) The increase in the mobile population has alleviated the labour shortage in the urban fringe. However, due to the complex background of the mobile population, as well as the absence of a unified management, difficulties occurred in public security and birth control.

In order to develop and control the urban fringe properly, the following problems should be taken into account:

(1) A complete survey should be adopted as a guiding concept. The development of the urban fringe should adhere to the overall planning of the central city or megalopolis, so that the performance might be facilitated.

(2) The readjustment of the industrial structure in the urban fringe should be subjected to unified planning and based on a comprehensive investigation. It should avoid a stereotyped pattern for all administrative units, so that better support can be received from and given to the central city.

(3) The infrastructure should be improved, so that a better environment and improved internal and external communication can be created for the development of the urban fringe.

(4) The disposal of waste water and refuse, as well as air pollution should be strictly controlled and the ecological environment improved.

(5) The social environment should be rectified, the limits of responsibility and power in administrative management must be clearly defined. Related propaganda and educational work should also be implemented.

In sum, the socio-economic and ecological conditions in the urban fringe attached to a metropolis or megalopolis should be properly improved.

Notes

1) All nationwide statistical data in this paper do not include Taiwan.
2) Xia Zonggan 1991, pp. 23 -30.
3) *Renmin Ribao*, Nov.7, 1990.
4) *Renmin Ribao*, Nov.8, 1990.
5) *Urban Planning Bulletin*, 1991, No.13.
6) Estimates based on statistical data of the 4th Census.
7) Yan Zhongmin and Lia Junde 1989, pp.8-14.

References (all in Chinese)

Gu Wenxuan, "General Description of Urban Development in the continent of China in the Last 40 Years", *Transaction China Urban Planning Society* 1991, pp.34-38
The People's Daily, Peking Nov.7, 1990
The People's Daily, Peking Nov.8, 1990
Urban Planning Bulletin 1991, No.13
Xia Zonggan, "The Progress of China's Urbanization", *Transaction China Urban Planning Society*, 1991, pp.23-30
Yan Zhongmin and Lia Junde, "An Inquiry into some Problems Concerning Urban Fringe", *Urban Economy Research*, 1989, No.12, pp.8-14
Zhou Guaji and Wang Jiazhen, *A Study on Remote Sensing Information about the Present Condition and Change of Land-use in Shanghai's Urban Fringe*, Nov. 1990

Beijing in "Open Door Policy" Breakthrough, Scope and Challenge[1]

by Zhaoliang Hu

1 The Space of Beijing

Different kinds of administrative, statistical, and historical criteria may be applied to define Beijing in six different ways. The following are listed according to size (see Map 1).

(1) Beijing City, founded within the Qing Dynasty wall.
(2) The four districts of Beijing Inner City (Dongcheng, Xicheng, Chongwen, Xuanwu).
(3) The Beijing City Planning Area.
(4) Beijing City and the near suburban districts, including the four Inner City districts and the four surrounding districts: Chaoyang, Haidian, Fengtai and Shijingshan.
(5) Beijing City and the near and far suburban districts, including the four Inner City districts, the four near and two distant suburban districts, namely Mentougou and Fangshan.
(6) Beijing Municipality, including 10 districts and 8 counties (see Map 2).

Covering an area of 16,808 square kilometers, making up 1.7% of the country's total area, Beijing Municipality extends over 160 km from east to west and over 170 km from north to south. By the end of 1991, Beijing Municipality had a population of 10.94 million, of which about 4 million residents populated the rural area. According to their residential status, there are five types of population in the municipal area:

(1) The permanent population of non-agricultural residents, who are supplied with grain and other essential goods by the government.
(2) The permanent population of agricultural residents, who are not supplied with grain and essential goods by the government.
(3) The temporary population composed of residents who work in the urban area for which permanent residential status is not required.
(4) The "floating" population.
(5) The "supplied" population.

The current calculations for the urban population published by the government includes the non-agricultural permanent residential population in the city and the

Map 1: Development of Beijing Municipality's Boundaries

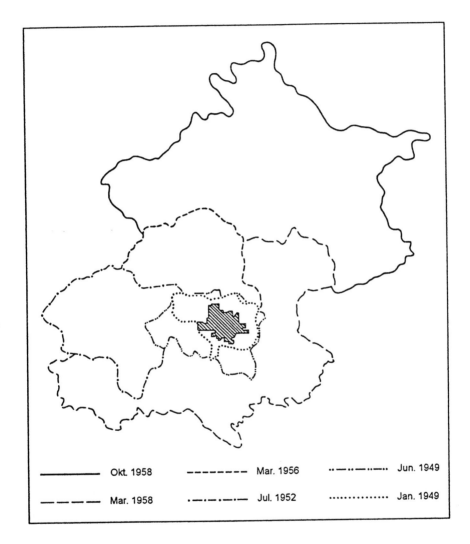

Map 2: Present Administrative Boundaries of Beijing Municipality

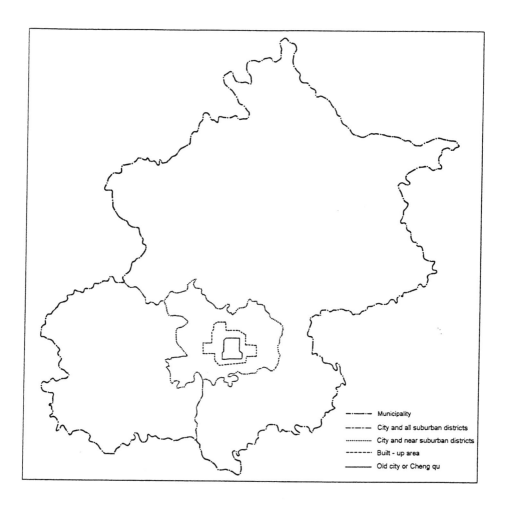

near-suburban districts. There were 5.7 million non-agricultural permanent residents in the city and the near-suburban districts of Beijing by the end of 1989.

Table 1: The space and population of Beijing (1989)[2]

	area (skm)	population (3) (1,000)
1. Beijing City	62	1,900
2. Beijing City districts	87.1	2,580
3. Beijing City Planning Area	750	6,000
4. Beijing City and near suburban districts	1,370	6,550
5. Beijing City and all suburban districts	4,568	7,470
6. Beijing Municipality	16,808	10,860

The Beijing City Planning Area, which covers 750 km^2, is the unit which government planning is based upon. It is not an administrative unit, for which statistical data could be attained. The permanent population including both non-agricultural and agricultural residents, combined with the temporary population, is the best basis for calculating the urban population. There were approximately 6 million residents in the Beijing City Planning Area by the end of 1989.

The best estimation of the population for which provision has to be made includes all five catogories of residents. By this definition, there were approximately 7 million residents in the City Planning Area of Beijing by the end of 1989.

In the beginning of 1949 Beijing Municipality covered an area of 707 km^2 and had a population of 1.56 million. Between 1949 and 1961, the administrative area of Beijing was enlarged five times. Its area increased by 16,101 square kilometers and its population by 2.8 million. The historical data demonstrate that one should focus on these complex changes.

2 Breakthrough to an International City

Beijing has progressed under the "Open Door Policy" in urban construction, and is increasingly becoming an international city.

In 1989, the GNP of Beijing was four times higher than in 1978. The tertiary industry grew even more rapidly. The proportion of teriary industry in Beijing was less than one quarter by 1978 and over one third by 1989. The first New

Technical Development Zone in China was set up in Beijing in 1987. Now there are over one thousand enterprises in the New Technical Development Zone.

The City's public facilities including communications, utilities, sewage systems, telecommunications and urban afforestation, have also progressed. In addition to the central gas and power supply systems, the City has constructed approximately 40 kilometers of subway, and more than 50 overpasses and bridges. More than 140 million m^2 of new buildings, including 85 million m^2 for residential quarters, have been completed; this is seven times the total space of housing in Beijing in 1949. 10 million m^2 of new buildings per year have been completed since 1986.

At the same time there are many obstacles for Beijing in the near future.

(1) The relative stagnation of the regional economy.
(2) Rapid growth of the urban population.
(3) Shortage of water resources.
(4) Preservation and renovation of the city of Beijing.

3 The Regional Economy

Table 2: A comparison of the three Economic Regions
(% of China's total industrial output)

	1978	1989	change %-points
Beijing-Tianjin-Hebei	13.8	10.6	-3.2
Beijing	4.7	3.4	-1.3
Tianjin	3.9	3.0	-0.9
Hebei	5.2	4.2	-1.0
Shanghai-Jiangsu-Zhejiang	24.9	26.1	1.2
Shanghai	13.0	7.0	-6.0
Jiangsu	8.7	12.4	3.7
Zhejiang	3.2	6.7	3.5
Guangdong-Fujian	6.4	10.1	3.7
Guangdong	4.7	7.6	2.9
Fujian	1.5	2.3	0.8
Hainan	0.2	0.2	0.0
Whole Country	100	100	

The most severe problem for Beijing is its relatively slow growth, compared to other areas. Due to the "Open Door Policy", the economic potential of the coastal areas in the South of China has been enlarged. The main centers of economic activities are steadily moving to the South of China. The Yangtze delta and Pearl River delta are the most dynamic regions in the entire country. Guangdong Province ranked top in economic development, investment, and foreign trade in 1987. From 1978 to 1989, the percentage of the total industrial output in Beijing-Tianjin-Hebei decreased by 3.2 percentage points. During the same period, an increase of 1.2 percentage points was reported for Shanghai-Jiangsu-Zhejiang and 3.7 percentage points for Guangdong-Fujian.

A number of factors, such as location, history, and policy are involved in the wave of economic development in South China.

(1) Location

The Guangdong-Fujian region is geographically close to Hongkong, Macao, and the international market. The region Shanghai-Jiangsu-Zhejiang is the second closest region. During the period from 1986 to 1989, foreign investment was three times as high as in Beijing-Tianjin-Hebei. Hongkong and Macao will be reunited with the Mainland between 1997 and 1999; the economic potential for South China will then grow further.

(2) History

In the last thousand years, Yangtze delta has been the most developed region in China, in terms of both its economy and culture. Beijing was chosen as the capital of the country primarily for military reasons. The local economy near Beijing could not supply the capital's demands. Therefore, it was necessary to construct the Great Canal in order to transport grain and goods from the South of China.

(3) Policy

The "Open Door Policy" is more developed in Southern China. All four Special Economic Zones and the Open Door Province of Hainan are situated there. China is currently implementing both a planned and a market economy. In the South of China the market economy is more powerful compared to the North. State-owned industries contribute 55% of the total industrial output in Beijing-Tianjin-Hebei, compared to 38 resp. 39% in Guangdong-Fujian and Shanghai-Jiangsu-Zhejiang. Due to locational, historical and political reasons, capital, labor, technology, and skilled laborers, all are moving from North to South. In sum, the center of the Chinese economy has shifted from North to South over a longer period of time. Beijing, situated in a relatively backward zone, will have more serious difficulties in the near future.

4 The Rapid Growth of the Urban Population

The census data show that the total population of the Municipality increased from 4.1 million in 1949 to 10.8 million in 1989, and that the urban population expanded from 1.5 million to 6 million.[4]

According to the Beijing city-planning, Beijing's population will comprise 10 million by the year 2000. Some planners have predicted that Beijing's population would be stabilized by the year 2020. On the basis of a more complete analysis, the growth in Beijing's population will not cease until the year 2050.

(1) Population factors in China

The natural population growth will remain a major factor both in urban and in rural areas. Meanwhile approximately 20 million residents migrate from rural into urban areas every year. It is supposed that this process will continue until the year 2050.

(2) Specific factors of Beijing

The growth of Beijing's population is closely linked with its existing social and financial systems, history, and cultural traditions.

In many Western countries, there are cities which function as political centers, for example, Washington, D.C in the United States. However, it is difficult for China to have this type of an attribute. In a socialist country, having a central planning economy, the political center also performs the function of economic management. Therefore, economic organizations engaged in service activities, such as finance, insurance, trust, communication, and mass media, all concentrate in the political center. International business negotiations are also conducted there. Throughout the modernization process, these activities have had a relatively rapid development. These forms of process have made a major impact on the growth of Beijing.

In the current financial system, approximately 73 per cent of the income of Beijing's local government stems from industrial profits and taxes. In order to support a large variety of functions, Beijing has had to adopt a so-called "industries support city" policy. The industrial population in the city accounts for more than two-fifths of the total workers, and industry occupies nearly one third of the total land. This is a well-noted indication concerning the expansion of Beijing.

In Chinese history, the cultural center has always been closely associated with the political center. Reputable universities and institutes, eminent libraries, gymnasiums, and theatres, are all located in Beijing. The Olympic Games many times were held in the U.S., but not in its capital Washington D.C. If China hosted the Olympic Games, Beijing would be the only possible location.[5]

In Beijing the provision of infrastructures is superior to those in Shanghai and Tianjin. The urban area of Beijing is two times larger than that of Shanghai and one half larger than that of Tianjin. The provision of telephone booths and the length of road per capita, are twice as high as those of Shanghai and Tianjin.[6]

5 Severe Shortage of Water Resources

The growth of Beijing is seriously restricted by the environmental capacity. First, water resources are limited. The average annual precipitation of Beijing is 630 mm and there is a great seasonal and annual variation. Currently, all the water resources have been utilized, while ground water is intensively exploited. There is a great depression cone of ground water in the urban area. Guanting Reservoir and Miyun Reservoir are two important water supply reservoirs in Beijing. Due to sedimentation of over 0.6 billion cubic meters and the increase in water use in the upper bays, the Guanting Reservoir water supply has decreased year by year.

There are two ways for maintaining the water supply in Beijing:

(1) Conservation of water

Raising the effectiveness of irrigation water utilization, raising the industrial water recycle rate and utilizing sewage are the main goals for water conservation. Since the beginning of the 1980's, conservation of water has been the only means of maintaining the water supply. The problem is that the conservation of water requires a lot of investment and raises the cost of water.

(2) Drawing water

The Yangtze River is the first river on the list for drawing water. Due to the long distance and complex physical environment, drawing water requires a great amount of investment and a long period for construction. As a rule the result is not satisfying. For example, Tianjin drew 1 billion cubic meters of water from the Yellow River in 1972, of which only 100 million cubic meters reached the urban area and only 30 million cubic meters entered the waterworks. 450 million cubic meters entered the Tianjin urban area from the Yellow River in 1981, of which only 150 million cubic meters entered into the waterworks. The average cost of water in 1981 was 1.9 RMB per cubic meter.[7] In the long run only a few industries with high profits will be able to utilize the water drawn from the Yangtze.

Due to the lack of water resources, some researchers have suggested that China should select a new political capital.

6 Difficulties for City Planning

There are mainly two difficulties for city planning. The first problem concerns the preservation and renovation of the Old City of Beijing. The Old City is the best preserved and largest feudal city in China. It has all the characteristics of traditional Chinese planning and architecture, a clear axis, neat symmetry, and magnificent features. Many buildings and gardens have a high artistic standard.

The down-town area of Beijing was renovated after 1949. The old city walls were pulled down and ring roads were built. The Changan Boulevard was expanded and the Tiananmen Square was reconstructed. Many high-rise buildings for public and residential usage have been built. Most of the renovation projects have produced both favourable and unfavourable results.[8]

During the renovation of the old city attention has to be paid to the preservation of its unique traditional features and surrounding environment. The most important sectors on the main axis, from Qianmen via Tianan Men, the Palace Museum, Jingshan, the Bell Tower, are key areas that have to be protected. Within certain areas both the size and height of the buildings should be strictly controlled. No building higher than six meters should be constructed. Typical residental areas, streets, and lanes will also be maintained. They demonstrate the ancient culture and traditional architecture of Beijing.

The next priority is the regulation of space structure. There are three fields of space structure in the Inner City which should be regulated.[9]

(1) The Central Business District should be prepared for further development.
(2) The population density of 30,000 people per km^2 should be gradually decreased. Reconstruction of the section close to the former city wall and the Temple of Heaven, where many pattry houses are located, should be prompted.
(3) It is necessary to adjust land use in the old city center. Enterprises causing pollution and units needlessly located in the Inner City should be removed. A variety of public structures and cultural facilities for daily life should be established.

Major satellite towns are to be constructed in the remote suburbs, according to the industrial development and location of the original county and district centers. Four satellite towns - Huangcun, Changping, Tongzhou, and Yanshan - will be built up in the near future. The satellite towns should offer ample opportunities for employment, complete facilities for daily life, and convenient traffic connections to the capital. The development of satellite towns surrounding Beijing in fact is in a very early stage. The largest satellite town, Tongzhou, has currently only 80,000 residents. It is, therefore, necessary to raise the level of the county in the administrative system and improve the quality and authority of urban planning.

Notes

1) This paper has been supported by the Doctoral Program Foundation of the Chinese Institution of Higher Education.
2) *Statistical Yearbook of Beijing*, 1990.
3) The population includes both the permanent population and the temporary population. There were 5,690,000 non-agricultural permanent residents in Beijing city and the suburban districts by 1989.
4) Sun Hongming 1990.
5) Hu Zhaoliang, Meng Xiaochen 1988.
6) Hu Zhaoliang 1988.
7) Lu Kebai 1990, p.40.
8) Hou Renzi 1982.
9) Wang Dong 1989.

References

Hou Renzi, "Beijing City - Historical Development and Renovation", *Historical Geography*, No.2, Shanghai Publishing House, Nov. 1982 (Chin.)
Hu Zhaoliang, "Expansion of Beijing City - Causes and Countermeasures", *China City Planning Review*, Vol.7, No.1, 1991, pp.63-71 (Chin.)
Hu Zhaoliang, Meng Xiaochen, "Socioeconomic and Political Background of the Growth of Large Cities in China", *Asian Geographer* (Hong Kong), Vol.6, No.1, 1988, pp.24-28
Hu Zhaoliang, "The Study of Mechanism for the Development of the Large Cities in China", *China City Planning Review*, Vol.4, No.3, 1988, pp.33-38 (Chin.)
Lu Kebai, *The works on Territorial Planning*, China Planning Publishing House, 1990 (Chin.)
Sun Hongming, "The Harmonious Development between Economic-Social and City Space", *Beijing Planning and Construction*, No.2, 1990, pp.14-16 (Chin.)
Wang Dong, "Some Opinions on the Development of Beijing", *Beijing Planning and Construction*, No.3, 1989, pp.19-22 (Chin.)
Wu Liangyong, "A Discussion on Beijing Planning", *Architectural History*, No.3, 1979 (Chin.)

Contributors

Bronger, Dirk, Professor, Department of Geography, University of Bochum/Germany

Druijven, Peter, Drs., Senior Lecturer, Faculty of Spatial Sciences, University of Groningen/Netherlands

Heberer, Thomas, Professor, Political Sciences, Politics of East Asia, University of Trier/Germany

Hu, Zhaoliang, Professor, Department of Geography, Beijing University, Beijing/China

Leung, Chi-Keung, Professor, Head of Department of Geography and Geology, University of Hong Kong/Hong Kong

Scharping, Thomas, Professor, Modern China Studies, University of Cologne/Germany

Shen, Bingyu, Mrs., Institute of Urban and Rural Development, Ministry of Construction, Beijing/China

Tan, Kok Chiang, Associate Professor, Department of Geography, University of Guelph/Canada

Taubmann, Wolfgang, Professor, Department of Geography, University of Bremen/Germany

Yan, Zhongmin, Mrs. Professor, Centre for Urban and Regional Development, East China Normal University, Shanghai/China

Yeh, Anthony Gar-On, Ph. D., Senior Lecturer, Centre of Urban Studies and Urban Planning, University of Hong Kong/Hong Kong